The Butler Way

The Best of Butler Basketball

David Woods

Blue River Press
Indianapolis

Edited by Mark Bast, MB Ink
Cover designed by Phil Velikan
Proofread by Heather Lowhorn
Packaged by Wish Publishing

Printed in the United States of America
10 9 8 7 6 5 4 3 2 1

Distributed in the United States by
Cardinal Publishers Group
www.cardinalpub.com

Acknowledgments

There are many people who contributed to *The Butler Way*, but four in particular were so influential that there would be no book without them: Jim McGrath, longtime sports information director at Butler University; Doug Carroll, journalism colleague and friend of nearly 40 years; Howard Caldwell, author of the Tony Hinkle biography, *Coach for All Seasons*; and Tom Doherty, a publisher who believed in this project from the beginning.

Also, there would have been no book without the assistance of Butler's Eugene S. Pulliam School of Journalism, which allowed the use of Room 216 of the Fairbanks Center. Nearly the entire book was written from that office.

Appreciation goes to all players, coaches, administrators, and media representatives interviewed in the course of covering Butler basketball regularly since 2001. The same goes to all Indianapolis journalists covering the Bulldogs over the years and to editor Mark Bast.

A Dawg Pound cheer for Mark Walpole, who proposed a book about Butler basketball as long ago as 2001. Special contributions were made by Dick Denny, Cathy Knapp, Herb Schwomeyer, John Parry, and Beverly Compton.

My heartfelt thanks to all.

Foreword
by Clark Kellogg

Over the last decade, Butler basketball has been one of the most successful basketball programs in the country. Unless you're an Indianapolis resident or an avid college basketball fan, you might find that surprising. In this book, David Woods gives you an up-close look at the *what*, *who*, and *how* of Butler basketball, particularly in the first decade of this century. He captures the DNA of Butler basketball and offers an entertaining, informative, and instructive account of the program that takes the reader behind the scenes and connects with all who've contributed to Butler's basketball history and success.

I love watching the game of basketball, and as a college basketball analyst, I appreciate and enjoy the way Butler teams play the game. Smart, tough, and unselfish. Disciplined, confident, and poised. Competitive, freely, and with great joy. Those characteristics have been on display through multiple classes of players and a number of head coaches, which speaks to the essence of Butler's sustained success. There is a process in place. A *values-based* process that prioritizes humility, thankfulness, servanthood, passion, and unity. There's nothing magical in the values themselves. However, the winning that has taken place there is a result of daily striving for improvement and embracing and practicing those values. Recruiting skilled players that will accept, grow, and thrive in such a culture is a contributing factor, too.

There are many ways to achieve championship-level success in D-1 college basketball, and Butler has found its own way—*The Butler Way*. Over the years, I've had the privilege of interacting with Butler University and the Butler basketball program on various levels. I've practiced and played pickup games at Hinkle Fieldhouse as an Indiana Pacer, I've called Butler games, commented on the team as a studio analyst, had a son recruited by the Bulldogs, and spent time with former players and coaches. And in all of my direct encounters, I've come away impressed and blessed.

Impressed because they believe and live their values on and off the court. They represent themselves, their university, and their program with class in every way. Blessed because I'm reminded that the values enumerated in the Butler Way are timeless, tried and true, universally available, and worth applying in all of our lives.

Table of Contents

The Butler Way:
How a Small School Wins Big

Drew Streicher stood at the foul line, cradled the basketball, bent his knees, and released. Good. He took the ball, repeated the same motions, and achieved the same result. Good.

The Butler University basketball player made both ends of a one-and-one, sending the Bulldogs ahead of Florida 54–53 with fewer than four minutes left in an NCAA Midwest Regional semifinal at St. Louis. The winner would be one victory from a Final Four appearance.

The 26,000 spectators inside the Edward Jones Dome, plus a national television audience, watched in amazement on the night of March 23, 2007. Florida was not only the defending national champion, but the team featured a roster of six future NBA players: Al Horford, Corey Brewer, Joakim Noah, Taurean Green, Chris Richard, and Marreese Speights. Representing Butler: a future doctor and dentist, plus four players whose basketball futures were at levels below the NBA.

No way something like this could happen?

There was a way. The Butler Way.

The words represent a doctrine that has allowed a small liberal arts college in Indianapolis to compete against those that have sports budgets 10 times greater. Butler, with an undergraduate enrollment of 3,900, is a college version of Milan, a tiny high school that won Indiana's state championship in 1954 and inspired the movie *Hoosiers*.

Yet Butler's program is the antithesis of Hollywood. It is more grit than glitz. Barry Collier, a former Butler player and coach who became athletic director, wrote the slogan for the school:

The Butler Way demands commitment, denies selfishness, accepts reality, yet seeks improvement while putting the team above self.

Tony Hinkle introduced a team-oriented style of play at Butler that has been embraced by 21st-century Bulldogs (Butler University Archives).

Collier's philosophy developed out of a 1995 summer retreat led by former coach Dick Bennett. A Butler coach, Thad Matta, coined the phrase "the Butler Way." Yet the roots predate the university, which was founded in 1855 by attorney and abolitionist Ovid Butler. The Butler Way's five principles—humility, passion, unity, servanthood, thankfulness—have been credited to Tony Hinkle, who coached basketball at Butler for 41 seasons and spent 70 years in service to the university.

Hinkle, toward the end of his life, was asked to identify the best basketball players that he ever coached.

"We never had any great players, only great teams," he responded. "The kids did what I told them, and we played as a team. That is why we could win so often."

Hinkle didn't invent the principles, either.

"These are tried and true," Collier said. "They have a biblical foundation. They have a societal foundation. They've worked for thousands of years."

They have worked for the Bulldogs, even if they couldn't pull off a momentous upset in 2007. Florida came back to beat Butler 65–57 in the Gators' toughest test on a road to a second straight national championship. Butler's future pros were Streicher (medical school) and Brian Ligon (dental school). A.J. Graves, Brandon Crone, Mike Green, and Pete Campbell were to become basketball pros in European leagues. What the Bulldogs had was "incredible toughness," Florida coach Billy Donovan said.

> I continue to be in awe of Butler. . .This is truly one of the elite programs, mid-major or otherwise, in America.
>
> —Seth Davis, *Sports Illustrated* and CBS Sports

How did the Dawgs respond after losing? They went 30–4 the next season, setting a school record for victories.

• • •

In 13 seasons, from 1996 through 2009, Butler reached eight NCAA Tournaments under four different coaches. In three seasons ending in 2009, Butler's cumulative record was 85–17. That ranked fifth in the nation behind Memphis (104–10), North Carolina (101–14), Kansas (97–16), and UCLA (91–18).

A program to which Butler is often compared is Gonzaga, a small private college (enrollment 6,923) in Spokane, Wash. Gonzaga has more national visibility, dating from its 1999 advancement to the Elite Eight. After a run of three straight Sweet Sixteens, Gonzaga had a 7–8 record in the NCAA Tournament from 2002 to 2009. In that same period, Butler was 5–4. In the teams' only meeting, Butler beat Gonzaga 79–71 for the 2006 NIT Season Tipoff championship at New York.

An unusual component of the Butler Way is that it has been furthered not only by coaches, but by a succession of players. They so internalize the system that they pass it on to newcomers like an inheritance. Summer gym is for instruction, not recreation.

"Regardless of what you're doing, you're going to do it the right way," said former Bulldogs player LaVall Jordan, an Iowa assistant coach. "And you're going to do it to win."

Butler players rarely speak about winning. They cite physical and mental toughness, doing their job, and accountability. The Bulldogs' style of play has been characterized by a stout defense—a man-to-man style that casts such a net that it is nearly a zone—sure ball handling, and accurate outside shooting. Butler is perennially among the nation's leaders in fewest turnovers and most 3-point baskets.

Basketball has brought an attention to Butler that's impossible to quantify. Student applications among freshmen increased to 5,923 in 2008. A *ButlerRising* capital campaign exceeded its $125 million initial goal months ahead of the deadline. The Butler Way has been proposed as the title of the university's mission statement. Butler Way is the name of a street running through the leafy campus.

"A lot of places will pay to have a brand developed," Butler President Bobby Fong said. "This is something that in some ways has grown organically out of what we do. We had a fortunate turn of phrase that encapsulates it."

• • •

When Collier arrived as coach in 1989, the Bulldogs had managed five winning seasons out of 19 following Hinkle's retirement. To hold Hinkle's immediate successors, George Theofanis and Joe Sexson, accountable for that would be to ignore the fact that college basketball changed and Butler did not.

Theofanis conceded that the Bulldogs had "zero" recruiting budget when he was coach in the 1970s. That later increased to maybe $3,000, certainly not enough to be competitive in Division I, the highest level of the sport. Average home attendance was no more than 1,000.

"They were trying to eat dinner on a dime. It wasn't a fair fight," Collier said.

It wasn't in the best interests of the university, in the estimation of Geoffrey Bannister, Butler's New Zealand-born president. He championed a $1.5 million renovation of Hinkle Fieldhouse, and he hired Collier.

"The university had gone into a quiet, retiring phase where people had forgotten its name," Bannister said in a 1991 interview with the *Chicago Tribune*. "Basketball is such a big part of our history, and it was a way to remind people we were back at work."

Collier's first team was 6–22. Butler had a steep climb. From 1980 through 1991, the Bulldogs did not win a single game in the Midwestern Collegiate Conference Tournament. That's 0–12.

By the time Collier moved on to become Nebraska's coach a decade later, Butler had five 20-win seasons. His we-over-me approach changed the culture. His final game as Butler coach, in fact, changed the culture. Coincidentally, the opponent was again Florida.

In the NCAA Tournament on March 17, 2000, 12th-seeded Butler led fifth-seeded Florida by seven points with four minutes to play. The game went into overtime, and Butler twice went ahead by three points. But with Butler ahead by a point and eight seconds left, LaVall Jordan missed two free throws. Next, Florida's Mike Miller took a pass, faked left, and drove right. He lowered his shoulder, leaned forward, and flicked a 5-foot shot that hit the rim, teetered . . . and dropped in as time expired. Butler lost 69–68.

As devastating as the defeat was, the outcome galvanized the Bulldogs. It was perhaps the most important game played by Butler in the 2000s because the ripple effect was felt in every subsequent season by every player and every coach. The game is often rebroadcast on ESPN Classic. It *is* a classic.

Senior co-captains Mike Marshall and Andrew Graves were in unity on the message they delivered to teammates afterward. "This program needs to be better than where it stands today," Marshall told them.

The next season, Butler was better. In the summer of 2000, players stayed on campus and practiced together without coaches' supervision, something that had not been routine until then. Matta stayed for that one season, 2000–01, or long enough for Butler to score its first NCAA victory since 1962. Other coaches followed—Todd Lickliter and Brad Stevens—but the system remained intact. No one stood above the team.

"You're not playing for your coach. You're playing for those other four guys on the court or your 14 teammates," said Streicher, who enrolled without a basketball scholarship.

Not only upperclassmen instruct new Bulldogs. So do ex-Bulldogs. Marshall became the athletic director at Brebeuf Jesuit, an Indianapolis prep school. He played with Butler's incoming freshmen in the summer of 2008. They didn't absorb everything, Marshall said, but they tried.

"They're playing for all the guys whose shoulders they're standing on who came before them," he said.

Informal games at Hinkle Fieldhouse include Bulldogs, other college players home for the summer, Indiana Pacers, plus present and future NBA players.

One measure of how remarkable Butler's rise has been is that it did so without any of the eight hometown players who began the 2009–10 season in the NBA. Indianapolis-area products Jeff Teague, Courtney Lee, Eric Gordon, Greg Oden, Mike Conley, George Hill, Josh McRoberts, and Rodney Carney all played college basketball elsewhere.

That contributes to a persistent myth that Butler wins without talent. Beginning in 1997, the Bulldogs had five Horizon League players of the year: Jon Neuhouser (1997), Rylan Hainje (2002), Brandon Polk (2006), Mike Green (2008), and Matt Howard (2009). Two others, Thomas Jackson (2002) and A.J. Graves (2008), were preseason players of the year but finished behind teammates in the postseason. In 2009, the collective scoring of Gordon Hayward and Shelvin Mack made them the most productive pair of freshmen in the nation, and both played for the U.S. national team that won a gold medal in the Under-19 World Championship in New Zealand.

Butler has sought players who are selfless, skilled in dribbling, passing, and shooting, and sometimes overlooked by the sport's traditional powers. Not that Butler is incapable of developing NBA talent—Green has received a long looks as a free agent and Hayward could end up in the NBA someday—but that is not what Butler is targeting. Recruiting analyst Dave Telep said it is a waste to get caught up in rankings of Butler classes or players. Someone like Joel Cornette, a 6-foot-10 center who became a passer/defender for the 2003 Sweet Sixteen team, fit Butler's system.

"That is the only thing that is important to them," Telep said. "And that's why they're successful. Not because of where their guys are rated.

"They know their program better than anyone else. I think that is the brilliance of Butler basketball."

• • •

As long as the sport remains basketball and not track and field, those who run fastest and jump highest will not always prevail. A case study was one Las Vegas summer tournament featuring top teenage prospects. A Georgia team, the Atlanta Celtics, had three future NBA players: Dwight Howard, Josh Smith, and Randolph Morris.

The opponent was a collection of Indiana kids who knew basketball, but nobody knew them. The Indiana coach was former Butler star Billy Shepherd. It was a mismatch in the making. Instead, the Indiana team won.

"We had a Butler-type team out there," Shepherd recalled.

Among those on the roster was Campbell. He was among four small-town Hoosiers who played for Butler's 2007 Sweet Sixteen team. The combined enrollment of high schools attended by Campbell (Yorktown), Graves (White River Valley), Streicher (Washington, Ind.), and Crone (Frankfort) was about 2,500. That's smaller than five high schools in Indianapolis alone.

Basketball in the 21st century is more city than country. The Norman Rockwell image of a boy shooting at a hoop nailed to the barn is surely outdated. Or maybe not.

Graves shot at a backyard hoop used by three older brothers, two of whom played for Butler. Indiana University is about 35 miles from Switz City (pop. 311), but IU didn't come calling. Few recruiters did. They didn't check out the outskirts of Muncie, either. That's where Campbell honed his shooting touch in the driveway.

New Castle (pop. 18,347) has been a Bulldogs nursery. The town is home to the Indiana Basketball Hall of Fame and features the world's largest high school gym

Florida's Joakim Noah drives against Julian Betko in a 2007 NCAA regional game at St. Louis. The Gators' collection of future NBA players had to come from behind to beat Butler 65–57 (Butler University Archives).

(capacity 9,325). Five guards from New Castle—Darnell Archey, Brandon Miller, Bruce Horan, Zach Hahn, and Chase Stigall—came to Butler in the 2000s. Horan, Archey, and Miller rank Nos. 1, 3, and 4, respectively, on Butler's all-time list for 3-pointers made.

Butler has a tradition of small-town boys making good. Bobby Plump, as much as anyone, personifies Indiana basketball. It was his last-second shot that gave Milan a state championship before Indiana divided its tournament into four classes. Plump went on to become Butler's all-time leading scorer. His records were surpassed by another small-school star, Cloverdale's Chad Tucker, in the 1980s.

Cornette has asserted that Butler's environment—big-time basketball on a small campus—is unequaled. The student in the Dawg Pound painting himself blue or chanting slogans might sit next to a player in class. Crone liked being "a regular Joe" when eating lunch at Atherton Union or walking along the south mall.

"This program doesn't give you a big head or let you think you're bigger than you are," Crone said.

•••

A couple of incidents during the 2003 NCAA Tournament helped dramatize the Butler Way.

In the first, Joel Cornette crashed into the bench and ruined his shoes with 3 ½ minutes left in the Bulldogs' second-round game against Louisville at Birmingham, Ala. Reserve forward Rob Walls unhesitatingly shed his shoes and gave them to Cornette. Walls didn't score in the game. He didn't even play. Yet he undeniably influenced the Bulldogs' 79–71 victory that propelled them to the Sweet Sixteen.

"Joel ran into a water cooler, and I guess some juice or something got on his shoes," Walls said. "Somebody said, 'We need a 15! We need a 15!' That's what I wear, so I took mine off. It was a no-brainer.

"That's the Butler Way. That's just a small example of what the Butler Way is. It's good to be in the spotlight a little for getting my shoes off. But anybody on this team would have done that. It's great to be part of a program like that."

Five days later, the Bulldogs were in Albany, N.Y., for the East Regional. They lost to Oklahoma 65–54, ending their season and Cornette's college playing career. He and Brandon Miller collected their thoughts, addressed the media afterward, and walked silently through a back corridor toward the locker room.

A janitor fumbled a load of garbage, littering the floor with empty boxes. Cornette stopped to help clean up the mess. So did Miller. Picking up the boxes revealed more about them than any box score.

"The basketball side of this is over," Cornette said upon reaching the locker room. "But we'll always be a team."

•••

Players can't grow outsized egos in Indianapolis, a city tepid in its support of the Bulldogs. Butler lags behind not only the NFL's Colts and NBA's Pacers in media coverage but also IU and Purdue. Yet it's not as if the Bulldogs' achievements have gone unnoticed. They have often received more publicity nationally than locally.

ESPN2's *First Take* program devoted unprecedented TV coverage in the 2007–08 season, selecting Butler as its official mid-major team. The weekday program presented a weekly Butler element. The Bulldogs have made frequent appearances on one of the ESPN networks. Jon

LeCrone, commissioner of the Horizon League, acknowledged that there have been complaints from other league members about Butler being on TV so often. (Programming decisions are made by ESPN, not the league.)

Burke Magnus, a senior vice president at ESPN, said viewers want to see the best teams. He tells teams that if they win, they'll be on TV.

"We love these guys," Magnus said. "They're a great program in a league we have a great relationship with."

Collier has called athletics the front porch to the university for many people, and such national TV appearances are of incalculable value. School president Fong likes using the Butler Way because the players don't confine it to basketball. He said it is a reason the slogan is consistent with the university's mission to "educate the whole person."

The 2008–09 team included two engineering students, Hayward and Avery Jukes. Howard, Graves, and Streicher have been Academic All-Americans. The Butler Way can be as easily applied to the university's elite pharmacy and dance programs as to hoops.

"There's never been this grand design 20 years ago to arrive at this point," Collier said. "Because we really don't think we've arrived. We're trying to get better than where we are now."

• • •

Butler might have the only college basketball program whose arena is better known than the team itself. People talk about Hinkle Fieldhouse with a reverence associated with places of worship. When the court is lit by sunlight filtering in from tall windows above, nothing is missing but the choir.

Butler Fieldhouse—the name was changed in 1966 in honor of Hinkle—is a red-brick hangar-shaped edifice built for $800,000 in 1928. The campus was then in the Irvington section of Indianapolis, and the big barn on West 49th Street was the first building finished at the new location.

The fieldhouse does not have the amenities associated with modern arenas but remains one of the best places anywhere to play or watch basketball. It has good sightlines. It has character. It has history.

"It's like the place is alive almost, with all the stuff that it does, and how you feel when you walk in here," Cornette said.

During an opening to a documentary televised on ESPN Classic, sportscaster Bob Costas called the fieldhouse the basketball equivalent of baseball's Wrigley Field or Fenway Park. Scenes from *Hoosiers* were filmed at the fieldhouse. It is a National Historic Landmark.

One reason for the designation is that the building hasn't been used only for basketball. Seven American presidents—Herbert Hoover, Dwight Eisenhower, Richard Nixon, Gerald Ford, Bill Clinton, George H.W. Bush, and Barack Obama—have appeared there. During World War II, the U.S. military used the fieldhouse as a barracks.

The most renowned athlete ever to perform there wasn't even a basketball player. Jesse Owens tied the 60-yard world indoor record of 6.1 seconds at the Butler Relays on March 23, 1935, crashing into bales of straw after the finish line. The fieldhouse has held a Billy Graham Crusade and a Sonja Henie ice show. It has been home to four pro basketball teams. It has been the site of the first U.S.-Soviet basketball game, the first ABA All-Star Game, tennis matches played by Bill Tilden and Jack Kramer, the 1987 Pan American Games volleyball tournament, the circus, the rodeo, roller derby, bicycle racing, and graduation ceremonies.

It was illogical that a university with fewer than 2,000 students would build a 15,000-seat arena. But that's what Butler did after the Indiana High School Athletic Association promised to play the state tournament there for the next 10 years. Indeed, the state tourney was played there from 1928 to 1971, with a brief interruption during the war years, 1943–45. When originally constructed, the arena had the largest capacity of any basketball arena in the United States.

"It had all of us somewhat in awe," recalled John Wooden, the former UCLA coach who played for Martinsville High School in the 1928 state tournament, the first at Butler Fieldhouse. "The size, it was so huge, so different."

Oscar Robertson led Attucks High School to state championships there in 1955 and 1956. Attucks became the nation's first all-black team to win a state championship. Robertson called the fieldhouse "the ultimate."

Badly needed renovations were made to the fieldhouse in 1990. The decrepit basement locker room was upgraded, windows were replaced, seatbacks were added, offices were installed, the parking lot was repaved, and the surrounding area was landscaped. Capacity was reduced to 11,043. Additional changes lowered that to 10,000.

It is an old building, and yet it is timeless. The university has no impending plans to replace it. Modern architects modeled the $183 million Conseco Fieldhouse, home of the NBA's Indiana Pacers, after the structure. *Sports Illustrated*'s Luke Winn proposed that the sport go retro and hold NCAA Tournament first- and second-round games there.

Postgame activity at Hinkle Fieldhouse is unlike anything anywhere. The playing floor is not off limits. Small children swarm onto it, sometimes bouncing and shooting basketballs in mimicry of heroes they just watched. Butler players linger around the floor's perimeter, mingling with family and friends, and replying to questions from reporters.

Butler's bulldog mascot, Blue, is a popular figure at Hinkle Fieldhouse (Photo by John Fetcho).

Before there was an NCAA Tournament, bracketology, recruiting rankings, or fantasy sports, Indianapolis erected a monument symbolizing a passion for a game born in America and loved in Indiana. The Butler Bulldogs are giving new generations reason to come and be as enraptured as fans long before them.

The 1920s Teams:
Two National Championships

The 1920s were a golden age for sports. The heroes started with baseball slugger Babe Ruth but didn't end there. There was Red Grange in football, Paavo Nurmi in track and field, Jack Dempsey in boxing, Johnny Weissmuller in swimming, Bobby Jones in golf, and Bill Tilden in tennis.

It was a golden era for Butler basketball, too. Before there was an NCAA Tournament, or even a National Invitation Tournament, Butler won two national championships. One was won on the court, the other via balloting. Both are commemorated with banners inside Hinkle Fieldhouse.

David Thompson, a 1939 Butler graduate, and older brother Phil were water boys for Butler teams during the 1920s. They lived near the campus, and their family housed some athletes. They were so close to the program that when the campus moved, their family did, too, to a house on Hinseley Avenue near the new fieldhouse.

"Unless you were there, you just cannot fully appreciate how really good the 1920s teams and players were," Thompson wrote in a 1998 letter as the university observed its 100th year of basketball.

Oddly, in six seasons under coach Pat Page, the Bulldogs' poorest record was 11–7 in 1923–24—and that is the season they won their first national title.

In the early 1920s, the campus was on College Avenue, and the fieldhouse had not been built. The Bulldogs played home games in the Exposition Building at the state fairgrounds.

Butler was 16–4 in 1922–23, including victories over four Big Ten opponents: Wisconsin, Illinois, Purdue, and Chicago. That season ended with a 26–22 loss to Franklin College, a small school (enrollment 350) located 20 miles south of Indianapolis. Franklin was 17–0 and declared the 1923 national champion. (Kansas was 17–1 and chosen national champion by the Helms Foundation.)

Franklin featured most of the players, including Fuzzy Vandivier, from the Franklin Wonder Five that won Indiana high school championships in 1920, 1921, and 1922.

"They had Vandivier, and we could never stop him," Bob Nipper, a former Butler player, said in a 1991 interview.

Finally, though, the Bulldogs did stop him. They started the 1923–24 season with a 4–7 record, including a 35–19 loss at Franklin. But on the final day of the regular season, the Bulldogs ended Franklin's 36-game winning streak, 36–22. Although Butler's record was 7–7, beating Franklin was such an achievement that Butler was invited to the national Amateur Athletic Union Tournament in Kansas City, Mo.

The Bulldogs defeated Schooley-Woodstock 34–29, Hillyards 35–29, and Kansas State Teachers 40–21 to reach the championship game against the Kansas City Athletic Club, made up mostly of former University of Missouri players.

"I tell you, it was a big deal," Nipper said. "Coach Page had special meetings in the hotel and then took cabs over to the arena."

It was big enough to attract 10,000 fans to the championship game. Nipper scored the go-ahead basket, and Haldane Griggs added another after the center jump. Griggs scored 12 points, as Butler won 30–26 to claim the national championship.

Team captain Wally Middlesworth became Butler's first basketball All-American. Griggs scored 54 points and Paul Jones 33 in the four games, and both were selected to the all-tournament team. Of Griggs, the Kansas City Athletic Club's publication reported, "Such playing as he did was uncanny."

Griggs, a graduate of Arsenal Tech High School in Indianapolis, is a member of the Indiana Basketball Hall of Fame and charter member of Butler's Athletic Hall of Fame. He was one of the school's greatest all-around athletes. Griggs was on a state championship relay team in track and later played pro football and for a touring baseball team.

"He outjumped all the other centers," Thompson wrote in his letter. "If Griggs had been playing today, the motion picture *White Men Can't Jump* would never have been made."

The Bulldogs came back in 1924–25 with a 20–4 mark, setting a school record for victories that lasted 37 years. They won a rematch with the Kansas City Athletic Club, beat Notre Dame twice, and defeated Big Ten foes Iowa, Wisconsin, Illinois, and Chicago. Butler split with Franklin College and lost twice to Wabash College, 22–19 and 35–31. Wabash was a power in college basketball (they won the 1922 national championship), finishing 18–1 that season.

Hinkle, at age 27, succeeded Page as head coach in 1926. Hinkle's first two seasons produced 17–4 and 19–3 records, prefacing Butler's best team to date.

The Bulldogs opened the 1928–29 season in their new fieldhouse against Pittsburgh, which was coming off a 21–0 season and a Helms Foundation national championship. Pittsburgh was led by Doc Carlson, an innovative and charismatic coach. Carlson and Hinkle both ended up in the Naismith Basketball Hall of Fame.

Butler ended up beating Pittsburgh 35–33 and then edged Purdue 28–27 in the game in which the fieldhouse was dedicated. The Bulldogs were 14–1—losing only at Chicago, 24–21—before Notre Dame beat them by the same score, 24–21.

Two weeks later, in a rematch at South Bend, Butler crushed the Fighting Irish 35–16 to end the season with a 17–2 record. Future major league pitcher Oral Hildebrand scored 11 points to lead Butler. (Hildebrand played 10 seasons in the American League for the Cleveland Indians, St. Louis Browns, and New York Yankees. He had a lifetime record of 83–78, an earned run average of 4.35, and started a World Series game for the champion Yankees in 1939.)

Butler player William Bugg said Hinkle's strengths were in teaching fundamentals and handling players. Hildebrand could be moody.

"If something went bad out on the floor not to his liking, he (Hildebrand) just took off and went up into the bleachers and sat down," Bugg said in a 1989 interview. "Somebody said something about it to Tony, and Tony said, 'Just leave him alone. He'll change his mind. He'll be back down. He's just a kid. He'll get over it.' That's exactly what happened. Tony just didn't make a scene of it."

At the end of the season, the Bulldogs reasoned that they were state champions. Turns out they were more.

The Veterans Athletic Association of Philadelphia announced on December 16 that Butler was the national champion. The Bulldogs' strength of schedule and rout of Notre Dame were both persuasive.

Hinkle and team captain Frank White traveled to Philadelphia in February 1930 for a banquet honoring all of the 1929 champions. Riding on the train with them was Notre Dame football coach Knute Rockne.

Hinkle wasn't sure his national champs were his best team. Indeed, two years later, in 1930–31, he coached another 17–2 team. And then there was his nationally ranked team of 1949 and the Sweet Sixteen year of 1962.

"The best season? That's a tough one to ask a fella . . . it was 62 years ago," Hinkle said in a 1991 interview. "We had a lot of fine teams. It's tough to say, but it must have been. The voters said so!"

The 1948–49 Team (18–5):
National Recognition Again

The Associated Press introduced its college basketball poll on January 20, 1949. Butler made that inaugural Top 20 at No. 19 and later climbed as high as No. 11 for three weeks. The Bulldogs weren't ranked again for nearly 53 years—until December 25, 2001.

Coach Tony Hinkle's fourth postwar team was his best of the era. Buckshot O'Brien, in his junior year, broke the Butler career scoring record.

"The 1948–49 team was one of the finest working, best passing, most defensive-minded teams we've had at Butler," Hinkle said. "They didn't have the size, but they more than made up for its lack by other qualities—spirit, determination, and will to win."

Butler opened the season with road losses to Big Ten opponents Illinois (67–62) and Ohio State (60–48). The Fighting Illini later finished third in the NCAA Tournament. In the final AP poll, before postseason games, Illinois was No. 4, Butler 18th, and Ohio State 20th.

The Bulldogs' other losses—also on the road—were at Notre Dame (60–58), Cincinnati (49–44), and Case Western Reserve (66–61). In the middle of the season, Butler won 16 of 17 games, taking its own Hoosier Classic by defeating Indiana 64–55 and Purdue 47–43. Butler split with Notre Dame, Cincinnati, and Case Western Reserve, beating all three opponents in Indianapolis.

Butler received its most national recognition when playing in New York City and defeating Long Island 63–54, behind O'Brien's 20 points. He led the Bulldogs that season in scoring (15.8), field-goal percentage (.410), and free-throw percentage (.785).

"We really should have finished about 20–3," O'Brien said. "Two or three ballgames were ballgames that we never should have lost."

Jim Doyle (14) teamed with Buckshot O'Brien to give Butler a potent backcourt combination. The Bulldogs climbed into the national rankings in 1949 (Butler Univeresity Archives).

He and Jimmy Doyle formed a potent backcourt combination. That team included four others later inducted into the Indiana Basketball Hall of Fame: John Barrowcliff, who played in the National Industrial Basketball League; Marvin Wood, coach of champion Milan High School in the 1954 state tournament; Charles Maas, who won 80 percent of his games in 11 years coaching at Tech High School in Indianapolis; and Bill Shepherd, who coached sons Billy and Dave at Carmel High School. Shepherd's sons became Indiana's Mr. Basketball in 1968 and 1970, respectively, and Billy set scoring records at Butler.

Other letter winners were Dee Baker, Ralph Chapman, Robert Evans, Walter Fields, and Robert Mehl.

"Those guys were neat and wonderful to play with," O'Brien said. "I've always thought you're only as good as your team lets you be."

Butler was not among the 19 teams selected for postseason play. Eight were in the NCAA Tournament, and 12 were in the National Invitation Tournament. Kentucky, coached by Adolph Rupp, played in both, winning the NCAA Tournament and losing to Loyola of Chicago in an NIT quarterfinal.

The 1961–62 Team (22–6):
Sweet Debut in the NCAA

Before it became fashionable to evaluate basketball teams based on athleticism, the 1961–62 Bulldogs had one of the nation's best collections of athletes—even if the lineup averaged only 6-foot-1.

"We're easy to underrate," coach Tony Hinkle told *Time* magazine in the February 2, 1962 edition. The headline of the piece: "Fierce Little Butler."

The fierce five, all returning starters, were all from Indiana. Except for Indianapolis' Gerry Williams, they were all from small or midsized towns:

- Jeff Blue, a 6-foot-6 sophomore, who was called "this kangaroo from Bainbridge" by Hinkle. Blue averaged 15.9 points and set a school record with 12.0 rebounds.
- Tom Bowman, a 6-foot-4 junior from Martinsville who led the team in scoring at 18.4 and was team MVP. He was the Indiana Collegiate Conference player of the year.
- Ken Freeman, a 6-foot-3 senior from Mishawaka, was a three-sport athlete in football, basketball, and baseball.
- Gerry Williams, a 5-foot-8 junior with spectacular speed and leaping ability, set a state record of 6-foot-6 in the high jump—10 inches over his head—as a senior at Shortridge High School. He once won a conference 100-yard dash for the Bulldogs' track team. He averaged 15.9 points.
- Dick Haslam, a 5-foot-9 senior and a top golfer, led Crawfordsville to runner-up in the 1958 high school state basketball tournament.

A top reserve was Larry Shook, an all-conference football player for Butler's 1961 unbeaten squad and the Bulldogs' top hitter in baseball.

Jeff Blue, left, and Indiana Collegiate Conference player of the year Tom Bowman helped Butler upset Bowling Green and reach the Sweet Sixteen in 1962 (Butler University Archive).

The Bulldogs started the season 3–4, losing on the road at Illinois (82–72), Purdue (65–57), and DePauw (85–69). A 77–72 home loss to Michigan State stretched the Bulldogs' losing streak to three.

Then Butler won a school-record 13 in a row, highlighted by an 83–67 victory at Notre Dame in which Blue and Williams scored 26 points each. The Bulldogs' streak ended at Valparaiso, 60–52, but they won the next four and clinched the conference championship with an 87–86 overtime victory at Ball State.

At 20–5, Butler's record was good enough to get into the National Invitation Tournament, in which it had played in 1958 and 1959. Butler had never been to the NCAA Tournament.

"We were hoping to get an NIT bid when we got the NCAA Tournament bid," Bowman recalled. "Coach Hinkle said, 'When the NCAA invites you, you go.'"

The NCAA field included 25 teams, and Butler was assigned to play No. 8-ranked Bowling Green at Lexington, Ky. Bowling Green featured future NBA stars Nate Thurmond and Howard Komives and was coached by Harold Anderson, who was to join Hinkle in the Naismith Basketball Hall of Fame.

Butler's campus—which then had an undergraduate enrollment of 1,900—was abuzz with excitement. There were rallies for the team, and a contingent of fans followed the Bulldogs to Lexington. There was significant media coverage for at least some of the teams.

"They didn't say much about Butler," Bowman said.

The Bulldogs took a 56–53 lead over Bowling Green on Williams' two free throws with 33 seconds left, then held on for a 56–55 upset. The 6-foot-10 Thurmond had game highs in points (21) and rebounds (14), but it was Butler going to the Sweet 16.

In the Midwest Regional at Iowa City, Iowa, the Bulldogs were within a point at halftime, 37–36, against No. 3 Kentucky. The Wildcats, led Larry Pursiful's 26 points, pulled away in the second half for an 81–60 victory. Williams scored 20 and Blue 19 for Butler.

There was a third-place game in the regionals at the time, and Butler and Western Kentucky played with as much intensity as the advancing teams. In the closing seconds of overtime, Freeman sent a full-court pass to Williams, whose layup gave Butler an 87–86 victory. Williams scored 23, Bowman 21, and Blue 18.

Bowman, Blue, and Williams all returned the next season, but an ambitious schedule left Butler with a 1–6 start. Four of those losses were to No. 8 Illinois, Bradley, Purdue, and a UCLA team that reached its first Final Four under coach John Wooden. Butler closed the 1962–63 season by winning 10 of 11 games, for a record of 16–10. By the end, Hinkle said, Butler was just as good as the previous year's Sweet 16 team.

Blue, Bowman, and Williams all finished their careers with more than 1,200 points. Of the 13 players Hinkle selected for his all-time team, four from the 1961–62 season—Blue, Bowman, Williams, and Haslam—were on it.

They make the extra pass. They enjoy the game. You can tell when you watch them play. They're tough. They just want to have one more point than the opposition. They don't care who gets it.

— Bobby Plump, 1958 Butler graduate and former all-time scoring leader, talking about the way the Bulldogs play

The 2000–01 Team (24–8):
Agony Becomes Ecstasy

Archives show that Butler's 2000–01 season didn't start until November 18, 2000. More accurately, the Bulldogs started eight months earlier.

For that's when a 12th-seeded Butler team played fifth-seeded Florida in the NCAA Tournament at Winston-Salem, N.C. It was a game Butler could have won and should have won. There were curious calls and noncalls, especially at the end.

The Bulldogs led by seven points with four minutes to play, and yet the game went into overtime tied at 60. The Bulldogs twice led by three points in the extra period.

As Butler clung to a 68–67 lead in overtime, LaVall Jordan was fouled with eight seconds left. He was an 83 percent foul shooter, nearly automatic. He missed twice.

Future NBA forward Mike Miller of Florida took a pass on the left wing and headed toward the hoop. He avoided a collision with Butler's 6-foot-11 Scott Robisch and shot from five feet. The basketball crawled over the rim as the clock expired. Butler lost 69–68, ending a school-record 15-game winning streak. Florida advanced as far as the championship game—held in Indianapolis, coincidentally—but none of that mattered in the moment.

Jordan dropped to the floor, disappointment piled on top of grief. On Selection Sunday, the day NCAA pairings were announced, his great aunt, Jetha Jeffers, died. She was 87. Her health had worsened in the year after suffering a stroke. On Tuesday, after Butler's practice, Jordan went home to Albion, Mich., for the funeral of the woman who raised him.

"She made all the difference in the world in my life," Jordan said. "She raised me like I was her own. Basically, she was my mother throughout my childhood experience. She taught me everything."

Coach Barry Collier told Jordan to stay home, take some time, and lean on family. Jordan wanted basketball to divert his attention. He attended the funeral on Thursday, then rejoined his team late that night for the Friday game. The one-point loss ended what was "the worst week of my life," he said later.

Jordan was consoled by Collier and teammates after the game. No one mentioned the free throws, other than to declare that those did not lose the game. Collier, a devout Christian, told Jordan things happen for a reason, even if the reason is not easily discernable.

Jordan said he thought about his aunt throughout the game. In despair, he had the presence of mind to reason that he had another season, another shot.

"But she won't be back," he said. "That's a loss I'll have to deal with forever."

The loss gnawed at the Bulldogs. It always will. Collier has said watching a rebroadcast makes him sick, and he doesn't particularly like to relive the game or talk about it. Joel Cornette, then a freshman for the Bulldogs, said he is bitter because the officiating changed late in that game. Jordan was told by ESPN analyst Dick Vitale that the Bulldogs were wronged. Mike Tranghese, of the NCAA selection committee and watching the game on TV, was irate. He vowed not to allow the assigned officials to work another game in the tournament.

"I thought we got hosed," Cornette said. "It's tough to look at it that way, but it's the truth."

Jordan received letters of support and sympathy from strangers. Gradually, he healed. After all, he said, his aunt was a strong person. She would never quit, so he would never quit.

The Bulldogs never quit, either. They were resilient when Collier left Butler for Nebraska and Thad Matta was promoted from assistant to head coach. They were resilient during an August trip to Finland in which the itinerary kept changing and accommodations were far from luxurious.

The challenges enhanced team cohesiveness and allowed Matta dress rehearsals for the season to come. The Bulldogs went 6–1 on the trip, led by—who else?—Jordan. He averaged 14.6 points in the seven games.

● ● ●

With sophomore Brandon Miller newly eligible—he practiced against the Bulldogs the year before after transferring from Southwest

Missouri State—Butler was set to start the season with an unconventional lineup of three guards. There was the 6-foot-2 Jordan, 6-foot Miller and 5-foot-9 Jackson. The 6-foot-10 Cornette and 6-foot-6 Rylan Hainje would have to carry the load inside. One of the first men off the bench would be another sharpshooting guard, 6-foot-1 Darnell Archey.

Matta's stateside coaching debut was made easier by Miller's Butler playing debut. In the opener at Hinkle Fieldhouse, Miller scored 26 points—including 14 of 15 free throws—as the Bulldogs defeated Eastern Illinois 90–73. His pent-up energy was manifested by driving to the basket, diving to the floor, and taking charging fouls.

"I had played this game a thousand times in my head," Miller said. "To have my return come at Hinkle Fieldhouse is something special."

After beating Birmingham-Southern 71–62 and Ball State 71–48, the Bulldogs headed to Evansville with a chance to become 4–0 for the first time since 1986. Butler had a four-game winning streak in the instate series, and Evansville was 1–3 under Jim Crews, who played for Indiana's unbeaten 1976 championship team. One cause for concern was the condition of Miller, who dislocated his shoulder in practice but was cleared to play.

Butler twice built 10-point leads in the first half and was seemingly in control. But after the Purple Aces scored the final seven points of the half to trim the deficit to three, they continued surging in the second half to go ahead by seven.

Archey came off the bench and scored eight points over the closing three minutes, including a 3-pointer that cut Evansville's lead to 74–73 with 45 seconds left. With 3.3 seconds left, Butler had possession out of bounds, and Jackson lofted the ball to the front of the rim. Hainje leaped for what would have been a winning dunk, but the ball grazed off the top of his hands. Despite 56 percent shooting and Hainje's 23 points, the Bulldogs endured their first defeat by that 74–73 score.

"Our offense wasn't the problem. We didn't defend," Matta said.

Miller soldiered on for 28 minutes but was ineffective, finishing with two points, four fouls, and three turnovers. He postponed shoulder surgery until after the season and continued to play in pain.

The Bulldogs had an even more difficult assignment next at Indiana State. The 4–1 Sycamores were coming off a 59–58 upset of Indiana and featured a 14-game home winning streak in the Hulman Center at Terre Haute.

Butler and Indiana State exchanged leads 16 times, and the score was tied eight times. At the end of regulation, Jackson missed the potential game-winner, and Cornette's tip-in was off at the buzzer. At 78–78, the game went into overtime.

With the Bulldogs trailing 88–85 and 20 seconds remaining in OT, Miller's 3-pointer tied the score again. Indiana State guard Kelyn Block darted to the basket and scored with three seconds on the clock, giving the Sycamores a 90–88 victory.

Forward Matt Renn led the Sycamores with 28 points. Hainje scored 22 for Butler.

Butler lost despite shooting 55 percent. The Sycamores were even better, shooting 61 percent.

"That's a tough opponent, but 61 percent . . . it's hard to win a game like that," Matta said.

• • •

The Bulldogs had a 10-day break for semester exams before the first of four successive home games, beginning December 16 with a visit by UNC-Wilmington. After a couple of last-second losses by Butler, the 2–4 Seahawks appeared to be an antidote for any lingering ills. Besides, Butler had an 18-game winning streak at Hinkle Fieldhouse.

But after shooting so accurately at Evansville and Indiana State, the Bulldogs couldn't locate the hoop in their own gym. Four guards—Jordan, Jackson, Miller, and Archey—were a collective 6-of-25. Butler defended well, committed a season-low eight turnovers, and didn't allow a free throw until 3.5 seconds remained. Yet the Bulldogs' late-game luck continued to be bad.

With the shot clock expiring and score tied, Wilmington's Barron Thelmon sank a 30-footer with 16 seconds left. The Seahawks' only two free throws padded the final margin to 53–48.

"Teams always hit shots like that against us," Jordan said. "It's like we now have a target on our shirts."

The Bulldogs were so distraught that they called a players-only meeting afterward. Two days after the Wilmington loss, they found relief.

Tennessee-Martin's team bus was caught in Indianapolis traffic during a winter storm, arriving a half-hour late. The Bulldogs didn't delay. They jumped to a 14-point lead in the opening minutes. Jordan scored 21 points, and Butler completed a 77–48 blowout.

"I liked our team's energy," Matta said.

There was plenty to like two days later in another blowout. True, Santa Clara was coming off the most lopsided defeat in its history, losing at Purdue 98–52. But neither the Broncos nor the Bulldogs could account for Butler's 59 percent shooting—17-of-29—from the 3-point arc.

"I'm not sure where that comes from," Matta said, "but I'll take it."

In their 84–60 victory, the Bulldogs broke the school record of 14 3-pointers, set February 4, 1993, against Detroit. Miller and Archey made five 3s each and Jackson four. Miller didn't miss from the arc. Archey started the game on the bench, then couldn't wait to play after his teammates starting bombing away. Jordan said he thought Archey made more than five 3s.

"He was always open," Jordan said.

Butler closed its four-game, eight-day homestand against Texas Christian, which brought an 8–2 record and nation-leading 101-point average to Indianapolis.

Butler produced the more explosive offensive, bolting ahead 10–0 en route to a 15-point lead in the first half. The Bulldogs led by 16 in the second half of an 86–73 victory.

The perimeter trio of Jackson (19 points), Jordan (18), and Miller (10) had a collective 12 assists and displayed steady ball handling. Jackson was "phenomenal," Matta said.

• • •

The post-Christmas game in Tucson, Ariz., was going to be challenging. The Bulldogs were paired in the Fiesta Bowl Classic against 12th-ranked Arizona, the preseason No. 1 team that had a 30-0 record in its own tournament. The Wildcats' roster included guard Jason Gardner, a former Indiana Mr. Basketball from Indianapolis, and five future NBA draft picks—Gilbert Arenas, Richard Jefferson, Loren Woods, Michael Wright, and Luke Walton.

As Butler prepared for the trip, the opponent loomed as the least of its problems. Matta received a phone call informing him that travel would be impossible because a flight was canceled. New arrangements were hastily made, so the team took a bus to Cincinnati and flights from there to Minneapolis and Phoenix. About half the team found transportation to Tucson.

Matta was eager to get to the Bulldogs' destination. He turned to Jackson and said, "Let's get out of here."

Jackson asked his coach if he had heard what happened. What now?

"The van's on fire," Jackson replied, never changing expression.

The Bulldogs paid $300 to rent a limousine to take the rest of the team the rest of the way. The Tucson resort where they lodged was a welcome relief, although Hainje couldn't enjoy it. He was hospitalized with flu-like symptoms and put on intravenous fluids.

Yet these Bulldogs were not easily rattled, not even when falling behind Arizona by 11 late in the first half. They closed to within 32–28 by halftime and led on three occasions in the second half. Arizona led 62–60 before the 7-foot-1 Woods scored six points during a 10–0 spurt that closed out a 72–60 victory.

"We're not afraid of anybody," said Hainje, who scored 18 points. "We come into every game thinking we're going to win it."

Coach Lute Olson and the Arizona players spoke respectfully about the Bulldogs afterward, although Matta said he wasn't seeking a moral victory.

"They asked if we were surprised, but I told them that this was Butler basketball, and we played the way that we wanted to," Matta said.

In the consolation game against Louisiana-Lafayette, former New Castle teammates Miller and Archey combined for eight of the Bulldogs' 10 3-pointers in a 74–63 victory. Miller equaled his career high of five 3s and scored 23 points.

The Bulldogs began the new year with a 72–56 victory over Lipscomb, a new NCAA Division I team from Nashville, Tenn. Archey scored a career-high 22 points, featuring one stretch in which he sank three 3-pointers in little more than a minute. He salvaged what had been an uncharacteristic day.

The Bulldogs were so unlike themselves that the normally silent Jackson was assessed a technical foul. During the first timeout after halftime, Matta shouted at his players. He conceded that playing seven games in 19 days, including the Arizona trip, might have affected them.

"For the first time this year, we weren't ready to play," Jackson said.

That would have to change as the Bulldogs prepared to begin defense of their Midwestern Collegiate Conference title.

● ● ●

Deflating finishes continued to dog the Dawgs when they started MCC play against Wright State at Dayton, Ohio. But Butler could blame beginnings, not endings, for a 62–61 loss to the Raiders.

The Bulldogs fell behind 13–0 in the first four minutes of the first half. They recovered to go ahead 34–30 at halftime, then saw Wright State score the first 14 points of the second half. Butler again reclaimed the lead but couldn't keep it.

Butler scored one point over the closing 2½ minutes, largely because Jackson had to sit out with a two-inch gash over his left eye. Hainje had struck him with an errant elbow.

With Butler ahead 61–60, Hainje missed a free throw with 30 seconds left. That gave the Raiders a chance, and they capitalized. Kevin Melson's 12-foot baseline floater over Jordan won it for Wright State.

"It's tough to come back from these holes, but we did, only to give it back," Matta said. "I can't believe it."

The Bulldogs' record sputtered to 8–5. Their next two were at home but against two of the MCC's best, Cleveland State and Detroit.

Cleveland State was coached by 66-year-old Rollie Massimino, whose legacy was secured when he guided underdog Villanova to a 66–64 victory over Georgetown in the 1985 NCAA championship game.

This was one of Massimino's best Cleveland State teams, and it had won five in a row.

The Bulldogs shot 26 percent in the first half but wouldn't let Cleveland State assert control. Massimino was assessed a technical foul with 10 minutes left, and his exasperation peaked when Butler's lead grew to 10 points. He benched his starters for the final two minutes, a move opposed by star Theo Dixon, who stomped off the court and declined to comment. There were at least two heated confrontations between Cleveland State and Butler players.

"They stepped it up in the last 10 minutes, and we didn't respond," Massimino said. "The game got out of hand down the stretch."

Jackson led the balanced Bulldogs with 18 points and nine assists. It was the Vikings' seventh straight loss at Hinkle Fieldhouse and the Bulldogs' 10th straight conference victory there.

Detroit's visit to Indianapolis represented a rematch of the previous two MCC championship games, and Detroit/Butler was the best rivalry going in the conference. Detroit's Rashad Phillips, a 5-foot-10 guard, had already been MCC player of the year once and was on his way to winning that award again.

Detroit brought out the best in the Bulldogs, and specifically in Jordan, a Michigan native. Jordan scored 14 of Butler's first 16 points, including one 3-pointer from 35 feet. He finished with a modest 21 points but had done enough damage early. Phillips was limited to 13 on 5-of-13 shooting.

Detroit coach Perry Watson complained that the Titans' guards, Phillips and future NBA player Willie Green, were horrible and allowed too many open looks. Butler shot 11-of-22 on 3-pointers.

"We made that rim look the size of the ocean," Watson said.

The Bulldogs next headed not to the ocean but past Lake Michigan for a two-game swing in Wisconsin. Jordan had never lost in nine games in Wisconsin during his college career.

The Bulldogs' 27 percent shooting left them trailing Wisconsin-Milwaukee by seven at halftime. Their 65 percent accuracy in the second half and rebounding superiority allowed them to pull away to a 60–51 victory.

In the second half, Hainje and Cornette combined to shoot 9-of-9 and collect eight rebounds. One of Cornette's dunks was a rebound in which he soared high to follow a miss by Miller.

"I was stunned for a minute," Hainje said. "I sat back and said, 'Did he just do that?' It was that impressive."

Jackson, who had the flu, was limited to one basket and six points.

Two days later, at Green Bay, the Bulldogs played one of the most peculiar games of this or any other season. At Brown County Arena, Butler started poorly . . . and proceeded to make it worse. Hainje was assessed a technical foul in the opening minutes. Green Bay led by 19 points at the half and expanded that to 29 with 12 minutes left. The Bulldogs went nine minutes in the second half without a field goal.

That drought was followed by a flood. The Bulldogs stayed afloat with outrageous 3-point shooting, chopping away at the 49–20 gap. Miller and Archey combined to sink nine 3s in those final 12 minutes, some from nearly 30 feet.

Yet it was hard to make headway, especially with such a makeshift lineup: Miller, Archey, and first-year players Ben Grunst, Rob Walls, and Duane Lightfoot Jr. With less than eight minutes left, Green Bay led 61–35.

The Bulldogs scored the next 12 points to creep to within 61–47. But by the time 2½ minutes remained, they trailed by 18. With less than 50 seconds left, they were down by 10. Even when the scoreboard made it look hopeless, Miller was defiant.

"We're winning this game!" he shouted in the huddle as his coaches watched in bemusement.

The finish went thusly:
- 2:28 left: Archey 3-pointer, 65–50
- 2:13: Walls fast-break dunk, 65–52
- 1:27: Miller 3-pointer, 65–55
- 1:10: two free throws by Green Bay's DeVan Blanks, 67–55
- 58 seconds: Miller layup, 67–57
- 48 seconds: two missed free throws by Green Bay's Chris Sager
- 44 seconds: Miller 3-pointer, 67–60
- 32 seconds: Archey 3-pointer, 67–63
- 27 seconds: one of two free throws made by Green Bay's Greg Monfre, 68–63
- 18 seconds: Lightfoot layup, 68–65
- 18 seconds: one of two free throws made by Green Bay's Blanks, 69–65
- 12 seconds: Archey 3-pointer, 69–68

Archey fouled out with nine seconds left, trying to stop the clock. Blanks missed two more free throws—Green Bay's eighth and ninth misses of the final three minutes—to leave an opening for Butler. Miller dribbled the length of the floor and floated through the lane for a scoop shot. But the weary Bulldog was foiled by a leg cramp, and he missed. Green Bay held on for a 69–68 victory.

"They went down like the champions they are, firing all their guns at the end," Green Bay coach Mike Heideman said.

Because of cramps, Miller had to be carried from the arena. Green Bay fans applauded respectfully, then walked onto the floor to stand on the spots where Miller and Archey launched long-range missiles.

Miller scored 20 of his 24 points in the second half, and Archey finished with 17. Miller said there was no satisfaction in coming so close.

"We came here to do a job, and we didn't do it," he said. "If you're happy with this, there's something wrong with you."

A Butler victory would have represented one of the greatest comebacks in college basketball history. The NCAA record for largest deficit overcome is 32 points: Duke trailed Tulane 54–22 before winning 74–72 in the Dixie Classic on December 30, 1950.

The record that counted for Butler: 11–6. Of its six losses, five had come by a collective 10 points.

•••

Butler's team had come to resemble an old Indiana homestead— rich farmland on the outside but few treasures inside. Scott Robisch's presence helped the Bulldogs' impoverished inside.

The 6-foot-11 Robisch, of Springfield, Ill., underwent knee surgery on November 9 and hadn't played all season. He endured so many injuries that this was his fifth year of college, and the NCAA eventually awarded him a sixth year of eligibility. In 1996–97, at Oklahoma State, he missed the entire year with a broken hand. The next year he developed a stress fracture after just six games. He played nine more games for the Cowboys before transferring to Butler in January 1999.

Robisch played 24 games in the Bulldogs' run to the 2000 NCAA Tournament, starting the final 15. He thus became the third member of his family to play in the NCAA Tournament. His brother, Brett, did so for Oklahoma State in 1998. His father, Dave, helped Kansas reach the 1971 Final Four.

Robisch and Cornette made sure there was no post-Green Bay demise. Their inside force contributed to a 76–69 victory over Illinois-Chicago at Hinkle Fieldhouse.

Robisch's shooting was off—he was 2-of-8—but he collected six points and six rebounds in 17 minutes. He conceded he was nervous about coming back from a knee injury.

"It definitely helps to have another big body in there," he said. "When I'm in there, we get more into our natural flow. It just adds another weapon."

UIC coach Jimmy Collins complained that the Flames allowed Cornette to have the game of his life: 12 points, six rebounds, five assists, and one highlight-reel play. Late in the half, Miller sent a pass that appeared headed out of bounds. Cornette leaped to guide the ball through the hoop and elicited a loud response from the crowd.

Jackson scored 21 points but injured his knee and ankle late in the game. He didn't practice the next day, requiring pain killers and ice treatments. By the Saturday game against Loyola, Jackson was his usual self. Well, except for a new 'do. His mop was matted. His style wasn't a retro Afro, but "a little 'fro," he said.

"It's a new look for me," Jackson said. "I had to do something different."

Matta would have let him wear a wig if he could produce as he did against Loyola. To score 25 points on 10 shots from the field is about as efficient as a point guard can be. He tied his career high and added four assists in a 71–57 victory over the Ramblers. It was Butler's 13th consecutive home conference victory.

With January nearly done, the Bulldogs weren't done with the state of Wisconsin. All they needed to complete the tour were stops in Lake Geneva, Door County, and the Wisconsin Dells. It would be no vacation in Madison, where the Bulldogs were facing Wisconsin's 10th-ranked Badgers. This was Butler's fifth game in 11 days, including visits to Milwaukee and Green Bay.

Matta scheduled Wisconsin after plans for a neutral-court game against Kentucky in Cincinnati fell through. The Badgers were always looking for games, Matta said, because no one wants to play them. Similarly, no one wanted to play Butler.

Wisconsin led the NCAA in scoring defense (56.4) and had won 11 straight at its year-old Kohl Center, as well as 20 straight nonconference home games. Wisconsin was fourth in Ratings Percentage Index—RPI is a formula used to help select and seed the NCAA Tournament field—and Butler 67th.

Wisconsin, under interim coach Brad Soderberg, had a size advantage but didn't fully exploit it against the Bulldogs. Butler, an eight-point underdog, led by seven points before Wisconsin evened the halftime score at 20.

"The thing we talked to our guys about was not to crack, not to break," Matta said. "They're such a good team, they get the lead on you, and it's hard to get it back."

The reverse occurred. Cornette dunked twice early in the second half, and Butler never trailed over the final 18 minutes. Butler shot 65 percent in the second half. With the Bulldogs ahead by four and less than eight minutes left, Miller and Jackson sank successive 3-pointers to expand the margin to 47–37. Miller scored 17 and Jackson 14 in

Butler's 58–44 victory over a team that reached the Final Four only 10 months before.

Wisconsin became the highest-ranked team beaten by Butler since a 79–64 upset of No. 3 Michigan on December 22, 1965, at Indianapolis.

If there was one play that typified Butler's night, it was by Miller. Caught in a belly-to-belly confrontation with Wisconsin defensive ace Mike Kelley, Miller tried to alert the official that he was being hand-checked. Receiving no satisfaction, and with the shot clock winding down, Miller backed up. And sank a 25-foot 3-pointer.

"I thought, 'Can I get by him, or do I just shoot it from here?'" Miller said. "I know he's a great defensive player, so my best look might have been just to shoot the ball. Lucky for me, it went in."

Inside the locker room afterward, Butler's players were delighted but not delirious. The Bulldogs' coaches were confident they could win, even if they didn't say so publicly. After so many close losses, they made sure.

"It feels good to finally get one," Matta said.

Soderberg said he was "embarrassed" by the outcome. He wasn't necessarily shocked. He feared the smaller Bulldogs would spread the floor and use their superior quickness.

"Sometimes the other team just does some things that you don't have an answer for," Soderberg said. "We didn't have anyone to defend Jackson."

• • •

Robisch's joy in victory was muted afterward. He had received news of the January 27 crash of an airplane carrying those affiliated with Oklahoma State's basketball program. Among the 10 dead were two players and six staffers and broadcasters connected to the team. The plane went down about 40 miles east of Denver while returning from a game in Boulder, Colo.

Robisch had been on that plane. He knew the pilot. He was a close friend of one of the victims.

"It definitely puts it all in perspective," Robisch said. "It just makes you focus on things. It makes you want to live your life right and dedicate yourself to doing things better. Life goes on, and you just have to make the most out of opportunities like we had tonight."

• • •

Matta didn't want the Bulldogs to be sabotaged by success. So he posted a list of past Butler victories over nationally ranked opponents. The next games were usually losses.

The Bulldogs were attentive to the chart, and they followed the Wisconsin upset by beating Wright State 59–48 before a national TV audience and season-high 8,277 at Hinkle Fieldhouse.

"Coach left it up to us to take care of business, and that's what we did," said Jackson, who led Butler with 15 points.

The victory avenged the Bulldogs' one-point loss at Wright State and pulled them, at 6–2, within a half game of first-place Cleveland State.

Cornette delivered a complete game: 14 points, 12 rebounds, four blocked shots, and three steals. Not to be outdone, Hainje excited the crowd with a dunk.

Butler headed on the road to face the two other conference contenders, Detroit and Cleveland State.

Detroit, where TV analyst Dick Vitale once coached, played at 8,295-seat Calihan Hall. Calihan, built in 1952, was the second-oldest arena in the conference (after Hinkle Fieldhouse) and did not resemble the nondescript multipurpose arenas elsewhere in the conference.

The Titans hadn't lost at home since January 16, 1999, when Butler broke a 23-game winning streak. Detroit took a 27-game home winning streak into this one. Successive 3-pointers by Archey put the Bulldogs ahead 53–50 with 6:22 left, but they didn't score again from the field until 22 seconds remained. With the Bulldogs behind 60–57, Hainje missed a layup that would have cut it to one with barely a minute to play.

As good as Butler was on 3-pointers, Detroit was better on 3-footers. The Titans punctured Butler's defense for eight second-half inside baskets—four of them dunks—and won 68–63. Butler fell to 0–6 in games decided by five or fewer points.

"When you come into this place, you want to be in position to win, and I thought we were there," Matta said.

There was a confrontation between Hainje and a Detroit fan afterward. Assistant coach Mike Marshall intervened, and Hainje walked away.

Detroit's guards, Willie Green and Rashad Phillips, scored 20 and 16 points, respectively. Phillips defended effectively against Jackson and, with 1,998 points, climbed into second place on the school's all-time scoring list.

A season-high crowd of 7,333 turned out at Cleveland State for one of its biggest home games since 1986, the year the Vikings beat Indiana 83–79 in the NCAA Tournament. The Vikings had a seven-game winning streak and were 10–1 at home.

Butler trailed by 10 in the first half but led most of the second half. Miller's 3-pointer gave the Bulldogs a 56–50 lead that they couldn't hold. Theo Dixon scored the next six points for Cleveland State—two on free throws with 33 seconds left—and tied the score at 56.

The Bulldogs called timeout but couldn't set up a high-percentage shot. With the clock running out, and Miller well behind the arc, he let it go. Three points. To punctuate his 24-footer, he raised a finger to his lips, signaling he had silenced the crowd.

"I wish that I wouldn't react like that," Miller said. "I wish I could just be calm. But I get caught up in the game, and I show my emotions when I play."

The Bulldogs caught up in the standings. There was a virtual tie, with Cleveland State 8–3 and Butler and Detroit both 7–3.

The Bulldogs had finally won a close one. Matta fretted that they were jinxed and turned to assistant coach Todd Lickliter and told him Cleveland State would send it into overtime with a tying 3-pointer. That did not happen.

"That felt good to hear our guys say, 'Hey, we got one,'" Matta said.

Back at Hinkle Fieldhouse, the Bulldogs beat Milwaukee and Green Bay, extending their MCC home winning streak to 16 and staying on a path toward a repeat regular-season championship.

Surprisingly, it was Milwaukee—loser of 16 in a row to Butler—that supplied the drama. Butler frittered away a 12–0 lead. Milwaukee led by seven points in the second half and by four with less than one minute left.

Jordan drove for a layup, trimming the Panthers' margin to 64–62 with 54 seconds on the clock. After Milwaukee's Clay Tucker missed two free throws, Miller made two, tying the score at 64. Tucker had a chance to win for Milwaukee but missed a 12-footer over Jordan.

Hainje started the overtime with a rebound basket, and the Bulldogs never trailed again. He had been urged to keep his cool, and he did.

Moreover, Hainje scored a season-high 26 points in Butler's 80–75 victory.

Hainje left for the locker room late in the first half to have a sprained ankle taped. He agonized after twice missing tap-ins following missed Butler free throws. He merely shook his head at the end of OT when he was wrapped up by Tucker as Matta pleaded for an intentional foul call.

"I was focused, I think, more than I've been in most games," Hainje said. "I remember Coach always telling me, 'Just go to the next play.' That's what I try do to, just keep moving on.

Butler followed up against Green Bay in a 78–52 blowout that was bittersweet. It was the last game at Hinkle Fieldhouse for Jordan, a senior whose Bulldogs were 52–5 at home in his career. He played infrequently as a freshman, started four games as a sophomore, and became a leader as a junior. As a senior, he guarded the opponents' top scorers and made many of Butler's biggest baskets.

"He's molded these guys, as he's been molded," Matta said. "That's what this program—that's what this university,—is all about. He has risen in his four years to the top of this university."

At the end of the game, Jordan raised his arms to acknowledge an ovation from the crowd of 7,566. He walked to center court, kneeled, and kissed the Bulldog painted there. If ever there was a kiss of true love, that was it.

"This is a great place to play," Jordan said. "It's going to be tough not to come back to Hinkle."

At 9–3, Butler was atop the MCC standings. The Bulldogs wanted to finish things right for Jordan. The Butler Way.

"We knew this was his last game, and we wanted him to go out with a bang," Jackson said. "He did."

• • •

Butler closed the schedule at Loyola and UIC. Loyola's home was the Gentile Center, built in 1996 along Lake Michigan and across a walkway from the university's historic Alumni Gym. The Ramblers played in Alumni Gym, built in 1923, when they won the NCAA championship in 1963—one year before the Civil Rights Act passed—and became the first predominantly black team to be champion.

Loyola's story was every bit as compelling as that of Texas Western, whose all-black team beat all-white Kentucky for the 1966 NCAA title.

Regrettably, Loyola's achievement is not as well known as that of Texas Western, whose season was chronicled in the movie *Glory Road*.

Loyola was far removed from its glory days. Against Butler, the Ramblers played without confidence, were short on close-in shots, made unforced turnovers, and lost their fifth straight. Jordan scored a season-high 23 points in a 66–62 victory. He also guarded an opponent six inches taller, 6-foot-8 Schin Kerr.

After going 0–6 in games decided by five or fewer points, Butler had three such victories in four games. The Bulldogs remained tied for first with Detroit heading to the final day.

"I don't know what Saturday is going to bring," Matta said, "but I know this: it's on us now."

Butler was assured of at least a co-championship when Detroit lost at Milwaukee 80–69. There was reason to believe the Bulldogs—ranked 40th in RPI—might get into the NCAA Tournament without winning the MCC tourney. To do that, they would have to secure an MCC title, and to do that, they would have to beat UIC.

The Bulldogs trailed UIC by six points in the first half. After Miller's 3-pointer put them ahead 52–49 midway through the second half, they never trailed again—and never were out of danger. Matta, who rarely quarreled with officials, disputed calls and once tore off his jacket and flung it in disgust.

The score was tied at 59 and 61. Hainje's three-point play lifted the Bulldogs ahead 66–61, but they missed five free throws in the final 35 seconds. Nothing was coming easily, as nothing had come easily all season.

A 3-pointer brought the Flames to within 67–66 with 11 seconds on the clock. Jackson made the second of two free throws, and it was 68–66. As time expired, UIC's Jon-Pierre Mitchom shot a 3-pointer. It was on line but rimmed off.

"Too close for me," Matta said.

Butler (20–7) had won another MCC title and extended its school-record streak of 20-win seasons to five. Improbably, the offensive force was Cornette, whose 20 points were 12 more than his average and six more than his previous high. The Bulldogs' celebration started on the court and continued in the locker room. Yet since a return to the NCAA Tournament was not assured, their response was muted.

"We persevered," Matta said. "As this team's done all year long, we showed great toughness. As I told them in the locker room, our backs were to the wall two weeks ago when we walked out of Detroit."

• • •

Matta was the conference's coach of the year in his first season after succeeding Collier. Wright State's Jesse Deister was selected newcomer of the year over Miller. Jackson made the all-MCC first team, but Jordan was shunted to the second team. Inexplicably, Jordan wasn't chosen to the all-defensive team, which included three of his teammates: Jackson, Cornette, and Hainje.

"I know this: to a man on our team, not one guy would trade in an individual honor for a conference championship," Matta said. "That's the beauty of our guys and why we've been successful."

The MCC chose its NCAA representative from a tournament, as was customary everywhere except the Ivy League, which used final standings. The tourney site was predetermined, so whichever team happened to be at home in a given year had an advantage. Surprisingly, only once in 21 previous MCC tournaments had the championship been won by the host school (Dayton in 1990).

Playing host in 2001 was Wright State, a more-than-capable team—its record was 17–10—and a No. 4 seed. If the top-seeded Bulldogs won their quarterfinal against Loyola, they likely would have to play the host Raiders in a semifinal.

Wright State was pushed by No. 5-seeded Milwaukee but survived 64–63 on Deister's 3-pointer with 36 seconds left.

Butler eliminated drama in the next quarterfinal, crushing Loyola 78–52. The Bulldogs led by five at halftime and started the second half on a 23–5 binge, featuring Archey's 10 points in the first four minutes. Wright State, 14–2 at the Nutter Center, was next.

"Wright State is a tough place to play, and we learned that early in the season," Cornette said. "But I think we've come a long way. I think we're prepared for what's going on."

The Butler/Wright State semifinal had a sub-plot. The Raiders were coached by 35-year-old Ed Schilling. His father, Ed Sr., played for coach Tony Hinkle and set a Butler scoring record in 1965–66. Before Wright State, the younger Schilling coached at two Indiana high schools, Western Boone and Logansport, and was on John Calipari's staffs at the University of Massachusetts and the New Jersey Nets.

A clamorous crowd of 6,181 gathered in Dayton in expectation of seeing the Raiders dispatch Butler.

The Bulldogs trailed by four at halftime but went ahead midway through the second half when Jackson assisted on three successive field goals. As they strained to protect their lead, Matta called timeout and told the players it was "Thomas time."

In the closing four minutes, Jackson maneuvered along the baseline for two reverse layups to blunt Wright State's rally. On the second sequence, he drove to the hoop and missed, but Jordan snatched the rebound. The 5-foot-9 Jackson then slipped through again to score.

Jackson and Cornette reversed roles, with Jackson scoring inside and Cornette outside. Cornette, a 39 percent foul shooter who heard "air ball" chants after missing the rim twice in the first half, made five straight free throws. His 16 points included a rim-hanging dunk in the last minute.

"I really think we have put ourselves in that position to get an at-large," Matta said. "I don't think these guys want an at-large, but we'll take an at-large."

Jordan finished a 17-point game with four straight free throws in the final minute of Butler's 66–58 victory over Wright State. He wasn't contemplating anything other than a championship. Jordan wanted a third ring so he would have as many as assistant coach Mike Marshall.

For the third straight year, the final was Detroit vs. Butler. The No. 2-seeded Titans won their semifinal over Cleveland State 91–81. Phillips scored 35 points, becoming Detroit's all-time leader, and set a tournament record with nine 3-pointers.

Rashad Phillips was essentially the MCC's answer to The Answer, Allen Iverson. Like his NBA counterpart, Phillips was small but quick, braided his hair, wore tattoos, wrote rap music, and featured the No. 3 jersey. He was called the "Excitin' Titan." He was "Jackie Chan in Nikes," according to former Butler coach Barry Collier.

The Bulldogs had been effective against Phillips—he averaged 12.2 points in four previous meetings against them—but had no assurance of duplicating that. Their only loss in the previous 12 games had been at Detroit, and Phillips was effective in guarding Jackson.

"I think everyone knows this matchup is going to be Butler against Rashad," Cornette said. "And that's no knock on their players. It's just that he does so much."

That is, Phillips did so much when he was not being guarded by LaVall Jordan.

In the championship game, the Bulldogs built a 29–19 halftime lead—a large margin for Detroit to overcome against a defensive-minded opponent. Nonetheless, the Titans did pull to within 31–28. But after Butler went on a 9–0 run to go ahead by 12, fewer than eight minutes remained. The issue was settled.

The Bulldogs went on to win 53–38, securing a fourth tournament title in five years. They held Detroit to 24 percent shooting in its lowest output of a 22–10 season.

When Butler students rushed the Nutter Center court to celebrate, they could have raised Matta onto their shoulders. After all, Matta's 23rd victory in his first season tied a record for the school's 109-year-old basketball program. The students could have lifted Hainje, who had 20 points, 11 rebounds, and multiple floor burns.

The students instead elevated Jordan. Hey, those kids attended college in Indiana. They understood basketball. They understood the influence Jordan had went beyond the 10 points he scored. Jordan, the tournament MVP, held Phillips to 11 points on 4-of-15 shooting. Jordan was on top of the heap and on top of the world.

"That was wonderful," Jordan said. "To cap off my senior year with another ring, it was just great. We've been hungry for this all year, after a tough loss in the first round. We've been wanting to get back to the NCAAs."

Matta waited his turn to cut down the Nutter net. He played to the cameras, whooped it up with his players, and climbed slowly down the ladder. Not that he ever really came down. He said the moment was exactly as he had dreamt it.

"This net is going in my office at home," he said, choking back emotions. "So I can look at it every single day. There's a long story that goes with this piece of net. It's the greatest moment of my life."

Detroit coach Perry Watson pointed not to a basket or defensive play that ignited Butler, but a loose-ball scrum won by Hainje. That showed that the Bulldogs were unwilling to be separated from a championship trophy.

"For us," Hainje said, "that's the Butler Way."

•••

Players, coaches, family, fans, and media gathered at Matta's home to watch the NCAA selection show. Players cheered even before Butler's pairing was announced, in apparent relief that they wouldn't be shipped to Boise, Idaho.

Butler was awarded a No. 10 seed—its highest ever—and placed opposite No. 7 seed Wake Forest in a Midwest Regional game in Kansas City, Mo. Butler could have been seeded higher, given its No. 29 standing in RPI. Butler players noticed that the winner likely would play No. 2 seed Arizona in the second round.

"We want to play them again. We've got a lot to prove," Hainje said.

Considering the Bulldogs had not won in the NCAA Tournament since 1962, they were in no position to look ahead. Coincidentally, the Bulldogs played in the first round the year before at Winston-Salem, the campus home of Wake Forest.

Matta said the Demon Deacons were defensive-minded, so the game would be "a lot like playing ourselves."

Indeed, the similarities between Wake Forest and Butler extended to their basketball heritages and universities. The best year for both in the NCAA Tournament was 1962, when Butler scored its only two victories and Wake Forest reached its only Final Four. The major difference was Wake Forest's membership in the Atlantic Coast Conference and participation in major college football.

Here's how they matched up:

	Butler	Wake Forest
Founded	1855	1834
Enrollment	4,168	6,258
Undergraduates	3,500	3,944
Tuition, room, & board	$24,340	$28,720
Academic majors	67	34
Average SAT	1,200	1,240–1,360

One difference between Wake Forest and Butler was recruiting strategies. While Butler's roster was confined to the Midwest, Wake's reach was worldwide. The Deacons had two 6-foot-9 European forwards, Darius Songaila of Lithuania and Rafael Vidaurreta of Spain. The 23-year-old Songaila, who went on to a long NBA career, won a bronze medal playing for his country at the 2000 Sydney Olympics.

Wake Forest finished the previous season by winning the NIT. The Deacons started 12–0 but were 7–10 after January 2. They bottomed out in a 71–53 loss to Maryland in the ACC Tournament. By contrast, Butler had won 12 of 13.

There was a sense of urgency on the Deacons' side—this was their first NCAA appearance since 1997—and a mission on the Bulldogs' side. Everywhere the Bulldogs went, they were reminded of Mike Miller's last-second shot for Florida.

LaVall Jordan was distraught after missing two free throws late in Butler's overtime loss to Florida in the 2000 NCAA Tournament. But he came back the next year and helped the Bulldogs beat Wake Forest for their first NCAA tourney victory since 1962 (Butler University Archives).

"Every time I turn on the television in my hotel room, I see that shot going in," Matta said.

Butler's team had to take a somewhat circuitous route to reach Kansas City. To accommodate the Bulldogs' travel party of 35, they flew first to Pittsburgh and connected to Kansas City. Their flight passed over Indianapolis.

At the Kansas City news conference, the Bulldogs said, over and over, that getting to the NCAA Tournament was not adequate. They were here to win. If the Bulldogs did win, coach Dave Odom said, it would not be because Wake Forest overlooked them.

Jordan opened the game by scoring on a 3-pointer and jump shot. Wake Forest then trimmed Butler's lead to 5–2.

What followed was a basketball counterpart to what King Louis XV famously was supposed to have said before the French Revolution: *Apres moi, le deluge.* That is, "After me, the deluge."

What a Dawg deluge it was.

Brandon Miller made a 3-pointer.

Jordan made his second 3-pointer.

Jackson made a 3-pointer and then another.

It was 17–2.

Matta turned to his coaches, including administrative assistant Brad Stevens, and asked the question: "Are we really ahead 17–2?"

"He said that four times in the first half," Stevens recalled.

Wake Forest scored again, on a free throw, but still didn't have a field goal.

Jordan made a jump shot.

Hainje made a 3-pointer.

It was 25–3. Butler had made 7 of 8 from the arc.

Broderick Hicks scored Wake Forest's first basket after nearly nine minutes elapsed, but the dam had long since broken.

Hainje made a jump shot.

Cornette converted a three-point play.

Midway through the first half, it was 30–5.

It was an unimaginable deficit for a team once ranked No. 4 in the nation.

The Bulldogs cooled thereafter, yet only slightly. At halftime, it was 43–10.

Wake Forest had shot 12 percent (3-of-25). Their 10 points were the fewest in one half of an NCAA Tournament game since 1941. Only three teams in the history of the tournament, which debuted in 1939, had scored fewer than 10 in a half.

"I think we played a little bit scared with that big lead," Matta conceded. "I know I was scared. I didn't know what to tell the team."

Miller was around to give him something to say. When the combustible guard ran to the sideline to complain about an alleged misdeed by the Deacons or the officials, Matta calmed him by responding: "Brandon, look at the scoreboard."

The Deacons cut the margin to 45–21 but soon sagged behind 54–23. Robert O'Kelley sparked a 13-0 run to bring them to within 54–36, but Wake Forest was never closer than 16 thereafter.

Final: Butler 79, Wake Forest 63.

For the first time in 39 years, Butler had won an NCAA Tournament game. Not since the Bulldogs, then coached by Tony Hinkle, beat Bowling Green 56–55 in 1962 had they advanced. Not only had none of Butler's players been born in 1962, neither was the coach.

Coincidentally, another historic Butler victory came in Kansas City. That's where the Bulldogs won their first national championship, beating the Kansas City Athletic Club 30–26 in the 1924 AAU Tournament.

At least the outcome meant people could stop asking Jordan about those missed free throws against Florida.

"Now we've given them something else to talk about," he said.

As was their custom, the Bulldogs changed tactics in the second half as circumstances warranted. When Wake Forest intensified its perimeter defense, Butler abandoned the 3-pointer (one second-half attempt) and drove to the hoop.

The Bulldogs featured scoring balance: Miller had 18 points, Hainje and Jordan 15 each, and Jackson 14.

In the ACC, Wake Forest never encountered an opponent like Butler.

"I guess they're kind of unique in a way," O'Kelley said. "I can't think of a team that we played that resembles them."

On hand to witness Butler history was Barry Collier, who was probably more responsible for this moment than anyone. Collier, in his first year as Nebraska coach and the one who hired Matta onto Butler's staff, sat among the cheering section of about 400 Bulldog fans.

In the other bracket, Arizona led by 22 at halftime and dispatched 15th-seeded Eastern Illinois 101–76.

If the NCAA had abided by its own guidelines, Butler/Arizona as early as the second round would not have occurred. The bracket was to be built so rematches could not be played until the Sweet Sixteen. An NCAA insider later told Butler athletic director John Parry that the Butler/Arizona pairing was a preventable mistake.

The reason that mattered to Butler—besides the fact that Arizona was a formidable team—is that those unaccustomed to the Bulldogs' style fared worse than familiar opponents. Arizona coach Lute Olson underscored that point, saying the Bulldogs "blew their cover" in the first-round blowout of Wake Forest. Butler almost certainly would have had a better chance against any of the three other No. 2 seeds: North Carolina (which lost to Penn State in the second round), Iowa State (which lost to Hampton in the first round) or Kentucky.

Besides coming close to beating Arizona the first time, the Bulldogs had reason for hope because of Arizona's bumpy rides in the NCAA Tournament. Although the Wildcats had been to three Final Fours since 1988, they endured an equal amount of futility. On five occasions since 1990 as a No. 4 seed or higher, Arizona failed to reach the Sweet Sixteen. As a No. 1 the year before, Arizona lost to Wisconsin 66–59 in the second around.

Olson steadied these Wildcats, who started 8–5 and then won 16 of 18. After the December 28 game against Butler, he took a leave of absence to be with his wife of 47 years, Bobbi, who had ovarian cancer. She died January 1. He didn't return for five games.

"Once he did come back, he did get the ship back together again," said Arizona guard Jason Gardner, the Indianapolis native.

Butler's ship had been sailing for weeks, and Arizona happened to be the storm ahead. For a while, the Bulldogs rode a wave.

Jordan's nine points pushed Butler in front 14–9, and Archey's 3-pointer expanded that to 22–15. Miller drove to the hoop but missed a layup that would have kept the margin at seven. Arizona cleared the rebound, and Gardner drilled a 3-pointer that trimmed Butler's lead to 24–22.

After that five-point swing—two points Butler didn't score and three that Arizona did—the Wildcats scored the final eight points before halftime and forged ahead 30–26.

About six minutes into the second half, the Bulldogs were within seven, 43–36. Then Arizona held them without a field goal for nearly seven minutes, and a 15–0 run created a 58–36 chasm.

"At times I found myself counting white shirts," Matta said. "I thought they had seven, eight, nine guys out there guarding us."

It seemed that way because of the Wildcats' length and height and because Gardner and Gilbert Arenas were every bit as quick as Butler's guards. Arizona finished off a 73–52 victory. No single Wildcat was responsible—Arenas led Arizona with 15 points—but all that NBA talent overrode Butler's system.

"We didn't have any answers today," Matta said.

Butler, ranked fifth in the nation in 3-point percentage at .415, started the second half 0-of-9 from the arc and finished 6-of-26 for .231. It was Butler's second-worst 3-point percentage all season. Miller and Jackson were an aggregate 3-of-17 from the field, 1-of-11 from the arc.

"I don't think there's any question that we wore them down," Olson said. "If the legs are not the same, the 3-point shot is not the same."

The Bulldogs' nine-game winning streak, and 24–8 season, was over. Although no one knew it at the time, Matta's coaching career at Butler soon would be over, too. On May 2, he decided to leave his alma mater and accept a higher-paying job at Xavier. Of course, there was no hint of what was to come in the game's aftermath. Matta said the hardest part of the outcome was that there would be no practice the next day.

"But what we accomplished, and the way this team came together, this is such a unique and special group," Matta said. "This goes down as one of the three best seasons ever in Butler history. And to lose eight games, two of them to Arizona, that's not too bad."

Butler's six other losses were by a combined 15 points. A case could be made that Arizona was the strongest opponent played by Butler in the 2000s—better than Florida's 2000 NCAA runners-up or 2007 national champions, better than Indiana's 2002 NCAA runners-up, better than 2003 Duke or 2008 Tennessee teams that were ranked No. 1 during those respective seasons. (Arizona lost to Duke 82–72 in the 2001 NCAA championship game.)

Jordan was part of 91 victories, then a record by a Butler player. He didn't complain about a tournament draw that pitted the Bulldogs against Arizona in a rematch that should not have been.

"If we played again tomorrow, we'd have a chance to win, no matter who we played against," Jordan said. "We're confident in our system and our program, and that's just the way we are at Butler.

"We always think we have a chance."

Before he was recruited by Butler, LaVall Jordan had never heard of the university. While there, he endured tragedy and triumph. By the time he left, he was an articulate spokesperson for the Butler Way.

The 2001–02 Team (26–6): Snubbed

For the second time in 13 months, Butler was looking for a head basketball coach. After losing Barry Collier to Nebraska in April 2000, Butler lost Thad Matta—after one season—to Xavier in May 2001.

Matta said he had "the greatest job in the world," but Xavier paid more. Butler athletic director John Parry said he made mistakes in managing the process, although there was probably nothing he could have done to retain Matta.

Matta had a four-year rollover that included the same financial compensation Collier had. The salary was about $180,000, or triple what Matta made as an assistant. Matta told Parry that security was his main concern, so the coach was offered a seven-year contract that included a buyout owed to Butler if he left in the first three years. Matta told Parry he thought Butler would be good for the next three years, and the seven-year contract was rejected.

"So much for security being the main issue," Parry said.

Parry said he misread Xavier's interest in a one-year head coach and underestimated the connection between Matta's agent, Michael Messaglia, the son-in-law of former Notre Dame football coach Lou Holtz, and Xavier athletic director Mike Bobinski. Messaglia and Bobinski were Notre Dame graduates. Moreover, Matta wasn't sure how supportive Parry was of him.

"The minute he went down to Xavier, he was gone," Parry said. "His feeling was he could go farther at Xavier."

Matta told Butler's players he was leaving at a team meeting one night, and he was introduced as Xavier's coach at a Cincinnati news conference the next day. Matta succeeded Skip Prosser, who left for Wake Forest.

Parry said he would listen to the views of Butler's players before hiring a new coach. The players, who strongly backed Matta the year before, were as united behind assistant coach Todd Lickliter. Both coaches were sons of coaches, graduates of Butler, and former Collier assistants.

"He's really the brains of the operation," center Joel Cornette said of Lickliter. Cornette also said he wouldn't rule out transferring to another school if Lickliter were not promoted.

Another former Collier assistant, Jay John, campaigned for the Butler job. John had served three years as an Arizona assistant coach. A letter representing 21 Butler basketball alumni was sent to Parry in support of John.

Butler's selection process didn't last long. On May 3, 2001, Matta was introduced as Xavier's new coach. On May 4, the decision was made to promote the 46-year-old Lickliter. He became the Bulldogs' third coach in 14 months.

"It's a lifelong dream for him," said Lickliter's wife, Joez, after he was introduced at a news conference the next day. "You just can't believe it."

Lickliter's voice broke several times as he expressed gratitude for the players' support. Parry expected to conduct a national search and had nine head coaches whose backgrounds he wanted to investigate. The opening attracted wide interest from head coaches, Parry said, in contrast to the mostly assistants who had applied the year before. In the end, the athletic director agreed with the players, who made a logical and "very cogent case" to stay within the coaching staff.

"If we brought in another coach, it's a whole new system you have to learn," forward Rylan Hainje said. "And usually it takes a year to get that system in. It's going to be a lot easier."

Not only was the system intact but, largely, so was Butler's lineup: Cornette, Hainje, and guards Thomas Jackson and Brandon Miller were back. The Bulldogs had Darnell Archey off the bench. They also retained 6-foot-11 Scott Robisch, who was awarded a sixth year of eligibility by the NCAA. Because of injuries, he had never played a full college season. He spent the off-season resting an ailing left knee and working out in a pool.

"This is definitely the most talent on the floor Butler's ever had," Robisch said.

The Bulldogs had all the ingredients of a preseason Top 25 team, except for the ranking itself. They returned all but one starter from a 24–8 team that recorded Butler's first NCAA Tournament victory since 1962. Jackson was the preseason player of the year in what was now the Horizon League, changed from the Midwestern Collegiate Conference.

The Bulldogs' slogan was simple: One more. That could be interpreted as one more NCAA Tournament victory or one more league championship. Their mission remained the same. They would have to prove themselves all over again.

•••

The Bulldogs started the season about as far from home as possible—3,000 miles—while remaining in the United States. They played in the aptly named Top of the World Classic in Fairbanks, Alaska, about 125 miles south of the Arctic Circle.

Fairbanks' mean temperature in November is 4 degrees, and the average low is -5. Players and coaches bundled up before heading to a local YMCA for workouts. Appropriately, for a bunch of Bulldogs, they went on one outing to see sled dogs.

Butler opened against Radford, which ended the previous season one game away from the NCAA Tournament with a loss in the Big South championship. Lickliter couldn't have scripted his debut better. The Bulldogs sank 12 3-pointers and had five double-figures scorers in a 73–56 victory.

Butler advanced to a semifinal against Delaware, which beat Wichita State 62–47. Bowling Green defeated pretourney favorite Mississippi 82–78 behind Keith McLeod's 33 points.

Robisch's years of patience and rehab paid off against Delaware. He scored a career-high 24 points on 11-of-14 shooting—mostly from outside—and led Butler to a 76–59 victory. That nearly equaled his entire output, 28 points, in 15 games the previous season. After Delaware pulled within eight points in the second half, Robisch made five consecutive baskets and outscored the Blue Hens 10–2.

"It's so nice to see him play basically pain-free and have the kind of energy he has," Lickliter said.

In the other semifinal, Washington beat Bowling Green 81–74, despite McLeod's 28 points.

In the championship, the weary Bulldogs played a third game within 50 hours against the rested Huskies. Washington had a day off between its first-round victory and afternoon semifinal.

Washington went on a 14–0 run, built a lead as large as 18 points, and led 42–28 at halftime on 67 percent shooting. At halftime, Hainje delivered a rousing address to his teammates, who somehow pulled themselves together. With 14 minutes left, the Bulldogs trailed by 17.

"As crazy as it sounds, we never felt desperate," Lickliter said.

Hainje scored six points, capped by a dunk off a pass from Miller, in a 15–2 spurt that trimmed Washington's lead to 57–53. Hainje's 3-pointer pulled the Bulldogs to within four again, 60–56. Miller's 3 tied the score at 62, and Archey's 3 with 57 seconds left put Butler in front 65–64. Hainje iced it with two free throws.

In a game in which they led for fewer than two minutes, the Bulldogs won 67–64, outscoring Washington down the stretch 29–9. Excluding postseason conference tournaments, the Bulldogs hadn't won a tourney title since the 1948 Hoosier Classic on their home court. They hadn't beaten a Pac-10 team since a 1965 victory over Southern California. Butler, and Lickliter, was 3–0.

"I've been around them so long that I would never, ever count them out," Lickliter said. "Not only do they have tremendous character individually, they have team character."

As a result of ballots collected at halftime of the championship game, the tournament's MVP was Washington's Doug Wrenn—who was scoreless against Butler in the second half. Jackson scored 19 and made the all-tournament team. Hainje scored 13 of his 16 in the second half and was omitted from the all-tournament team. No complaints.

"I got what I want, Coach. A championship," Hainje told Lickliter.

• • •

Elements contributing to Butler victories—teamwork, stout defense, accurate shooting, crisp ball handling—were publicly displayed in every game. What the public didn't see was what happened in every practice.

Lickliter often said that outsiders would be surprised by the ferocity of those practices. Fists weren't thrown, but arguments were frequent.

"It's just like you get into a fight with your older or younger brother," Hainje said. "You do it because you love them. You're trying to show them how to get tougher. We push everybody, from top to bottom."

Mike Moore, a 6-foot-10 backup center, said practices could be as intense as games. He was responsible for one dramatic moment.

In one November scrimmage, the first and second teams were tied at 17. It was late, so the game was suspended until the next day. The second team had the ball under its own basket with 2.9 seconds left. Moore took the inbounds pass about 80 feet from the other basket. His heave banked off the glass and through the hoop: Butler II 20, Butler I 17.

Miller walked around, hands on hips in disgust. Cornette lay down at midcourt in frustration. Moore said it was a play you'd see in postseason tournaments. That the losers' reaction was so great underscored what Butler opponents learned: the Bulldogs hate to lose.

"I don't think there's anybody on this team who would come in and say, 'If you put these five on the floor, they're guaranteed a win in practice,'" Lickliter said. "I don't think that's going to happen."

The coach's recurring problem was restraining players from jumping off the bench to cheer teammates. Officials repeatedly turned to Lickliter, asking everyone to sit. Lickliter said he didn't really try to restrain them.

"I act like I do," he said. "It's a great feeling to know that you've got people in your corner and especially people who are close to you and spend a lot of time together."

• • •

Upon returning to Indianapolis from Alaska, the Bulldogs dispatched Indiana State 69–49. They were 4–0 for the first time since 1986. It was Butler's 12th straight win at Hinkle Fieldhouse and Indiana State's 10th straight loss there.

During a pregame ceremony, Butler raised a league championship banner from the previous season. Lewis Curry was on that team but rarely on the court. He missed 20 games because of a knee injury. So the 6-foot-8 junior from Fort Wayne, Ind., was gratified to contribute 12 points in eight minutes against the Sycamores.

"I don't care if I play five minutes or 35 minutes a game," Curry said. "It's all about producing when you're called on."

Two days later, the Bulldogs completed their November schedule at Purdue, which was 12–0 in the previous 12 meetings of an intermittent series. It was a meaningful game for Hainje, who was born in Lafayette, Ind., and attended one year of high school there at Central Catholic.

As they had in Fairbanks, the Bulldogs fell far behind, almost hopelessly. Hainje scored all nine Butler points in the closing two minutes of the half to trim the Boilermakers' lead to two. Purdue surged ahead by 14 with less than 13 minutes left and led by 10 at under the seven-minute mark.

"There were a lot of times it looked bad for us," Lickliter acknowledged.

The Boilers began to bend against Butler's trapping defense, and they finally broke. Butler went on a 10–0 run to go ahead for the first time, 61–60, on Hainje's 3-pointer. Hainje spun in the lane and found Cornette for a dunk. Another Hainje 3-pointer and his assist to Robisch made it 70–66 with 41 seconds on the clock.

Rylan Hainje was the Horizon League's 2002 player of the year. Hainje, and the Bulldogs, were never as potent after he injured his ankle (Butler University Archives).

Hainje finished with 25 points in a 74–68 victory at Mackey Arena—where the Boilers win nearly 90 percent of nonleague home games. The Bulldogs hadn't won at Purdue since 1953 and hadn't beaten Purdue since 1967.

For the first time since 1930, Butler was 5–0.

Jackson, closely guarded near the arc, foiled Purdue's strategy by slicing to the hoop for seven layups, four left-handed. He scored 21 points and sank the four free throws that secured the outcome.

"We love the big arena, the packed house," Jackson said. "We love coming in and breaking people's bubble."

The Bulldogs were halfway toward a 10–0 start but needed to be vigilant ahead of a December 19 visit to nationally ranked Ball State. There could be no slipups against the likes of Birmingham-Southern and Lipscomb—two teams new to NCAA Division I—or Evansville,

Northern Iowa, and Mount St. Mary's. By season's end, Butler would be penalized for playing such opponents.

Butler climbed to No. 9 in the Sagarin computer rankings and 27th in RPI (Ratings Percentage Index). After a 70–34 victory over Birmingham-Southern, visiting coach Duane Reboul was a believer. He didn't agree that the Bulldogs should be a Top 25 team. "Higher than that," he said.

"They have all the pieces. They have no weaknesses," Reboul said. "Their defense is their constant. That's what all great teams have."

The visitors' 34 points were the fewest by a Butler opponent since a 52–30 victory over Canterbury in 1947.

The Bulldogs' 12 3-pointers against Birmingham-Southern were followed by 13 more in a 76–56 victory over Lipscomb in Nashville, Tenn. The Bulldogs were left open so often that they set a school record with 32 attempts from the arc.

Darnell Archey and Miller made five 3s apiece, and Archey scored a career-high 26 points.

Back at Hinkle Fieldhouse, the Bulldogs beat Evansville 101–65. It was their most points scored in a 13½-year stretch through March 2009 and as dominant as any Butler performance of the 2000s. In the first half, the Bulldogs shot 59.5 percent, had a 16-to-1 assist-to-turnover ratio, caused 14 turnovers, and led 58–24.

Butler finished with 14 3-pointers. Hainje was so efficient that he took only six field-goal attempts and scored 18 points. Jackson had 19 points, 11 assists, and zero turnovers.

"Butler, maybe they'd win the Big Ten. I don't know," said Evansville coach Jim Crews, a former player and assistant for Indiana's Bob Knight.

Butler completed the climb to 10–0 with a 77–65 home victory over Northern Iowa and a 66–46 victory over Mount St. Mary's at Emmitsburg, Md. The Bulldogs had matched Tony Hinkle's 1930–31 team with the best start in school history. Butler and Oklahoma State (Robisch's former school) were the only 10–0 teams in the country.

"We're 10–0 by living our motto: 'One more,'" Lickliter said.

• • •

Butler players could maintain they weren't looking ahead to the December 19 showdown at Ball State, but there's no denying they were. Years later, Brad Stevens, an assistant coach for those Bulldogs, recalled they were "amped up" for the game.

It was the most anticipated major/mid-major matchup imaginable in a regular season. All 48 seats on Ball State's press row at sold-out Worthen Arena were assigned, including credentials to six NBA scouts.

As spectacularly as the Bulldogs started, Ball State had exceeded those achievements. The Cardinals rose to their highest ranking ever, 15th, after beating No. 4 Kansas and No. 3 UCLA in the Maui Invitational. They were 6–2 and ranked 21st. They led the nation in 3-pointers, were second in scoring (89.9), and were six-point favorites as they prepared to meet Butler in Muncie, Ind.

"Ball State is for real. Ball State can beat anybody," ESPN analyst Jay Bilas said.

Until the midpoint of the first half, Butler and Ball State played evenly. Then Hainje produced the most sensational 11 minutes of a 127-game college career. His 3-pointer and fadeaway jumper, followed by a basket off the glass, sent Butler ahead 17–14. Before the half ended, he added back-to-back 3s, another fadeaway, and a driving left-handed layup. In 11 minutes, he outscored Ball State 17–16 and carried the Bulldogs to a 35–26 halftime lead.

The charged atmosphere was evident when tempers flared early in the second half after Hainje dove on a loose ball. Players shoved each other at midcourt before referees separated both teams.

The incident aroused the fans and the Cardinals, who scored 13 straight points to trim Butler's 14-point lead to 40–39. Archey's 3-pointer from the left corner ended that run, and when Ball State pulled within three again, he made another 3. The Bulldogs' lead grew to 15 before their 75–66 victory was completed. It was Butler that had the most 3-pointers: 12, to the Cardinals' five.

"They might have played Kansas and UCLA," Hainje said, "but they hadn't played Butler."

He scored 19 of his 23 points in the first half. Three guards—Jackson, Miller, and Archey—accounted for 32 of the Bulldogs' 40 in the second half. At 11–0, the Bulldogs were off to the best start in their 110-year basketball history.

The outcome begged the question: if Ball State was ranked, and Butler was 11–0, why wasn't Butler ranked? It didn't take long for voters to supply an answer.

Lickliter arrived home from Sunday holiday shopping to find an early Christmas present for his Bulldogs. Butler was ranked for the first time in 53 seasons. Butler was 24th in the *USA Today*/ESPN coaches' poll and the next day was 23rd in the Associated Press media poll. Not since 1949, the first year of the AP poll, had Butler been in it.

"I think it's a tribute to what the kids have done," Lickliter said. "It's very nice for Butler to get the recognition and for our guys. I guess the challenge would be: could you stay here?"

Computers were enchanted by the Bulldogs. One such rating had them No. 2, another had them at No. 7. There was an ominous sign, however. RPI, a computer formula used to help select and seed the NCAA Tournament, placed Butler 48th.

The Bulldogs' new status heightened anticipation for Indiana's upcoming Hoosier Classic at Conseco Fieldhouse. Although the venue was in Butler's city, Indianapolis, the fans would overwhelmingly favor the Hoosiers. From 1948 to 1960, Butler held a Hoosier Classic in its own fieldhouse, usually drawing Indiana and Purdue. That tourney had long since been discontinued, and the Hoosiers had a 38–0 record in the reinstated version and a 25-point average victory margin.

To set up a so-called state championship game, Indiana and Butler would have to win Friday's openers. Coach Mike Davis' Hoosiers advanced easily, using 23 points each from Jared Jefferies and Dane Fife to beat Eastern Washington 87–60. The Bulldogs, after nine days off, labored to beat Samford 45–37.

The unranked Hoosiers were 7–4 but clearly favorites to go 40–0 in their tournament. Hainje said it would be "huge" to beat Indiana. Fife said being best in the state was hardly the Hoosiers' goal.

"We're competing nationally, as far as I'm concerned," Fife said. "We want to compete with the 1s and 2s in the country."

The championship game was not televised. So the walk-up crowd exceeded 5,000, a last-minute figure unheard of, according to organizers. That swelled attendance to 16,471.

The game featured seven lead changes and 10 ties. Early in the second half, Hainje crumpled to the floor after reinjuring his left ankle. He was sidelined for all but a few minutes thereafter—he

> They're ranked right now, so it's not like they're in the witness protection program, but I find it funny people at the end of the year call Butler the Cinderella team. How many years to they have to be good for people to realize they're good?
>
> — Jay Bilas, ESPN analyst

didn't score in the closing 30 minutes—and played the rest of that season with what turned out to be a bone chip.

The Hoosiers pulled ahead 51–42 and were pulling away. Butler responded with a 10–0 run, accented by successive 3s by Notre Dame transfer Mike Monserez, who replaced Hainje.

The turning point might have occurred with 2:10 on the clock and Indiana ahead 60–59. Indiana's Tom Coverdale fouled Jackson, and Davis received a technical for arguing the call. Archey made two technical free throws, and Jackson made one of two to push Butler ahead 62–60. Jackson made two more for a 64–62 lead, but Indiana's Jeff Newton tied the score with 17 seconds left.

Lickliter did not call a timeout. Instead, Jackson dribbled the ball upcourt, halted near the top of the key, then drove toward the goal.

"I had total confidence that he would make the right decision and the right play," Lickliter said.

Jackson penetrated deep enough to attempt a five-footer. The ball hit the glass, then the front of the rim, before bouncing high. Cornette was there to slam the ball through the hoop with 3.4 seconds left.

Butler defeated Indiana 66–64. The Bulldogs were 13–0 and 30–4 in the 2001 calendar year.

Butler fans were mostly confined to the upper levels of the arena. But they were audible all night, especially so as they celebrated and watched a mass of jubilant Butler players spill over into the courtside press row.

"They were all on top, and we could still hear them over the IU fans," Hainje said.

Jackson was the tourney MVP, collecting 14 points and seven assists. He was third in Michigan's 1998 balloting for Mr. Basketball, behind winner Fife, who scored 12 points for Indiana. Jackson never thought about that. Butler fans excoriated Fife on Internet message boards, saying the IU player would not shake hands with the Bulldogs.

"The Mr. Basketball thing is over and done with," Jackson said. "I'm moving on to other things."

It was difficult for Davis to move on. The second-year IU coach complained bitterly about the officiating. The comments detracted from the Bulldogs' victory, although Davis said he didn't want to take anything away from them.

"They played a great game, they hit big shots, they did everything they had to do to beat us," Davis said.

Even though it was merely December 29, the night represented a peak for Butler and a valley for Indiana. For the Bulldogs, perception—and computer data—never caught up to reality. For the Hoosiers, the defeat was a bump on the road to the Final Four.

• • •

The new year brought an old challenge to Butler: finish first in the conference. A change of the calendar also brought a change in questions about the Bulldogs: could they go 32–0?

The 20th-ranked Bulldogs had a better chance to be unbeaten in their league than No. 1 Duke did in the Atlantic Coast Conference, ESPN analyst Dick Vitale suggested. Excluding Loyola, which was 5–0 in an abbreviated 1979–80 season, two teams from the Midwestern Collegiate Conference had achieved perfect league records: Xavier (14–0) in 1995 and Wisconsin-Green Bay (16–0) in 1996. Both lost in the conference tournament but made the NCAA field.

RPI was hurting the Bulldogs because the Horizon's computer rating slipped to 21st out of 32 conferences. Any loss by Butler would be deemed a "bad" loss.

In preparing for a January 2 home game against Wright State, the Bulldogs couldn't practice at Hinkle Fieldhouse because facilities management shut off the power to fix electrical lines. They ended up working out at nearby Marian College.

Neither Butler's team nor administration was prepared for the overwhelming response on a campus where students were gone for semester break. For the game, there was traffic congestion, long lines at ticket windows, and long waits in bathrooms. Concession stands ran out of food. The near-capacity turnout was 9,056, the largest crowd at Hinkle Fieldhouse in more than eight years—since Indiana played there in 1993.

Wright State went on an early 11–0 run and built a 36–27 halftime lead. Butler caught up quickly in the second half, and from there, neither side could distance itself from the other. With the score tied at 72 and time expiring, the gimpy Hainje missed from in close, and the teams went to overtime. And then another overtime.

Jackson's 3-pointer sent the Bulldogs ahead 85–80 in the second OT, but they couldn't protect the lead. Butler trailed 88–87 when Jackson drove for a potential game-winning layup with 2.8 seconds left. He missed, and there was no Bulldog there, as Cornette had been against Indiana. Two free throws cemented Wright State's 90–87 victory, ending Butler's 13-game winning streak. Hainje missed a leaning 3-point attempt at the buzzer.

Hainje (31) and Jackson (26) scored career highs, as did Cain Doliboa (28) and Vernard Hollins (27) for Wright State.

"We caught them at a good time," Wright State coach Ed Schilling said of the Bulldogs.

Lickliter was so deflated after the defeat, his first as a head coach, that some in the athletic department were genuinely concerned about depression. Publicly, the coach reiterated what he had said before. That is, it would be hard to win a third straight title. Making it more so was the fact that Butler faced three road games, all in six days.

Perils of the road were manifested in the Bulldogs' trip to Cleveland. Their Sunday charter flight was delayed, leading to a late practice and postponing dinner until 10:30 p.m. When 14 players boarded a hotel elevator, they were stuck between floors for a half hour.

Wright State capitalized on two weeks of preparation to upset the Bulldogs, and Cleveland State coach Rollie Massimino said he was aiming at them even longer—since September 1. Butler stayed in the rankings at No. 24 and stayed the course by beating Cleveland State 62–45.

The Vikings shot 31 percent and needed an 8–0 run at the end to avoid a school record for fewest points. Hainje moved gingerly on his tender ankle but scored 14 points on 6-of-9 shooting. Robisch had a career-high 13 rebounds.

"They certainly played like a nationally ranked team," Massimino said.

Detroit had lost five in a row, all on the road, but had a 35-game home winning streak to protect when the Bulldogs arrived at Calihan Hall. Inflaming the rivalry was the fact that Butler or Detroit had played in each of the previous six league championship games, the last three against each other.

"Things have gotten pretty heated as far as the games go," Cornette said. "And it carries over the next year."

The Titans, playing at home for the first time in nearly a month, didn't allow their recent slide to continue. They built a 10-point lead midway through the first half, then saw Butler surge to tie the score at

47. Inexplicably, the Bulldogs crumbled and were outscored 16–2 in a three-minute span.

Detroit's 63–54 victory dropped Butler to 1–2 in the league. The small but passionate crowd of 3,036 chanted the inevitable, "*over*rated, *over*rated," to the Bulldogs. Frustration was evident in the faces of the Butler players. Hainje said the Bulldogs must concentrate on what they were doing, not what critics were saying.

"It's not Butler basketball. We're not focusing on the task at hand," he said. "As you saw, we came out lackadaisical; we didn't give ourselves a chance to win the game until the end."

Butler had season lows in shooting (31 percent) and assists (six). The formula for defeat was similar to that against Wright State. The Bulldogs were cold from the arc (7-of-26) against Detroit and received little production beyond Hainje and Jackson.

"I think we look for the 3-point shot early on too much," Jackson said. "We need to look inside in the beginning and then come out."

Youngstown State, new to the Horizon League, was the target of the Bulldogs' frustration. After the game was tied at 30 late in the first half, Butler went on a 20–2 run extending into the second half and rolled to a 68–50 victory.

Hainje had 14 points and 11 rebounds, and Monserez came off the bench for four first-half 3-pointers. Jackson said the Bulldogs played as they should.

"We just asked everyone to be more active tonight," Lickliter said.

• • •

The Bulldogs returned home for three games—Green Bay, Milwaukee, and league-leading Loyola—and a chance to ascend to their customary place at the top of the standings. They stayed on top of the nation's defensive statistics by squelching Green Bay 64–41.

The Phoenix scored 18 points in the opening nine minutes and 23 in the following 31 minutes. Butler lowered its defensive average to 56.6, first in the NCAA.

Milwaukee traveled to Indianapolis with a new coach, Bruce Pearl, who took over after Bo Ryan left for Wisconsin. Pearl knew the city well from his Division II days. During nine years at Southern Indiana, he played Great Lakes Valley Conference games annually at the University of Indianapolis. Pearl won 200 games at one school sooner than any coach in NCAA history—he was 231–46 (.836)—and coached a national champion in 1995.

Pearl's Panthers were coming off an overtime victory at Wright State and were 4–1 in the league, so Butler was forewarned. Pearl was respectful of Butler because he said winning in middle Division I was the hardest coaching job in America.

"What's more difficult? Finishing first in the Horizon League or seventh in the Big Ten?" he asked rhetorically. "They've got the money, they've got the facilities, and if they go above .500 in the league, they go to the NCAA Tournament."

After an even first half, Butler spurted to a 13-point lead with fewer than 13 minutes left, mostly due to Jackson's brilliance shooting and passing. Milwaukee mounted a comeback with 3-point shooting, as Wright State had done, and cut the margin to two. The Bulldogs led 70–64 with 2½ minutes on the clock but couldn't close it out.

With a 72–70 lead and less than 30 seconds left, the reliable Jackson mishandled the ball while trying to hand it to Miller. The resultant turnover gave Milwaukee one last chance. Pearl designed a play sending Clay Tucker to the hoop, and Tucker's father was signaling "two" from the stands. Instead, Tucker faked, let defender Rob Walls leap past him, and sent a high-arching shot from 25 feet.

Wham. The 3-pointer beat Butler 73–72. It was the Panthers' only lead of the second half. After 17 straight losses at Hinkle Fieldhouse, they had beaten a Top 25 team for the first time ever. Tucker's shot made ESPN's top 10 plays of the week.

"There was no way I was going to shoot a two-point basket and go into overtime," Tucker said.

There was no way Butler could have envisioned a 3–3 league record after its historic 13–0 start. The Bulldogs fell three games behind Loyola and two behind Milwaukee. It was a season on the brink.

"We're good, but we're not that good," Hainje said. "We can't just turn it off and on."

Jackson was 5-of-9 on 3-pointers and scored a career-high 27 points, one more than he had against Wright State. Tucker scored 24 for Milwaukee.

Lickliter spoke with restraint afterward, reasoning that it took a great shot to beat Butler by one point. Jackson suggested opponents were coming after the Bulldogs harder, and maybe they weren't ready.

Thomas Jackson set a Butler career record with 540 assists from 1998 to 2002 (Butler University Archive).

"You make your own future," Hainje said. "Right now, we've put ourselves in a hole. It's going to be tough to climb out playing the way we're playing."

Loyola traveled to Indianapolis with a 6–0 record that represented its best start ever in this league. Jackson called the game a do-or-die situation, and the Bulldogs acted the part.

Hainje scowled as he was introduced before the game and didn't exchange the customary chest bump with Cornette. Robisch shouted at a Loyola player on an early play and was cautioned to settle down by the flammable Hainje. Cornette and another Loyola player had to be separated after a heated postgame exchange.

These guys were serious.

Butler wrecked the Ramblers, 78–48. David Bailey, leading the league with a 23-point average, scored six. Ryan Blankson, another league leader with a 10-rebound average, had two rebounds.

"Against Illinois, a very physical team, we were not manhandled like we were tonight," Loyola coach Larry Farmer said, referring to an 87–72 loss to the No. 9 Illini.

In the first half, the Bulldogs began by shooting 5-of-22, and still they were ahead. In the second half, they shot 58 percent.

They played more like the team that rose to 20th in the national rankings than the one losing two home games in the Horizon League.

"We had to prove to the nation that this isn't over," Robisch said. "We've got goals in mind for the rest of the season."

•••

Do-or-die didn't end with the Loyola victory. The Bulldogs hit the road for three games that would determine whether they were in the league race or out of it.

Lickliter encouraged his players to accept challenges, and they encountered a new one at Illinois-Chicago. Jackson fouled out for the first time in 116 college games, leaving Butler without its floor leader. He picked up two fouls in the opening two minutes and two more on the same second-half play. Official Sam Lickliter (no relation to coach Lickliter) called Jackson first for a foul, then a technical.

So with 17 minutes left, Jackson was on the bench with four fouls. Soon thereafter, the Flames expanded their lead to 10 points. Coach Lickliter reminded the Bulldogs about other second-half deficits they had erased—17 against Washington, 14 at Purdue, and nine against Indiana.

Jackson sat for 80 seconds, and his return sparked a 10–0 run that pulled Butler even at 53. The score was tied at 64 when Jackson fouled out with seven minutes left, so he became a cheerleader and Miller a point guard.

"When I look over and see Thomas rooting me on, I can see that he believes in me," Miller said. "It gave me confidence."

Miller gave the Bulldogs an 82–73 victory. He scored nine consecutive Butler points in the closing 3½ minutes and finished with a career-high 29. He was 5-of-7 on 3-pointers and 12-of-12 on free throws. Hainje scored 20 but said Miller got it done basically by himself.

Besides Jackson's technical, Cornette received his second technical of the league season. Monserez might have saved Hainje from a "T" by tackling him along the sideline so Hainje wouldn't retaliate after being kicked in the head.

The Chicago-based Fox Sports team of David Kaplan and Norm Van Lier spent much of the UIC broadcast chiding Butler players for quarrelling with officials. Lickliter minimized the incidents and said that passion sometimes spills over. He said he was unconcerned about his players' attitudes, regardless of others' perceptions. Indeed, he liked the Bulldogs' state of mind.

"I feel there's a real sense of purpose," Lickliter said.

The Bulldogs headed to Milwaukee with one purpose—payback. Milwaukee, at 7–1, had a two-game lead over the Bulldogs and could practically eliminate them with another victory.

Hainje and Monserez sank four 3-pointers apiece in the first half, pushing Butler's halftime lead to 12. The Bulldogs expanded that to 13, matching their lead from the first matchup. But just as before, Clay Tucker rallied the Panthers. He scored 12 points in the closing nine minutes as Milwaukee closed to within one, 59–58.

With time running out, Tucker again had the ball in his hands. He dribbled past Hainje down the left side of the lane. That's when Jackson hedged off Jason Frederick enough to cause Tucker to pass instead of shoot. Frederick was apparently so surprised that he shot an air ball on a 3-point try. Cornette seized the ball as the clock ran out, and Butler seized a 59–58 road victory.

Hainje expected Tucker to shoot, as did almost everyone else among the 5,015 packing Milwaukee's on-campus Klotsche Center.

"I knew it was just me and him," Hainje said. "Either they were going to win again, or we were going to."

Butler finished the three-game road swing with such a dominant 72–57 victory at Wright State that the loss a month before seemed like a pairing of different teams. The victory was the Bulldogs' 20th, extending their streak of 20-win seasons to six.

The Bulldogs' biggest relief was what they found for Archey before the game. Doctors diagnosed his monthlong sluggishness as asthma, prescribing an inhaler. After shooting an aggregate 5-of-22 on 3s in league play, Archey came off the bench at Wright State and went 3-of-3. His 11 points came in seven minutes, and he invigorated Butler's fan contingent by throwing his arms in the air after his first 3-pointer.

"The only way he's not going to make shots is when something's wrong," Lickliter said. "We found out there was."

If there was something wrong with the Bulldogs before, there wasn't any more.

Their 61–48 home victory over Detroit was the third in a row over an opponent that had previously beaten them. Coupled with Milwaukee's loss at UIC, Butler pulled into a first-place tie at 8–3. The Bulldogs' 21 victories led the nation.

After the score was tied at 25, Jackson scored 10 consecutive Butler points, mostly on drives to the hoop. He scored 22 points on 9-of-13 shooting in what Cornette called an "amazing" performance.

Jackson was "the trump" for the Bulldogs, Detroit coach Perry Watson said. "They're still one of the best teams in the country. And they've got time to prove it. They've got another month."

• • •

There is no such thing as perfection, even in a five-game winning streak. Against Detroit, Miller was scoreless and Hainje was challenged by his coach to play harder after scoring six points.

"This is the thick of the season for us," Hainje said. "We want to hit that incline, not the decline."

The Bulldogs extended their winning streak to six with a 70–45 home victory over Cleveland State. Hainje responded to his off-game with 25 points and 10 rebounds.

The only off-key note was an incident in which Hainje and Cleveland State's Tahric Gosley bumped bodies and exchanged trash talk. A referee intervened, but Hainje said he didn't like Gosley sticking a finger up to his face.

The Bulldogs headed to Green Bay, where they had fallen behind by 29 the year before in a one-point defeat. Although Green Bay's record was 6–16, this visit was as close as that one. It was the Bulldogs' final game at Brown County Arena because the Phoenix were moving into a new arena.

The Bulldogs escaped with a 77–74 victory, watching a potentially tying 3-pointer bounce off the rim. Uncharacteristically, Butler's defense was punctured by 62.5 percent shooting. Two Green Bay players who were scoreless in the first meeting, Greg Babcock and DeVante Blanks, combined for 40 points.

"I don't care where you play, playing Green Bay is tough," said Lickliter, who was more prophetic than he wanted to be.

The coach continued to gently nudge Hainje, reminding him in a morning shootaround that he was running out of games in his career. Hainje felt Lickliter's disappointment at halftime, and he came out to score 15 of his 20 points in the second half.

"He didn't say anything, but I felt it," Hainje said. "I knew I had to step up and do something."

The Bulldogs ran their winning streak to eight, and Youngstown State's losing streak to 12, with a 75–50 victory at Hinkle Fieldhouse. The victory was Butler's 24th, tying a school record set the previous year. At 11–3, Butler moved into first place by a half game over 10–3 Milwaukee.

Archey came off the bench to score 22 points on 8-of-9 shooting— 6-of-7 on 3-pointers—and Robisch added 14 on 6-of-9 shooting. Both had been feeling the effects of the flu for two weeks, so their return to health strengthened an already deep team.

"This gives us the confidence we need heading into the last stretch of the season," Archey said.

It wasn't confidence that the Bulldogs lacked in their final league road test. It was energy.

Loyola, crushed by 30 points in the earlier meeting, applied unrelenting pressure in the rematch. Jackson, feeling lethargic for reasons he couldn't explain, twice called timeout to escape turnovers before Butler had scored a point.

The Ramblers led by as many 14 before winning 60–56 in a game that wasn't as close as the score. Jackson was burned for 20 points by league scoring leader David Bailey, who usually struggled against Butler. Jackson shot 1-of-6 and committed three turnovers.

"He wasn't himself," Lickliter said.

No Butler starter scored more than 10 points. It would have been worse if Monserez hadn't contributed 14 off the bench. The Bulldogs shot, rebounded, and defended poorly. They were tired.

● ● ●

Butler's seniors were awarded a gift before senior day.

The day after the Bulldogs lost at Loyola, Milwaukee lost at Cleveland State 69–67. That dropped Milwaukee to 10–4, so Butler had a chance to secure a share of the league championship by beating UIC at Hinkle Fieldhouse. It had been a long, hard pull from when the Bulldogs were 3–3 and three games out of first place.

"It was real tough to hang in there, to tell you the truth," Jackson said.

The Flames made it tough on Butler. There were a collective 53 fouls, 70 free throws, and two technicals in the bruisefest. But with so much at stake and 8,853 in attendance, there was an inevitability about the outcome. The Bulldogs took the lead for good midway through the first half, then rolled toward an 85–61 victory.

With a minute left, Jackson was the first of the three seniors to follow tradition, kneeling and kissing the Bulldog logo at midcourt. Simultaneously, Robisch was hugging teammates, so he missed out on the smack. Officials signaled for play to resume, so he touched the logo with his hand and ran off. When it was over, student fans poured onto the court to celebrate with players. Hainje reveled in all of it.

"This tops every game I've ever been in," he said.

It was the seniors' day. Hainje had 21 points, Robisch 14 points, and Jackson 12 points, seven assists, and seven rebounds.

Late in the game, the public announcer reported a score from Detroit: Detroit 94, Milwaukee 61. So, for the third straight year, it was an outright championship. Never in the 23-year history of the league had a team achieved that.

Lickliter said the Bulldogs showed character by not only winning this game but the others leading up to it. At 25–4, they broke the school record for victories.

"We were down, but we never quit," Lickliter said. "They epitomized what we call 'the Butler Way.'"

• • •

When the league announced award winners a few days later, Hainje was honored as player of the year over Jackson, the preseason player of the year. Both Bulldogs made the all-league first team. Despite Butler's title, Milwaukee's Pearl was coach of the year over Lickliter.

Cleveland was the site of the postseason tourney determining the league's representative in the NCAA Tournament. The Bulldogs had a resume worthy of selection even if they didn't secure that automatic berth. They were first in the nation in victories away from home (15), second in points allowed (57.4) and fewest turnovers (10.2), fourth in victories (25), and seventh in winning percentage (.862).

But all those numbers were offset by another: 66. That's where Butler was in RPI, a ranking in which strength of schedule was a component. Only one team with a worse RPI, New Mexico (74th) in 1999, had ever been selected as an at-large.

On the minus side: Butler was 7–0 against teams in the bottom 50 of RPI. On the plus side: Butler was 4–1 against those in the top 100: Indiana (18th), Ball State (79th), Detroit (86th), and Purdue (95th).

It was all a bit bewildering to those who weren't stat geeks or computer freaks. The bottom line: Butler would have to win the league tournament to validate all it had done and be certain of an NCAA berth.

"It's so hard when you feel you have to defend yourself. Why should we have to defend our league?" Lickliter asked.

Nevertheless, the Bulldogs arrived in Cleveland intent on adding a tournament title to one from the regular season. "One more," to quote their slogan. The Bulldogs earned NCAA berths that way in 1997, 1998, and 2000 and could surely do so again.

Less than 12 hours before tipoff against eighth-seeded Green Bay, basketball became an afterthought to Butler players and coaches. At about 3:30 a.m., a phone call brought news that the mother of junior forward Rob Walls had died. Walls' mother, Maxine, was 50.

If the players weren't so close—they spent more time with each other than with their own families—perhaps they could have postponed grieving or blocked it out. But they *were* that close. It was an emotionally draining night. There wasn't much sleep. Players met at 7:45 that morning for breakfast.

Walls chose to stay with his team rather than head home to the Chicago area. Life went on and so did the Horizon League Tournament. Those who didn't know about the shared grief watched a Butler team that was barely recognizable. With fewer than two minutes left in the half, Green Bay led 23–10. Ten points for almost an entire half? Something looked wrong, even if no one outside the Butler team could identify it.

The Bulldogs righted themselves, scoring the final 10 points of the half to pull within three. In the second half, they could pull away and get this quarterfinal out of the way. They continued facing stubborn resistance but finally asserted control. Successive 3-pointers by Miller and Monserez expanded Butler's lead to 48–40 with less than two minutes on the clock. Butler was utterly dominant during what was a 38–17 run since late in the half.

Before the Bulldogs could begin thinking about the next day's semifinal, Green Bay countersurged. Green Bay's Greg Babcock dunked, Monserez missed a 3-point try, and Cornette fouled on the rebound. Two free throws cut Butler's lead to 48–44.

In the closing 64 seconds, Miller missed the front end of a one-and-one that rattled in and out. Jackson twice missed front ends. Six potential points resulted in zero.

Trailing 48–47, Green Bay called timeout with 25 seconds left. DeVante Blanks drove toward the hoop and scored with three seconds left, completing a 9–0 run that shocked Butler 49–48.

Could three and a half months of work be destroyed in a minute and a half?

Lickliter addressed the media afterward and revealed details of the preceding hours. As he spoke, Hainje, who shared a hotel room with Walls, fought tears. Robisch said the Bulldogs were tight and "just didn't play like ourselves."

In answering questions, Lickliter asked one of his own: would Butler have to win every game to get into the NCAA Tournament?

Miller said he felt bad about losing, then looked at Walls and felt bad for feeling that way. Miller later confided to Lickliter that if victory meant the Bulldogs must be too callous to share in a friend's grief, then he would rather lose.

"If that's why we lost—and I'm not saying that's why we lost, there could have been a million reasons why we lost—but if that's why we lost, I'd lose again 100 times over," Miller said.

• • •

Five days after losing to Green Bay, Butler coaches and players traveled to Chicago for the funeral of Walls' mother. Meanwhile, as they awaited the decision by the selection committee, which met at NCAA headquarters a few miles from Butler's campus, debate raged about whether the Bulldogs were in or out. The passion, pontificating, and politicking were of a level associated with a national crisis.

Butler embodied what helped make the NCAA Tournament a billion-dollar enterprise, one of the small schools scoring big upsets and entertaining TV audiences. ESPN analysts Dick Vitale and Jay Bilas were among those coming to the Bulldogs' defense. They'd play anybody, Vitale said, "but the bigger names usually dodge them." Jon LeCrone, commissioner of the Horizon League, said he felt strongly that Butler deserved to be in and would be.

The league issued a two-page release touting Butler's credentials, including the fact that it was one of two teams to beat every opponent on its schedule at least once. The other? No. 1-ranked Duke (29–3). Yet a fifth loss caused Butler's RPI to plummet to 77th.

Butler players and coaches watched CBS' Selection Sunday telecast in a private gathering at Lickliter's north side home. Media representatives were not invited, as they were the year before at Thad Matta's home when the Bulldogs knew they were in.

Butler administrators watched pairings unfold in the Wildman Room of Hinkle Fieldhouse. Region by region, the bracket was revealed. Southern Illinois (26–7) showed up on the TV screen as a No. 11 seed in the East. The Salukis hadn't won the Missouri Valley Conference Tournament and made it as an at-large, so that was a good sign. Hope was dwindling, though. Shortly before the last pairing was announced, the Bulldogs' fate became obvious. Their concerns were confirmed.

"We're done," athletic director John Parry said.

Lickliter said at an informal news conference that he was numb from the committee's decision and that the players were devastated. The 2002 NCAA Tournament would go on without Butler. On Butler's campus, this edition would forever be referred to as the Snubbed Team.

• • •

The Bulldogs had more games—the NIT was surprised and delighted to have them—but effectively the season was done. A year that started with bright hope in Alaska ended in despair on a dreary night in upstate New York.

In the NIT, Butler (25–5) and Bowling Green (24–8), another snubbed team, had a better aggregate record than all but seven of 32 NCAA first-round pairings. Hainje scored 28 as Butler overcame a 14-point deficit to win 81–69 at Hinkle Fieldhouse. Butler players wore black patches on their jerseys in honor of Walls' late mother.

The Bulldogs were dispatched to Syracuse for a second-round game in which seven 3-pointers lifted them to a 13-point lead in the first half. Syracuse, behind Preston Shumpert's 36 points, came back for a 66–65 overtime victory in the cavernous Carrier Dome. Jackson dashed to the basket as time was expiring in OT and passed to Hainje, whose layup missed and was too late to count anyway.

Developments elsewhere furthered the Bulldogs' exasperation. Two mid-major brethren, Kent State and Southern Illinois, reached the NCAA Sweet Sixteen. Indiana, beaten by Butler, made it to the national championship game. If the Bulldogs had beaten Syracuse, they likely would have had a home quarterfinal against Richmond and perhaps reached the NIT's final four. It wouldn't have been as satisfying as the NCAA Tournament, but playing in New York City would have been some consolation.

Syracuse coach Jim Boeheim had been around college basketball long enough to care about issues beyond those affecting his own team, and he was outspoken about Butler. He called RPI nonsensical. If there was one team that wasn't selected for the NCAA and should have been, he said, it was Butler. Five of the Bulldogs' six losses were by a total of 10 points, two in overtime.

"They could have won all their games," Boeheim said.

In many ways, the Snubbed Team changed the sport more than it could have by making the NCAA field. Butler was a plaintiff in a selection process that went on trial. Even though this case was lost, Butler set a precedent. Eerily, in his bio for Butler's media guide, Walls gave this advice to youngsters: "Things happen for certain reasons; God works in mysterious ways."

There was so much lingering indignation about the snub that Butler leaders didn't have to say much publicly. Others took up the cause. *Sports Illustrated* called the NCAA selection committee "Big Losers," commenting that the "exclusion of Butler and Bowling Green exposed the panel as unrepentant big league sycophants."

NCAA insiders acknowledged to Parry that Butler's omission was a mistake. The RPI formula was amended to give more weight to road victories. Also, Butler, and especially the Missouri Valley, became more sophisticated about scheduling in order to enhance RPI. The Horizon League changed its tournament format to reward the regular-season champion with home-court advantage. Brad Stevens, an assistant coach who succeeded Lickliter as head coach in 2007, said recognition grew about how difficult league play—any league—could be.

None of Butler's biggest victories—Washington, Purdue, Ball State, Indiana—was televised. The Snub Team predated ESPN's "BracketBuster" series, which paired mid-majors and televised featured games.

An argument could be made that the Snubbed Team was Butler's best of the 2000s, maybe the best in school history. Butler has rarely had a twosome as talented as Rylan Hainje and Thomas Jackson, especially not in a group that won so many games or whose whole was greater than the sum of the parts. A committee gave three of the 15 slots on Butler's all-sesquicentennial team to Jackson, Joel Cornette, and Brandon Miller—and Hainje had a better year than all of them. The Bulldogs also beat the NCAA runner-up, Indiana.

If this was not the Bulldogs' best team, it is because they lost three of their last five, lacked the consistency to win at home over lesser opponents (Wright State and Milwaukee), and were at their best in December—before Hainje's injury.

The Snubbed Team wasn't solely responsible for subsequent changes in college basketball, but it was influential. It left a legacy exceeding that of championship teams.

"I think that team did something for college basketball," Lickliter said.

The 2002–03 Team (27–6): Redemption at Last

Butler began the 2002–03 season without Rylan Hainje and Thomas Jackson, one of the most talented duos in school history. Moreover, the Bulldogs were stinging from the NCAA Tournament snub of the preceding season.

"You just have to let it go," coach Todd Lickliter said. "It's not that you would want revenge. What's that statement? He who seeks revenge must dig two graves. If you don't let it go, you're going to destroy yourself."

The Bulldogs did let it go . . . and yet they did not. If it is possible to remain edgy—to perform in an agitated state—every day, for four months, then they did. That came naturally to someone with the combativeness of Brandon Miller.

The same with Joel Cornette. Away from the court, he vigorously debated Darnell Archey. What would Cornette and Archey argue about? Name the subject, and it was on. On the court, Cornette vexed opponents with multiple skills.

Rather than carry the snub around like a weight attached to their feet, the Bulldogs used it as a ship uses coal. They burned, and they steamed ahead.

On paper, the lineup looked good, not great. Cornette remained at center, and Miller succeeded Jackson at point guard. When the Bulldogs opened the season at Indiana-Purdue-Fort Wayne (IPFW), two other seniors, Archey and Lewis Curry, made their first collegiate starts. Also moving into the lineup was forward Mike Monserez, a fourth-year junior.

The youngest was Cornette, at 21. Monserez and Curry were 22; Miller and Archey 23. They had been at this a while and knew what they were doing.

"Now we have to carry it on," Curry said. "But it's a different team."

Curry, back in his hometown of Fort Wayne, contributed 13 points toward a 69–53 victory at IPFW. Archey was 5-of-9 from the 3-point arc and scored 15.

The revelation, though, was Duane Lightfoot Jr., a left-handed forward who totaled 39 minutes as a sophomore. He had not made a field goal in a college game in almost 21 months. He repeatedly slashed to the hoop and scored 12 points in 20 minutes.

Not only did Lightfoot have the appropriate name, he had the appropriate game: float like a butterfly, sting like a bee. He and Muhammad Ali came from Louisville, Ky. As a 10-year-old, Lightfoot met the boxing icon through a mutual friend.

"That's something I cherish," Lightfoot said.

He said he never considered transferring, even after sitting for two years. Hainje and Lightfoot paired off daily in practice the year before, iron sharpening iron. Off-season workouts took off 10 pounds, although Lightfoot's developed upper body made him appear bigger. His nickname: Dee-Light.

"I waited my turn," he said. "I played behind some great players."

• • •

With no Thanksgiving tournament, Butler players went home for the holiday. Or, in the case of Cornette and Monserez, went to the bedside of a 2 ½-year–old boy undergoing chemotherapy.

The boy's father, Lance McAlister, was a 1988 Butler graduate and sports talk show host in Cincinnati. His son, Casey, was diagnosed with leukemia.

McAlister spoke about his family on the air. That resulted in hospital visits from sports figures, including baseball slugger Ken Griffey Jr. of the Reds. Cornette and Monserez, both of Cincinnati, heard about Casey's plight and spent a half hour with him Thanksgiving morning. They delivered a hat, autographed poster, and T-shirts to the boy.

"If I look back on it, me and Mike got more out of the visit than he did," Cornette said. "It kind of makes our problems seem miniscule."

In an age in which there is cynicism about athletes, McAlister said, he wanted to make the Bulldogs' visit publicly known.

"When this kid makes it through this disease, he's going to help this world out," Cornette said. "I think he's destined for great things."

Casey underwent a successful bone marrow transplant in June 2003.

Butler players (from left) Joel Cornette, Brandon Miller, and Darnell Archey share a lighthearted moment during a news conference before an East Regional semifinal game against third-ranked Oklahoma (Butler University Archive).

● ● ●

When the season resumed, Lightfoot shot 6-of-7 again and scored 16 points as the Bulldogs crushed Ball State 71–45 at Hinkle Fieldhouse. Ball State had lost 6-foot-8 Theron Smith, a future NBA player, to knee tendinitis and was clearly impaired. The Cardinals fell behind 23–4. Miller guarded Chris Williams, who had been averaging 28 points and was limited to nine.

"They beat us physically and they beat us mentally," Ball State coach Tim Buckley said. "They laughed at us."

The Bulldogs would do no laughing when going on the road against two more instate opponents, Indiana State and Evansville. In coach Royce Waltman's five years at Indiana State, neither the Sycamores nor Bulldogs had won on the other's court. The Sycamores had gone into decline since beating Oklahoma in the 2001 NCAA Tournament, but winning at Terre Haute had never been automatic for Butler.

That was dramatized when the outmanned Sycamores climbed to within 42–34 midway through the second half. Plenty of time remained to overtake Butler. Miller would have none of it.

Butler, flailing on the defensive boards and tapping balls out of bounds, finally controlled a rebound—by Miller. Soon afterward, he was fouled and made two free throws. His defense caused an illegal dribble. He drew a charge, drove the lane for a left-handed layup, made a pull-up jumper, and passed to Monserez for a basket. He scored 11 of his 18 points in the closing 11 minutes of a 65–45 victory.

The Bulldogs weren't at all welcome in Evansville. Heated words between the teams began during warm-ups. Witnesses said Evansville coach Steve Merfeld shoved Butler freshman Bruce Horan and pointed at him as the teams passed through the Roberts Stadium tunnel at halftime. (Merfeld wouldn't comment on the incident.)

The Purple Aces were called for two intentional fouls and two technicals. After one of the hard fouls, in which Lightfoot was taken down, Butler teammates wrapped his arms to keep him away from Evansville's Jordan Watson.

"All the hostility stays between the lines once the game's over. It's normally over," Lightfoot said. "Not today, though. Today it kind of carried over into the handshakes."

The Purple Aces excited the crowd of 6,550 when they trimmed Butler's 19-point lead to 70–64. Archey responded with a 3-pointer that extended the lead to nine, and Butler went on to a chippy 77–64 victory. Two Butler staples—defense and 3-pointers—made the difference. Butler was 14-of-30 from the arc.

In the postgame, one Evansville player was asked what it was like to play Butler, and his response could have been echoed by hundreds of opponents over hundreds of games: "They know they're going to win."

• • •

Bradley traveled to Hinkle Fieldhouse as a 16-point underdog, but the Braves had a talented twosome in Danny Granger and Phillip Gilbert. Granger eventually left Bradley, transferred to New Mexico, and became an NBA All-Star for the Indiana Pacers. Gilbert was an all-Missouri Valley guard in 2004 and a pro in foreign leagues.

The Bulldogs, as usual, had to match that individual brilliance with a collective effort. They led the nation in scoring defense (48.8), and Bradley was fourth in scoring (89.0). Bradley led the Bulldogs 42–39 at halftime.

"I asked them at halftime, 'Can we get some resolve here?' Make a decision and see if we can play 20 minutes and defend, and see if we can overcome this," Lickliter said.

Monserez made key plays down the stretch. His left-handed drive put the Bulldogs ahead 63–62, and his assist to Lightfoot gave them the lead for good, 69–68. Butler sank eight consecutive free throws to secure a 75–70 victory.

Granger scored 26 points and Gilbert 25. Miller kept Butler close in the first half, scoring 15 of his 21. With the Bulldogs misfiring from the arc—3-of-19—they drove to the basket, drew fouls, and made 26-of-32 free throws.

"It's nice to have intelligent players who can adjust during games," Lickliter said.

Miami (Ohio) coach Charlie Coles reinforced that theme after the Bulldogs beat his RedHawks 59–42 at Oxford, Ohio. Butler had 16 assists on 22 field goals, made just seven turnovers, and limited Miami to 16 first-half points.

Coles was the lone head coach at any of the nation's 150 biggest schools to teach a course in basketball theory, so the fundamentals of the sport had long been of interest to him. He found himself watching Butler rather than his own team.

"I don't think I've ever coached against a more intelligent team than Butler. And I've been coaching a long time," the 60-year-old Coles said.

Butler closed its pre-Christmas schedule at 8–0 by beating St. Louis 68–46 at Hinkle Fieldhouse.

St. Louis coach Brad Soderberg had seen it all before. He was the Wisconsin coach when the Bulldogs beat the 10th-ranked Badgers 58–44 on January 30, 2001.

"They smoked us very similarly in Madison," Soderberg said. "The pieces have changed a little bit, but the system is still the same."

Beginning January 1, 2001, and continuing through two calendar years, Butler's record was 51–10. That .836 winning percentage was No. 3 in the nation behind Duke (61–7) at .897 and Gonzaga (55–10) at .846.

•••

The Bulldogs traveled 4,340 miles to end 2002, playing in the Rainbow Classic in Honolulu. The Bulldogs started swiftly in their opener against Texas-Pan American, sinking their first six 3-point attempts from the experimental distance of 20 feet, 6 inches. Archey scored 14 of his 16 points in the first half of Butler's 67–48 victory.

Butler was seemingly in control of its semifinal against Western Kentucky, leading by 15 in the first half and by 10 with 13 minutes left. The Hilltoppers rallied fiercely though, tying the score at 60.

On the final possession, the Bulldogs went into their weave, a sequence of dribbling and handoffs. When a defender backed away, Miller backed up and shot from 25 feet. After an 0-for-8 night, his 3-pointer with 2.4 seconds left won it 63–60.

For the second season in a row, Butler was a perfect 10. The 10–0 Bulldogs advanced to play host Hawaii, which had won 18 in a row at home.

The crowd of 7,925 witnessed another Butler shooting spree in the first half. Little-used freshman Bruce Horan—who went on to make a school-record 314 from the arc in his career—made five 3s in the first half as the Bulldogs built a 21-point lead.

The Rainbow Warriors cut that to 11 by halftime but fell behind 64–49 with four minutes remaining. What happened thereafter depended on your point of view: Hawaii clamped down on the Bulldogs with a withering press, or the Bulldogs were undone by officials who would not call a foul as Hawaii defenders bumped and hacked away. Either way, Hawaii forced enough turnovers to effect a 66–66 tie through regulation time.

"It was the worst 'homer' job I have ever seen," longtime broadcaster Chris Denari said of the officiating. "They were making stuff up."

Archey's 3-pointer pushed Butler ahead 69–68 in overtime, but Hawaii reclaimed the lead and never relinquished it. Hawaii coach Riley Wallace called the Rainbow Warriors' 81–78 victory the greatest comeback in the tournament's 39-year history. The outcome ended Butler's streak of 26 regular-season wins outside the league.

One streak that stayed intact was Archey's. He made two free throws, extending his three-season streak to 73 in a row and tying the Division I record.

Lightfoot scored a career-high 18 points on 9-of-9 shooting. Hawaii's Michael Kuebler scored 25 of his 29 points after halftime. Hawaii scored 32 points in the final nine minutes against Butler, which led the nation in defense (53.7).

Hawaii was no paradise.

"There are a lot of teams in the Top 20 who aren't coming to Hawaii and winning, I tell you that," Lickliter said. "This is a tough place to play. Hopefully, we'll be better for it."

Although the itinerary allowed little sightseeing, Butler players and coaches arose at 6:30 the next morning to visit Pearl Harbor. Japanese warplanes attacked the base on December 7, 1941, bringing the United States into World War II. Lingering resentment about the previous night's defeat vanished as the Bulldogs walked through the USS Arizona Memorial.

"It was something I think greatly impacted our players," said Brad Stevens, then an assistant coach.

"It certainly put things into perspective, and it made you think about the big picture."

• • •

To Darnell Archey, basketballs are like snowflakes. None is exactly alike.

So when he couldn't get accustomed to the feel of the brand of ball used in the 2001 Hoosier Classic, he did what any perfectionist would do. He took a ball home. And slept with it.

"I'm kind of obsessed with it," he conceded.

It was a magnificent obsession. There was no magic formula for his free-throw streak. Credit repetition, routine, and relaxation.

Butler coaches marveled at the hours Archey spent in the gym. If they stopped by Hinkle Fieldhouse at 10:30 on a summer night and heard the ball bouncing, they knew who was there without looking.

"He's a guy who's just addicted to touching a basketball," Stevens said.

> **B**ut the greatest among you shall be your servant. And whoever exalts himself shall be humbled, and whoever humbles himself shall be exalted.
>
> — Matthew 23:11–12

Villanova's Gary Buchanan set his Division I record streak of 73 free throws over 21 games from November 17, 2000 to February 12, 2001. An unusual element of Archey's 73 was that it spanned 52 games, beginning February 15, 2001.

Often, Archey didn't shoot free throws unless a technical was called on the opposing team, coming off the bench cold to do so. It should be hard to establish a rhythm with such infrequency, but Archey was as precise as digital technology.

The more distractions, the better. Opponents asked what number he was on. A fan in Hawaii shouted that he wanted to see history—by seeing him miss. Archey looked over and smiled.

"I'd rather shoot on the road than at home," he said. "It's so quiet here, you can hear anything. I like people booing me and talking to me. It helps me focus in more."

Archey's father, Dennis, started him off right by requiring his son at age seven to establish a pattern. Archey dribbled three times, took a deep breath, bent his knees, and followed through. When he shot, he was thinking about all the free throws taken in the backyard or in an empty gym.

When he was a high school sophomore in New Castle, Ind., he made 96 in a row in practice. He shot 89 percent as a senior and made 40 in a row—short of the school record of 64 set by Steve Alford in 1982–83.

Some of Archey's feats were legendary. In one Butler workout, he made eight 3-pointers in a row. Then he missed. Then he made 35 in a row, several from a step or two beyond the arc.

"It was pretty incredible," Stevens said.

Archey contended his form wasn't textbook perfect, that his left hand is crooked rather than straight on the follow-through. He rarely shot more than 50 or 60 free throws a day.

"I hope what he does from the free-throw line would be a window of what we would like to do," coach Todd Lickliter said. "He takes it one free throw at a time."

• • •

The Bulldogs knew they would be challenged as they sought a fourth straight Horizon League regular-season title. Over two calendar years, Butler had won at a higher rate outside the league (27–3) than inside (26–8).

"People don't even understand the Horizon League," Lickliter said. "They have no clue as to how difficult it is. And I don't really care. It's something that we know."

The Bulldogs stumbled at the beginning of three other championship years. They started 1–2 in the league in 2000, 3–2 in 2001, and 1–2 in 2002.

After three games in three days and travel from Hawaii, Lickliter was concerned about the players' health. The team arrived on a Wednesday in Indianapolis, practiced Thursday, traveled Friday to Chicago, and had a game Saturday. Illinois-Chicago had a week to prepare, featured a 7–3 record, and had won 14 of 16 at home. The Flames won the league's automatic NCAA Tournament berth in 2002 after Butler's Snubbed Team was eliminated.

"We're going to get everybody's best shot because we're Butler," Lightfoot said.

UIC was motivated by a string of eight straight losses to Butler. The Flames trailed 40–33 at halftime and 58–45 in the second half, but they rallied behind Armond Williams' 26 points.

Cornette fouled out with six minutes left, and UIC pulled into a tie at 65. Uncharacteristically, the Bulldogs clanked away at the foul line, making 3 of 8 over the final 10 minutes. They were rescued by an unlikely source in Lewis Curry.

Curry's tip-in with 17 seconds left put the Bulldogs ahead 67–65 and was their only basket of the final seven minutes. Curry played 26 minutes and scored a career-high 17 points in Butler's 68–65 victory. Illustrating Butler's difficulty was that all other teams visiting Hawaii lost their first games back on the mainland.

Archey's free throw with 2:23 left in the first half broke the national record, prompting an ovation from Butler fans in attendance. He made two more, extending the record to 76. He acknowledged that his palms were sweaty on No. 74 and that he was relieved when it was over.

"My parents and teammates were more nervous than I was, actually," Archey said. "I had a lot of pressure on me. I just smiled through it."

Butler's January 9 game against Loyola was its first at home in 19 days. As the Bulldogs had done against Western Kentucky (15 points), Hawaii (21), and UIC (13), they built a big lead. Late in the half, they were pouring it on the Ramblers 44–20.

The script stayed the same, and Butler couldn't protect the lead. Loyola outscored Butler 17–1 in the closing seven minutes of regulation, tying the score at 67. Loyola's Corey Minnifield scored 23 of his 28 points in the second half, sinking seven 3-pointers.

Again, Butler's recovery was made possible by an unlikely source. This time it was Avery Sheets. The freshman guard scored six of his 14 points in overtime, helping Butler to an 81–74 victory. Sheets needed six stitches afterward to close a cut on his right eyebrow. His clutch, hard-nosed play was reminiscent of Miller.

We're trying to be the toughest team in America. And the smartest.

—Butler guard Darnell Archey

"There's no player that I'd rather learn from," Sheets said. "On and off the court, he's been in every situation possible and knows how to handle it."

The Bulldogs seemingly did not know how to handle a lead. Lickliter downplayed that shortcoming, saying teams were going to make runs.

Butler didn't have to worry about that issue as long as it had this recurring theme: another game, another hero. In running their league record to 3–0, the Bulldogs beat Detroit 76–68 behind a career-high 24 points by Monserez. His 8-of-9 shooting came on an array of 3-pointers, fadeaways, and post moves.

In Game 4 of the Bulldogs' tour through the league, Lightfoot was their fourth hero. He scored a career-high 23 points in an 81–70 victory at Wright State. He had 17 in the second half, including 13 of Butler's last 17. And he did it all in 20 minutes.

"Are these minutes correct?" Lickliter asked in amazement afterward.

Youngstown State came to Hinkle Fieldhouse as a 21-point underdog and loser of 23 in a row on the road. Yet nothing was coming easy for the Bulldogs, whose 14-point lead shrank to 63–60 with 17 seconds left. The Bulldogs held on for 64–60 victory; their 15–1 record was the nation's best and represented the best start in school history.

"They weathered the best storm we could give them in this scenario," Youngstown coach John Robic said. "We made some shots that, eh, they were kind of lucky."

With 3:42 left, Archey made a free throw to extend his streak to 85. But he felt winded, and he didn't bend his knees on his next attempt. As he arched the ball toward the rim, he had a sense of foreboding.

"It didn't feel good at all," he said.

The ball was a bit short and rolled off to the right. The streak was over.

Fans gave him an ovation after he missed, then another after the game. He pointed toward his parents before approaching center court to acknowledge the applause. At Cornette's urging, he went back to the foul line to try a ceremonial free throw. Swish.

"I actually had more pressure on that one," Archey said.

• • •

The first-place Bulldogs next faced a pivotal game against Wisconsin-Milwaukee, which was 4–2 in the league. The outcome would give Butler control or set up a season-long fight for supremacy among Butler, Milwaukee, and UIC.

Milwaukee was going to be the site of the league tournament deciding the Horizon's NCAA Tournament representative.

The league tourney was set for the downtown U.S. Cellular Arena, although this game was played before a loud sellout of 5,007 at the on-campus Klotsche Center. The Panthers had won seven in a row there.

Butler didn't play like a team leading the nation in fewest turnovers per game (10.4) and committed a season-high 24. The Panthers' press was designed more to disrupt Butler's offense than to create turnovers. It did both.

"If you let them walk it up the floor and let them get into a rhythm, there aren't too many teams in the country that can beat Butler," Milwaukee forward Clay Tucker said.

Through it all, the Bulldogs overcame a six-point halftime deficit and reclaimed the lead, 48–43. They were positioned to maintain an unbeaten league record. But an 8–0 spurt, ending in 3s by Tucker and Ronnie Jones, propelled the Panthers ahead 62–54.

"That was basically the game right there," Lickliter said.

Milwaukee missed eight free throws in the final three minutes but held on for a 69–65 victory. Butler trailed 67–60 with 25 seconds left but had a chance to send the game into overtime. Horan missed a 3-pointer from the left corner with three seconds left that would have tied the score.

"This was a 'must' win for us," Tucker said. "We came out and played like it."

It was an awful outing by Cornette, who had five points, two rebounds, and six turnovers. He called the defeat "inexcusable" and lamented that he hadn't shown up when needed.

Miller scored Butler's final 10 points and finished with 18. It was too late to salvage this one, but it prefaced what was to come two days later.

Wisconsin-Green Bay led Butler by as many as eight points—equaling Butler's largest deficit of the season—and by 26–23 at the half. In the second half, the Bulldogs responded with one of their most complete performances, outscoring the Phoenix 45–27 in the second half of a 68–53 victory.

The second of successive Miller 3-pointers was measured at 29 feet, and soon thereafter he swished a 3-point fadeaway. Miller scored 24 points.

"I know Brandon Miller is a good player, but the shots he was hitting tonight, you can't tell me he does that on a consistent basis," Green Bay coach Tod Kowalczyk said.

Miller and Sheets were each 3 of 3 from the arc in the second half. Sheets scored all of his 13 points in the second half. The victory restored Bulldog boldness before a visit to Duke.

"Now that we've got a win under our belts, we can get excited about the Duke game," Sheets said.

• • •

Conventional wisdom was that Butler (16–2) was in a no-lose situation in playing No. 5-ranked Duke (13–2) at Durham, N.C. RPI, the computer rating system, was heavily dependent on strength of schedule. Merely playing Duke would boost Butler's RPI.

Yet a poor showing could reinforce a perception that a mid-major like Butler did not belong in a tournament against teams like Duke. In 55 seasons of the Associated Press poll, the Bulldogs had played top-five teams just 16 times and were 1–15.

"If they want any shot at an at-large bid, it's huge," said Jerry Palm of the collegerpi.com Web site.

Duke had won 22 in a row at home and 145 of 148 against nonleague opponents. Since 1986, the Blue Devils had been to the Final Four nine times and won three NCAA championships. They were ranked No. 1 at some point in each of the past six seasons, something that hadn't happened since the UCLA dynasty's run of 12 from 1964 to 1975.

"We're going to play the team that's had the top program since I've been alive," Cornette said.

Duke coach Mike Krzyzewski said he scheduled Butler because it is the kind of opponent the Blue Devils could meet in the first or second round of the NCAA Tournament.

Lickliter prepared as he did for any other game. He watched film, took notes, and assessed strengths and weaknesses. He chuckled as he cited the "scouting help" received from his brother, wife, and children, who had seen Duke on TV.

However, as Cornette stated afterward, preparation doesn't do it against a team like Duke.

The Bulldogs were once within six, 26–20, but shot 27 percent in the first half. Duke scored the final six points of the first half, and first six of the second half, and it was 38–20. Play continued, but the outcome was decided. Duke won 80–60.

The Bulldogs simply could not defend two future NBA players, 6-foot-6 Dahntay Jones (25 points) and 6-foot-10 Shavlik Randolph (24). It didn't matter that two other future NBA players, J.J. Redick and Chris Duhon, scored six and zero, respectively.

Krzyzewski gave Duhon one assignment: guard the point guard. Miller scored 12 points, but he had only three in the first half.

Duke's student fans, known as the Cameron Crazies, taunted Archey. They chanted, "Smeagol, Smeagol," after the sallow, gaunt character from the movie epic *Lord of the Rings*. Archey sank a 3-pointer and ran downcourt screaming at the fans, asking for more. He meant it. He sank four 3s and scored 14 points.

"People can think what they want to think after tonight," Archey said. "Our next goal is to win the conference tournament. We're going to win that and get a shot maybe to play them again."

Krzyzewski spoke respectfully of the Bulldogs and met privately with them afterward.

"This was, for us, really an NCAA-type atmosphere," he said. "Butler is a tremendous school—beautiful kids, well coached. It was an honor for us to play them. We weren't doing anyone any favors by playing this game."

•••

No matter how well the Bulldogs represented their league, they had to be ready for challenges inside the Horizon. When they returned home, awaiting them was Cleveland State, which had never won at Butler in eight tries. The undaunted Vikings led by six points in the first half and played evenly until an incident in the second half.

Cleveland State's Jermaine Robinson fouled Miller, and the two became entangled, with Miller on the floor. One witness said Miller wouldn't release Robinson's foot and that Robinson shook it loose. Butler players said Robinson kicked Miller. Miller said he was at the bottom of a pile and felt a blow to his abdomen that he thought was a kick. When he stood up, he was grabbed by teammates.

"I know it definitely got my adrenaline going a little bit," he said.

After both players were assessed technical fouls and officials separated the teams, Miller sank two 3-pointers that were 35 seconds apart. He extended Butler's lead to 49–40 in a 73–57 victory.

"It was hard to see Brandon get disrespected like that," Cornette said. "When you mess with a teammate, it's like messing with family."

Miller scored 22 points, including 4-of-7 shooting from the arc that raised his 3-point percentage in league play to .594.

A week later, Butler climbed into first place at 8–1, two games ahead of 9–3 Milwaukee in the loss column. The Bulldogs led UIC by three points with eight minutes left before pulling away to a 61–47 home victory. Cornette carried an unusual offensive load, scoring 12 of his 16 points in the second half.

• • •

Although the Bulldogs were on top of the standings, the schedule left them in catch-up mode. They had six games in 15 days ahead of a climactic March 1 home game against Milwaukee.

The closing stretch could not have begun worse. While Butler was losing at Loyola 73–63, Milwaukee was beating UIC 81–78. That put Milwaukee in first place at 11–2, ahead of Butler's 8–2.

Loyola's 5-foot-8 David Bailey came up big against Butler, scoring 21 of his 25 points in the second half. Cornette continued his offensive surge with 18 points, but Miller shot 1-of-9 and scored a season-low four points.

The Bulldogs had gone 80 games without losing two in a row, an achievement that would be jeopardized at Detroit two days later. Butler had lost there three times in a row. Until recently, the Titans had a 39-game winning streak at Calihan Hall.

Future NBA guard Willie Green had averaged 31 points over Detroit's previous six games. He scored 16 points in the first half. Butler, as it did so often, countered with a collective: Sheets came off the bench to make four straight 3-pointers, Cornette had 15 points and 11 rebounds, and Lightfoot swished four free throws in the final 11 seconds.

Butler survived 66–63 after Green's 35-foot attempt over Miller at the buzzer hit the back rim. Green finished with 23 points, but Miller had enough help to restrain him in the second half.

"Our backs are against the wall, and we really showed a lot of heart and a lot of toughness," Miller said. He scored 14 of Butler's 18 points in the closing 10 minutes of a 79–64 home victory over Wright State. When Wright State crept to within 69–61, he applied the finishing touches with back-to-back 3s from 25 feet. It was the Bulldogs' 16th home win in a row and, at 20–4, gave them seven successive 20-win seasons.

Butler left Indianapolis for a long weekend in northern Ohio, beginning on a Saturday at Youngstown State. As with other league opponents, the Penguins were intent on crowding Butler at the 3-point arc. That left Cornette guarded one-on-one, and he responded accordingly. A career 8.6 scorer, he had 18 of his career-high 24 points in the first half of a 69–60 victory.

"He makes them a different team that way," Youngstown coach John Robic said. "Now they're a five-headed monster."

The Bulldogs shot 59 percent, and yet Youngstown was within six in the final minute. No gimmes in this league. That became evident two nights later in Cleveland.

Cleveland State had lost 10 of 11 under beleaguered coach Rollie Massimino and was one away from its 20th defeat. Only 1,229 spectators showed up at the Wolstein Center, holding little hope of upsetting Butler.

The Vikings bolted to a 10-point lead, but by midway through the second half, they trailed 50–40. Then the Bulldogs started unraveling. Cleveland State scored 14 uninterrupted points and carried a 54–50 lead into the final four minutes. When Modibo Niakate rolled in a basket to expand the lead to 60–54 with 45 seconds left, Cleveland State was on the verge of damaging Butler's résumé.

"Am I thinking, 'We're in trouble, and we're going to lose?' No, definitely not," Miller said.

Up stepped Sheets, a freshman playing with the steely resolve of a senior. His 3-pointer trimmed the margin to 60–57 with 36 seconds left.

"I was like, 'Dang, I'm surprised he shot it,'" Archey said later.

After the Vikings missed two free throws, Butler regained possession, and Miller drove in for a left-handed layup with nine seconds left: 60–59. Cleveland State's Percell Coles made the second of two free throws, and it was back to Miller. His 15-footer tied the score at 61 with three-tenths of a second on the clock. Overtime.

With Butler trailing 68–67 and 5.3 seconds left in OT, Miller had two free throws. He made the second, tying it again at 68. After Lightfoot stole the ball, Miller was bumped on a 3-point attempt at the buzzer, but an official waved it off as a no-call. Another overtime.

Successive 3s by Archey overcame a four-point deficit and sent Butler ahead 74–72. Coles' 3-pointer temporarily gave the Vikings a 75–74 lead. Miller's straightaway 3-pointer from 28 feet made it 77–75 with 70 seconds left, and he secured the 79–75 victory with two free throws.

Miller scored 10 of his 23 points in the closing 10-plus minutes. Sheets' 14 equaled a career high.

A loss would have shocked the computer—Cleveland State was 262nd in RPI—but the fact was that Butler had not badly underperformed. The Bulldogs shot 51 percent and made 10 turnovers in 50 minutes. There was parity in the sport, said Lickliter, who was not surprised by the Vikings.

"We expected it. We really did," he said.

Butler, at 22–4, had the fourth-best record in the nation and was unranked. That didn't matter as much as the first-place tie between Butler and Milwaukee at 12–2. It was down to the last week.

• • •

Butler and Milwaukee made sure the story line didn't deviate. Clay Tucker's 40 points carried Milwaukee past Wright State 98–65. That was more points than the entire Green Bay team produced in a 58–37 loss at Butler.

Butler and Milwaukee were still tied at 13–2.

"It couldn't have been scripted better," Miller said.

It was probable that only the winner of the Butler/Milwaukee game—and champion of the regular season—would merit an at-large bid, if that were needed. Lickliter repeatedly stated that Butler was not

> This Butler program and its obnoxious-yet-effective 'Butler Way'—as their increasingly yet understandably cocky fans will tell you at length—is a whole different beast. Because there's no sign of slowing down.
>
> — Mark Lazerus, *Post-Tribune* of Northwest Indiana

playing for an at-large. To belabor its fragile status would "cripple you," he said.

Though the city of Indianapolis often regarded Butler as a sideshow—media and casual fans focused winter attention on the NBA's Pacers, IU's Hoosiers, and Purdue—the stakes this time were too compelling to ignore. An expectant crowd of 11,043 turned out on a Saturday afternoon in a fieldhouse that was a week away from its 75th birthday. It was Butler's first sellout since November 27, 1993, in a game against the Hoosiers.

The Bulldogs attempted to remove any drama. They led by 15 points in the first half and 16 in the second. But Milwaukee had erased a 13-point deficit in winning at Butler 73–72 the year before, so there was no security.

"They make runs at you. Our guys just would not wilt," Lickliter said. "And they wouldn't, either."

Milwaukee chipped away, gradually at first. Then they went on a 10–0 run to go ahead 65–64. Cornette scored six successive points that allowed the Bulldogs to reclaim a 73–70 edge with two minutes left. Milwaukee's Justin Lettenberger scored on a rebound, trimming that to 73–72. Butler's Curry missed a 3-point attempt, but Milwaukee's turnover returned the ball to Butler with 45 seconds left.

The Bulldogs killed the clock as long as they could but had to call timeout as Miller stumbled. There were two seconds on the shot clock, 12 on the game clock. Monserez didn't connect with Cornette on the pass inbounds, and Milwaukee had a chance for the game-winner. Cornette fouled with 4.2 seconds left, fouling out. Lettenberger's two free throws gave Milwaukee a 74–73 lead.

Butler called timeout. Twenty-eight games had been reduced to four seconds. The Bulldogs survived overtimes against Loyola and Cleveland State and escaped defeat at UIC and Detroit. Yet it could all go for naught if they could not win this regular-season title. On the

Milwaukee bench, coach Bruce Pearl was warning his Panthers about the shooting range of Miller and Archey.

Monserez was to throw the ball inbounds. From the baseline, he ran from side to side, searching for an open teammate. With little choice, he passed to Sheets on Butler's side of halfcourt, and Sheets dribbled ahead. . .

•••

If Sheets were not authentic, he would be the Hoosier of our imagination. He was raised on an Indiana farm in which days were divided between chores and hoops. One basketball rim outside, two more in the barn.

Darnell Archey dribbles against Oklahoma in the NCAA East Regional. His 26 points led the Bulldogs to an upset victory over Louisville, propelling them into the Sweet Sixteen for the first time in 41 years (Butler University Archives).

Not only that, Sheets was "absolutely fearless," according to Jeff Knoy, one of his coaches at McCutcheon High School.

Sheets might have been a freshman, but with Milwaukee ahead by a point and a season on the line, Butler had placed the ball in the hands of the right man at the right time. There was no defender to impede him as seconds ticked away.

Sheets kept dribbling until he was outside the 3-point arc, to the left of the top of the key. He stopped because he didn't want a layup blocked. Instead, he shot the ball. It went right through the net.

Butler 76, Milwaukee 74.

Fans swarmed the court faster than floodwaters in a winter thaw. The Bulldogs had won a fourth consecutive league title, a steep climb requiring five wins in 10 days. They won in a way no one in attendance would forget.

"That had to be one of the greatest games ever played here," Miller said, without exaggeration.

Lettenberger was jostled by some fans but didn't comment on the incident. He stayed until the end of Lickliter's news conference to apologize for a hard foul against Cornette in the first half. Cornette fell on his left wrist, and he emerged from the locker room afterward with it heavily taped. Pearl didn't complain, either, saying crowd control was adequate.

What wasn't adequate were words with which the principals tried to express themselves. Sheets said it was probably the best feeling he ever had. Pearl said it doesn't get any tougher in sport, all the while trying to sound as if he weren't making a basketball game too important.

Yet this felt like more than a basketball game. Sheets walked among fans nearly two hours after his shot. He was still wearing his uniform, as if taking it off would make the magic vanish. Milwaukee fans wept in the visitors' corner of the fieldhouse. Cornette choked back tears as he reflected on the occasion.

"People from both sides cried today. You can't tell me this was just a game," Cornette said. "It's so much more. People left here affected. That's unforgettable."

• • •

Whether it was jealousy, an affinity for statistics, or an endorsement of Butler's collective play, voters for Horizon League postseason honors dismissed the Bulldogs. Pearl was coach of the year, not Lickliter. No Butler player made the all-league first team.

Although the Bulldogs claimed to be fresh for the postseason—they had a week off before a league semifinal—they weren't entirely healthy. Cornette sprained his wrist and bruised his hip in the fall against Milwaukee. Miller was ill.

No. 5-seeded Detroit moved into a pairing against No. 1 seed Butler, riding Willie Green's 36 points to a 98–84 victory over No. 4 Loyola. Against Butler, Detroit led 16–6 as the Bulldogs endured an 0-for-8 half from the 3-point line. Miller was so sick that for much of the half he sat with a towel around his neck and a bucket in front of him. The Bulldogs trailed 23–19 as they retired to the locker room. Cornette challenged his teammates in a halftime oratory, reminding them they could celebrate afterward or plan for the NIT.

"Joel carried us. The guy would not let us lose," Miller said.

Neither would Miller. He scored all 12 of his points in the second half. His 3-pointer put Butler ahead for good, starting an 11–0 run. Green wasn't finished, scoring 11 of his 21 points in the final three minutes for Detroit. Archey's two free throws secured Butler's 58–55 victory. Cornette scored 19 on 8-of-8 shooting.

Detroit coach Perry Watson complained about the officiating, saying Butler was slighted the year before but that this was no way to correct that. The Bulldogs' victory was their seventh in a row, four by four or fewer points. Miller said the Bulldogs were "seeing the finish line" and didn't want their fate in someone else's hands

"I don't know if you can feel any more pressure than we've felt all along," Lickliter said. "No one knows the pressure that our level knows."

Butler faced a rematch for the championship against Milwaukee, which trailed for much of the other semifinal before beating UIC 75–73. If the Panthers had lost—and they nearly did—the title game would have shifted to Indianapolis.

College basketball had its storied rivalries: Indiana vs. Kentucky, Duke vs. North Carolina, UCLA vs. Notre Dame. For drama, however, no teams had surpassed what Butler and Milwaukee had done over 25 months. Their previous five meetings had been decided by a total of 13 points, four times on the final shot.

It was a grand occasion for Milwaukee, which was in its 13th year of Division I and had never played in the postseason. Clay Tucker said he could remember when as few as 300 attended games. For this championship, a sellout of 10,115 showed up, many of them rowdy students wearing school colors. The environment was "phenomenal," Pearl said.

If the Bulldogs had to do it over, they might have returned home after the Saturday semifinal, practiced there, slept in their own beds, and bussed back to Milwaukee for the Tuesday game. Day after day in a hotel room didn't do them any good, Lickliter acknowledged.

Milwaukee fans were treated to a nightlong celebration. The Bulldogs were squished so quickly that they didn't get the plate number of the truck running over them. Before four minutes elapsed, Milwaukee led 14–0. Then it was 21–4, and later 38–16. This was worse than Duke.

"It seemed like at times we were lacking the toughness that we showed in the past 25 wins," Archey said. "And it hurts to say that."

Tourney MVP Tucker scored 23 points, and the Panthers finished off a 69–52 victory that sent them to the NCAA Tournament. It would be another agonizing Selection Sunday for Butler. The sickly Miller, who had lost 14 pounds, was off form. He finished with four points, one assist, and four turnovers. Cornette was tearful afterward and alluded to the previous year's snub.

"I really hope this isn't it," he said. "I hope people really take a look at what we've done and put us in the dance. Because we deserve it."

• • •

The days leading up to the NCAA announcement were fretful. Even when Lickliter gave players two days off to relax, there was no way to do so. When Cornette went home to Cincinnati, there was his mother acting as bracketologist, laying out a mock bracket and telling her son what were good wins and what weren't. Never had Miller watched so much college basketball, rooting for teams in conference tournaments that would aid Butler's cause. Archey said he kept telling himself Butler was in, just so he could sleep.

Butler was 25–5, as in 2002, but had numbers working in its favor that it did not in 2002. RPI was 37th, or 40 places higher. Butler's five losses—to Duke, Hawaii, Milwaukee (twice), and Loyola—were on the road to teams that were an aggregate 50–3 at home. Most projections had Butler in the NCAA field.

Lickliter felt secure enough to invite media representatives to his north side home to watch the selection show along with players and coaches. The Dawgs packed onto an L-shaped couch, and stood behind it, watching the telecast. When *Butler* appeared on the screen, the eruption rivaled that for Sheets' winning shot against Milwaukee. Players shouted, hugged, and shook their fists. In that instant, they didn't care that Butler was a No. 12 seed in the East Regional, or that they were playing No. 5 seed Mississippi State, or that the game was in Birmingham, Ala.

After perhaps being the last team out in 2002, Butler was perhaps the last one in. Butler and Brigham Young, both 12th seeds, were the two lowest at-large teams. Butler benefited earlier by the voluntary withdrawal of Michigan, Fresno State, and Georgia for various misdeeds.

The Bulldogs began preparing for Mississippi State but weren't prepared for the backlash against them. In an interview with ESPN Radio, Pittsburgh coach Ben Howland suggested that the selection committee had taken care of the mid-majors. He asked how Boston College could be out and Butler in. ESPN.com placed Butler on the "not hot" list.

"Was Butler worth all the lobbying?" asked Indiana-based columnist Mike Lopresti of Gannett News Service.

It was not a debate Mississippi State wanted to join. Guard Timmy Bowers was solemn when he saw the bracket. A 12th seed beats a No. 5 almost every year, he said.

"Butler seems to be one of those teams that always pulls off the upset," Bowers said.

• • •

Butler and Mississippi State were both nicknamed "Bulldogs," but the resemblances ended there. Mississippi State was touted as a potential Final Four team, coming off a 64–57 loss to No. 2 Kentucky in the SEC Tournament.

All-SEC center Mario Austin, who sat out six games while the NCAA revisited his high school transcript, led the team in scoring (15.4) and rebounding (7.6). The backcourt of Bowers and Derrick Zimmerman was the most athletic that Butler had faced.

Butler planned to work out before its allotted 50 minutes at Birmingham-Jefferson Civic Center but couldn't find a local gym available a day before the game. These Bulldogs had been on the road so often, however, that they weren't disturbed by inconveniences or itinerary changes.

One change they did make was in hairstyles. Players featured close-cropped haircuts. Cornette had grown out his hair for 15 months but reluctantly agreed to shave it off in solidarity with teammates.

In contrast to the early knockout at Milwaukee, Butler was an aggressor against Mississippi State. Archey sank two 3-pointers as Butler went in front 12–3. Butler led 28–25 at halftime, but Mississippi State dominated most of the second half.

The pace was deliberate and possessions few. Toward the end, baskets were as infrequent as goals in soccer. Mississippi State built its biggest lead, 42–38, with eight minutes left but scored once from the field thereafter. Monserez sank a 3-pointer—Butler's only one of the half—to create a 45–44 lead with 1:54 left. Two free throws returned the lead to Mississippi State, 46–45.

Miller was caught in the air with the shot clock expiring and passed out of bounds with 1:04 left. But after a Mississippi State miss, Miller grabbed the ball and kept it. Lickliter looked down and paced the sideline in his first NCAA Tournament game as a head coach and did not call timeout. Not with the ball, game, and season in Miller's hands.

Bowers was caught in a screen, and Miller had an opening in the lane for a running one-hander. He arched in the shot with 6.2 seconds left, returning the lead to Butler, 47–46. Bowers' 3-point attempt missed at the buzzer, and Butler had won. Miller ran around the court pumping his fist in the air, and Monserez jumped onto a press table waving his arms at Butler fans.

"To hit a shot like that in the NCAA Tournament, nothing compares to it," Miller said.

He scored 14 points. Austin had 18 for Mississippi State, whose backcourt produced only three field goals. Coach Rick Stansbury said Mississippi State couldn't run and score in transition.

"They did what they do best," Stansbury said of Butler's Bulldogs. "They ran the shot clock and had control of the game."

It was the most notable upset of the first round. (More so than No. 13 seed Tulsa beating No. 4 Dayton 84–71.) Butler's 47 points were a season low and fewest by a winning team in the tournament since No. 13 seed Princeton beat No. 4 seed UCLA 43–41 in 1996 at Indianapolis.

No. 4 seed Louisville (25–6) awaited the Bulldogs in the schools' first meeting in nearly 30 years. On December 8, 1973, Louisville won 91–81 at Indianapolis. Marty Monserez, father of Mike, scored 10 points for the Bulldogs that day.

This pairing was especially meaningful for Lightfoot, a Louisville native. He grew up cheering the Cardinals.

"I've got some friends over there that I want to make a good impression on, too. And some coaches," Lightfoot said.

Louisville coach Rick Pitino publicly praised the Bulldogs, even if he thought privately that the Cardinals had a clear path to the Sweet Sixteen. He had an impeccable NCAA Tournament record, 27–7, and had taken Providence to the Final Four in 1987 and Kentucky in 1993, 1996, and 1997. Pitino suggested the mid-major label be dropped forever, calling Butler "a major, major basketball power."

The styles of play could not have contrasted more. Louisville's pace was that of a bluegrass thoroughbred. The Bulldogs were more like racewalkers. Pitino was worried less about their tempo and more about their template—a collection of four senior starters and a fourth-year junior.

"It's all about experience and talent. And Butler has it," Pitino said.

The previous year's experience continued to fuel the Bulldogs. Let the snub go? Not a chance. Miller said they were playing not only for themselves, but for the three seniors—Hainje, Jackson, and Robisch—from 2002.

"We feel like we were owed one from last year anyway, getting snubbed," Cornette said. "So this is our second game, and we're making up for lost time."

Soon after tipoff against Louisville, the Bulldogs had considerable making up to do. Five minutes into the game, Monserez pointed toward an official that the possession was Butler's. He slammed his hand to the floor when the call went against Butler and was assessed a technical foul. Francisco Garcia's two free throws began a 10–0 run, expanding Louisville's lead to 18–5. Soon, the margin grew to 24–9. This is what Butler skeptics expected and what Butler fans feared.

Butler players were resilient, though. Sheets, as fearless as ever, sank a 3-pointer to make it 24–12. These Bulldogs were on the endangered list, but at least they weren't extinct. They switched to a zone defense that muddied Louisville's offense. On defense, Louisville kept attacking Butler ball-handlers, mostly Miller, but in doing so allowed open shooters behind the arc. Miller didn't make a field goal. But he made the difference.

"Brandon controlled the entire game with his play at point guard," Monserez said later.

The Bulldogs went on a 12–0 run—a spurt that began and ended on 3s by Monserez—to climb to within 26–24. Archey's 3-pointer and Cornette's basket closed the half, and stunningly, Butler was ahead 34–33.

The Bulldogs sank their first four 3-pointers of the second half, two by Archey, and led 50–39 with less than 14 minutes to play. Butler's problem was that no one could guard All-America swingman Reece Gaines. The 6-foot-6 Gaines scored all of Louisville's points in a 13–2 run that tied the score at 52. Gaines matched Archey shot for shot.

Yet the Bulldogs never trailed in the second half, scoring an atypical 45 points. Repeatedly, Butler screened off the Cardinals as Archey scurried into the left corner. When he received the ball, even before releasing it, Louisville fans gasped. They knew it was going in.

Monserez said he kept going to the hoop in the second half, expecting to rebound an Archey miss. Except Archey never missed. A lifetime of preparation—thousands of shots taken in New Castle and Indianapolis and elsewhere—had prefaced this moment. This was Michael Jordan in the NBA playoffs against Portland.

"Like Michael Jordan said, 'There was a big ol' hoop out there.' It felt like Michael in '92 against the Blazers," Archey said.

Jordan once filmed a Nike commercial with Spike Lee in which Lee's character claimed, "It's gotta be the shoes." Coincidentally, the shoes became a subplot to Butler's story. Late in the game, Cornette pursued a rebound, diving over his bench and into the crowd. Along the way, he leveled two water coolers, one filled with a sports drink that left his shoes squishing out blue liquid.

"We need a size 15! We need a size 15," someone shouted.

Reserve forward Rob Walls, without hesitation, pulled off his 15s and passed them to Cornette. Butler called a 20-second timeout so Cornette could pull them on. He later called the shoes Cinderella's slippers. Walls never left the bench, and yet he influenced the outcome with his heady gesture.

"That's the Butler Way. That's just a small example of what the Butler Way is," Walls explained afterward.

The shoes changed, but otherwise nothing else did. This was a Sunday shootout Gaines could not win by himself, even in scoring 22 of his 26 points in the second half. Monserez sank a 3-pointer to push Butler's lead to 70–66, and after Gaines answered in kind to make it 70–69, Archey's eighth 3-pointer restored the lead to 73–69 with 90 seconds left.

Lightfoot's basket against his hometown team kept Butler safely ahead, 75–71. Two free throws each by Archey and Monserez in the final 13 seconds secured a 79–71 victory.

Butler was in the Sweet Sixteen, 41 years after Tony Hinkle took the Bulldogs there in the only NCAA Tournament in which he coached. In beating No. 14 Louisville and No. 20 Mississippi State, the Bulldogs beat ranked opponents consecutively for the first time ever. Their 27th victory broke the school record set in the snub season.

Archey scored 20 of his 26 points in the second half, featuring 6-of-6 accuracy from the arc. Butler was 14-of-22 on 3-pointers for 63.6 percent. Of Monserez's career-high nine assists, six were to Archey for 3s.

With Butler's media audience growing, Cornette revisited the snub theme. It was a bone the Bulldogs never would release.

"On paper, people think we're nothing and can't match up with anybody and shouldn't be here," Cornette said. "You watch TV, we barely knew we were playing today. Nobody talked about it, nobody cared, nobody gave us a shot.

"And we're still playing for a national championship, and we are still *here*."

Next up: No. 3-ranked Oklahoma.

• • •

On the Bulldogs' charter flight to Indianapolis, some players relaxed, but others opened books to study. The flight was delayed, so about half of the 1,000 fans gathered on the Hinkle Fieldhouse parking lot left before the team arrived. Hundreds cheered when the police-escorted buses rounded the curve onto 49th Street. Inside the fieldhouse, under a Sweet Sixteen banner, the team huddled as fans surrounded them.

"You made it possible for us to get where we are now, but we're not finished," Lickliter shouted to the crowd.

The lowest seed and smallest school in the Sweet Sixteen unleashed a media blitz that was harder to handle than Mississippi State or Louisville. The Bulldogs were darlings not only of the city and state, but of the entire country.

Archey was all over the airwaves doing radio interviews. Sports information director Jim McGrath received 10 times as many media requests as he did when Butler cracked the Top 25 the season before. The Bulldogs were the cover feature in Monday's *USA Today* sports section. They merited large headlines in the *New York Times* ("Butler Shows Louisville the 3, and the Door) and *Chicago Tribune* ("Best in Show: Butler").

Reporters wanted to collect quotes from Cornette, who was so good in a freshman speech course that the instructor invited him back to help teach the class. Archey, Cornette, and Mike Moore—all business interns—were at the fieldhouse and on the phones selling tickets to fans traveling to Albany, N.Y., for the East Regional. Cornette gave informal tours to those unfamiliar with the historic fieldhouse. Lickliter wasn't around for the day after. He had such a bad case of the flu that a doctor ordered him to rest at home.

Lightfoot was so giddy that he said the words *Sweet Sixteen* in virtually every sentence he spoke. He wrote it on chalkboards in classrooms. He started all instant messages to friends with those words. It wasn't only him. There were signs and posters and banners all over campus. Some professors called off class because they were traveling to Albany.

The bookstore in Atherton Union was bustling. It stocked NCAA bracket T-shirts, then *Road to the Final Four* shirts, then *Sweet Sixteen* shirts. They sold as fast as they came in, and the store manager kept reordering. Cameron McGuire, vice president for university advancement, found his voice mailbox full. He cleared the 20 calls, went to an hourlong meeting, and again checked voice mail. Full again.

"It's buzzing," Cornette said. "You go to class and you see people who shaved their heads to try to show their team spirit. It's amazing. It means the world to us."

It was exposure money could not buy. A sponsorship evaluation firm estimated that if the school were to buy all the media mentions since the selection show, it would cost about $2.8 million. President Bobby Fong was happy to point out that Butler's 86 percent graduation rate for basketball players was highest in the Sweet Sixteen and third out of the entire tourney field of 65.

At a send-off for the team, with blue and white balloons decorating the fieldhouse, broadcaster Chris Denari was master of ceremonies for an energetic crowd exceeding 2,000. It was far removed from 1989, when Denari arrived as the school's sports marketing director and sold tickets out of a shoe box.

When the Bulldogs arrived in Albany to play Oklahoma, the joyride continued. On the bus ride to the arena, the driver pointed to a skyscraper to show what a big city Albany was. He obviously didn't know Butler's campus was in Indianapolis.

"He might have thought we were from Milan," Archey said.

It was inevitable that Butler would be compared to 1954 Milan or to the fictional Hickory team from *Hoosiers*. Miller said he didn't mind the analogy because, in the end, Hickory won. However, all those media images didn't blur the vision of Oklahoma coach Kelvin Sampson.

"I can see where Cinderella would beat Mississippi State last week," Sampson said. "But Cinderella doesn't come back and beat Louisville in the same trip. I'm an old-school guy. I like Butler's team. If I wasn't playing them, and I had a chance to watch, I'd watch Butler play."

Not many viewers would watch Butler play. CBS, not expecting a contest, was televising the game to 19 percent of the country and Texas/Connecticut to 81 percent. After all, Butler began the tournament as a 300-to-1 shot. Yet as formidable as the Sooners were, they were concerned for reasons not attributable to Butler. Hollis Price, the Big 12 player of the year, had a sore groin. Ebi Ere's left (nonshooting) wrist was broken.

The Bulldogs weren't cheered only by fans lucky enough to purchase one of the 1,250 tickets allotted to the school. About 2,500 showed up at Hinkle Fieldhouse to watch the game on large-screen TVs. Soon after tipoff, the Sooners' strategy became obvious: don't let Butler's 3-point shooters shoot.

With the Sooners crowding the arc, that left the scoring load to Cornette. He scored seven points, two on a dunk, as Butler played Oklahoma to a 20–20 standoff through 16 minutes. In the closing four minutes of the half, Oklahoma outscored Butler 12–3 to go ahead 32–23. Ere scored 10 in the surge, including two 3-pointers.

The game was slipping rapidly away from Butler when the Sooners built their lead to 40–28. Cornette picked up his third foul within the first two minutes of the second half but didn't allow that to restrain his aggressiveness. He scored 11 of Butler's next 13 points, trimming Oklahoma's lead to 46–41. Finally, with eight minutes left, he picked up his fourth foul. He didn't score again.

Others stepped in. Monserez grabbed a loose ball at the arc and sank a 3-pointer to make it 50–47. Curry followed with another 3, and it was 57–52. Three minutes left, and Butler was in it.

Butler regained possession after a missed free throw by the Sooners, but Miller and Cornette missed connections on a possession that could have made it a two- or three-point game. Soon after that, Archey missed on only his third 3-point attempt of the night.

Ere finished with 25 points, and Oklahoma finished off Butler 65–54. Cornette scored 21, not nearly enough to compensate for Butler's 4-of-13 shooting from the arc.

"We were well aware on a given night this could happen," Lickliter said. "The tough part of it is that it did. I'm so thankful this team prolonged it for as long as they could."

Sampson's strategy worked. He discarded film of the Mississippi State and Louisville games, saying those teams did not know how to play Butler. Instead, Oklahoma coaches studied league games against Milwaukee, which beat Butler twice and lost on a last-second shot. Sampson was so singularly impressed by Cornette that the coach bearhugged the opposing player afterward.

"I think we played smart," Sampson said. "To play a team like Butler, playing hard's not good enough. Because they're going to play as hard as anybody."

No. 1-seeded Oklahoma went on to lose to No. 3 seed Syracuse 63–47 in the Elite Eight. Oklahoma couldn't solve Syracuse's zone defense, which did nothing to soothe Butler's wounds. The Bulldogs had played at Syracuse in the NIT the year before and would have known what to do. In the Albany aftermath, the Bulldogs were teary-eyed not only because they lost, but because they believed they could have won.

"It was not a dream. It was a goal," Monserez said. "Not just to get to the Final Four, but to win the whole stinking thing. Why would you set your goal to lose?"

Butler's final numbers were to be treasured, if not immediately, then upon reflection. The Bulldogs were 27–6, setting a school record for victories. The seniors won 100 games, nearly unimaginable at Butler. Archey finished 72-of-74 on free throws, a .973 percentage that would have broken the NCAA Division I record except for the technicality of insufficient attempts.

The grieving process began. It is more than basketball when young men live and labor and laugh and cry together for an entire season. For several seasons, in the case of the seniors. These were not teammates, Cornette reiterated. These were brothers.

Butler's players had been part of something special. They knew it and said so. Miller and Cornette embraced in front of the bench and walked off the floor, arm in arm, past the stands, into the tunnel, and out of sight.

"The basketball part of this is over," Cornette said back in the locker room. "But we'll always be a team."

The 2006–07 Team (29–7):
New York, New York

Overnight success never occurs overnight. It might have seemed that way to those following Butler's storybook season of 2006–07, featuring a championship in the NIT Season Tipoff and culminating in a near-upset of the eventual NCAA champion. However, a foundation for that was built earlier and can be traced to two important dates.

The first was August 24, 2005, the first day of classes for that academic year. That's when transfers Mike Green and Pete Campbell formally became students at Butler, where they would have to wait one season before becoming eligible to represent the university in basketball.

The second was January 21, 2006, a nadir in coach Todd Lickliter's tenure. That's when the Bulldogs lost to Youngstown State 64–62, dropping their record to 9–8. In 2½ seasons since reaching the 2003 Sweet Sixteen, Butler had a cumulative 38–37 record. Virtually no one noticed Butler's descent because no one was paying attention by then. After a 13–15 season in 2004–05, four players left the program.

Dynamics inside any team aren't necessarily evident to those outside. In this case, it was impossible not to notice. The cohesiveness and competitiveness of Butler's 2005–06 players caused lasting results. Not only that season, but going forward.

Forward Brandon Polk, the 2006 Horizon League player of the year, said the Bulldogs were together on and off the court. The previous two seasons were tough to take, according to Brandon Crone, a junior forward on that team.

"We just had a lot of guys who didn't have a winning mindset," Crone said. "At the end of the '05–06 season, we really started establishing ourselves."

After Youngstown, the Bulldogs, despite a 2–3 record in the league, resolved to make a run at the championship. They had been fifth in the preseason poll, and early results indicated that was appropriate. Instead, beginning with a 55–51 victory at Cleveland State, the Bulldogs went on a six-game winning streak.

Butler could have earned a league co-title and brought the Horizon Tournament to Hinkle Fieldhouse by winning the finale at Detroit. The Bulldogs, behind by 10 with two minutes left, tied the score before falling 73–71 at the buzzer. They made 18 3-pointers, a school record. Butler's bid for a return to the NCAA Tournament ended in an 87–71 loss at Milwaukee in the league championship. The season ended in a 67–63 loss at Florida State in the NIT.

For Lickliter, defeat wasn't reason to despair. What hurt was to see careers end for 1,000-point scorers Bruce Horan and Avery Sheets—holdovers from the 2003 Sweet Sixteen—and also for Polk, who accomplished so much after playing the previous season with an injured shoulder. The Bulldogs were 20–13, winning more games than any other Division I team in Indiana.

"I've enjoyed this team so much," Lickliter said. "They're fun to go to practice with, they're fun to travel with, they're fun to compete with."

The fun had only begun.

• • •

Butler went into the 2006–07 season having lost three senior starters. So it was understandable that the coaches and media forecasting the outcome of the Horizon League standings voted Butler sixth. Oddly, the last time the Bulldogs lost three senior starters, in 2002, they advanced to the Sweet Sixteen a year later.

The previous season's practices had been spiced by red-shirts Mike Green and Pete Campbell. They became roommates after transferring from Towson University and Indiana-Purdue-Fort Wayne (IPFW), respectively. Green was a city native of Philadelphia and Campbell a small-town Hoosier. Green was a distributor, Campbell a 3-point shooter.

They complemented those who had played for the Bulldogs before: junior guard A.J. Graves, tough-minded senior forwards Brandon Crone and Brian Ligon, and sophomore wing Julian Betko.

The 6-foot-6 Betko, of Ruzomberok, Slovakia, transferred from Clemson to Butler in January 2004. Two knee surgeries had essentially kept him out of two college seasons, and though he lost some athleticism, he was a valued reserve in '05–06.

The Bulldogs were included in the 2006 NIT Season Tipoff—formerly the Preseason National Invitation Tournament—but before that played in New Orleans for the first time ever.

Their opening opponent, Tulane, was a creditable Conference USA team that would go on to a 17–13 season. But on this night the Green Wave were as overrun as the city was by Hurricane Katrina. Butler shot 52 percent and led by 24 at halftime of a 77–37 victory. Crone scored all of his 18 points in the first half.

The preseason NIT, now organized by the NCAA, had a new format with four teams from each of four regions. Four regional champions would advance to New York's Madison Square Garden for semifinals and the championship.

The Midwest Regional was set for Conseco Fieldhouse in Indianapolis and offered Butler a rare chance to play a team like Notre Dame on a neutral court. Notre Dame discontinued a long series with Butler after 1995, largely owing to a streak of five straight losses.

The Fighting Irish led Butler by seven points in the first half, sparked by freshman forward Luke Harangody. Graves was without a 3-pointer until nearly 19 minutes had elapsed, but then he made two to push Butler ahead 31–27 by halftime. He was getting warmed up. So was the action.

The Irish started the second half by scoring the first 10 points. After Butler regained the lead briefly, the Irish went ahead and stayed there. With Graves firing 3s from outside, and Green driving inside for baskets or kick-outs, the Bulldogs stayed with them.

Over the closing seven minutes, the teams were never separated by more than three points. The score was tied at 60, 62, 64, and 67. Green made the first of two free throws to send the Bulldogs ahead 68–67, then missed the second. Harangody's jump hook put Notre Dame back in front 69–68.

What happened after that gave Butler more than a momentary lead in a single game. A Green-to-Graves play set in motion everything that was to follow. Without such an occurrence, there would have been no NIT championship and possibly no NCAA Tournaments in seasons immediately thereafter. Dominoes were ready to fall, but it took Green and Graves to push them.

Brandon Crone drives against Notre Dame in the 2006 NIT Season Tipoff. Crone's skill and grit helped revive Butler's program (Butler University Archive).

With 90 seconds left in the game, Green passed into the right corner. Graves caught the ball behind the arc and arched it over Harangody's reach, and the rippled nets signaled that Graves had made his eighth 3-pointer. Butler led 71–69. Notre Dame's Russell Carter had a 3-point attempt to win the game, but Betko deflected the ball. Butler had won by that 71–69 count.

Graves' eight 3s—six in the second half—would be the most of his college career and were one off the tournament record set by Duke's Shane Battier in 2000. Green scored 19 points, and his 12 assists, in his second game for Butler, would be the most of his college career. The eighth 3 and 12th assist added up to more than three points.

Green played on losing teams before small audiences at Towson, and he spent the postgame news conference smiling and speaking about how "big-time" the scene was.

Butler moved on to play Indiana, which defeated Lafayette 91–66 in Kelvin Sampson's first game as the Hoosiers' coach. Sampson was at Oklahoma when the Sooners eliminated Butler from the 2003 NCAA Tournament at Albany, N.Y. He devised an effective plan for that game, but this time Sampson was confronting Butler on a night's notice.

Despite 24 percent shooting, Butler managed to be within three, 26–23, at the half. Graves started 0-of-6 from the 3-point arc, and the Bulldogs struggled to score. With Green on the bench with four fouls, Indiana lengthened the lead to 12. Lickliter was assessed a technical after throwing his coat in response to a foul call, and Indiana's Lance Stemler made two free throws to make it 47–35.

Next stop for the Hoosiers: New York? Not yet.

Unable to score from outside, Graves went inside and drew fouls. His six free throws, around a 3-pointer by reserve guard Marcus Nellems, trimmed Indiana's lead to three. Freshman forward Willie Veasley, playing with his left hand padded to protect a broken bone, tipped in a miss to push Butler ahead 50–49. Crone's two jumpers, the second a 3-pointer with 91 seconds left, made it 57–53. Green missed twice at the foul line, and Stemler's basket pulled the Hoosiers within two, 57–55. There were 41 seconds left, so one defensive stop would allow Indiana a shot to tie or win.

With the Bulldogs in possession and 16 seconds left, they called one timeout and then another. They had none left. With the shot clock expiring, Graves forced an attempt from the top of the key. The ball banked off the glass and went in with five seconds to play. After going 1-of-9 from the arc, Graves' 3-pointer had the Bulldogs bound for Broadway.

Butler 60, Indiana 55.

"We just didn't play smart," Sampson said, pointing to the Hoosiers' 20 turnovers. "It's not a hard game. We have to play smarter."

Graves finished with 20 points, shooting 10-of-10 on free throws. He was 4-of-18 from the field.

• • •

No Butler team had played at Madison Square Garden, once the Mecca of college basketball, in nearly a half century. The Bulldogs lost to Bradley 83–77 in their most recent appearance, March 14, 1959, in the postseason NIT.

They would have to wait a little longer to reach New York. For the pretourney news conference at the Marriott Marquis, located in the middle of the theatre district, coaches and players from North Carolina, Gonzaga, and Tennessee assembled. The Bulldogs' flight from Indianapolis was delayed, and they missed the event altogether. They missed about half of their scheduled practice at Baruch College in Manhattan.

The Bulldogs kept missing the hoop when they took the floor against 22nd-ranked Tennessee. Coach Bruce Pearl's Vols built a 21–8 lead, probably prompting tourney organizers to wonder how they ended up with Butler instead of Indiana or Notre Dame. Butler scored the final seven points of the half to close within three, 25–22.

As dreadfully as the Bulldogs shot the ball in the half (25 percent), the Vols were correspondingly as bad handling it (14 turnovers). Butler proceeded to score the first seven points of the second half for a 29–25 lead and never trailed again—for the rest of the tournament.

The unlikely source of a second-half outburst was Betko, who in 37 games for Butler had averaged fewer than three points. He scored 11 successive Butler points—nine on three 3-pointers—as the margin stretched to 46–38.

Meanwhile, the Vols treated the hoop as if it were the circumference of a coaster. They shot 10 percent—3-of-29—in the second half. Over the final 27 minutes, Tennessee scored 23 points. Butler moved into the championship game with a 56–44 victory. Graves and Betko scored 15 points each. Green endured 1-of-12 shooting and five turnovers, but none of that mattered.

"I felt like I was open almost the whole game," Betko said. "I just knew this year Coach expected me to, if I'm open, to shoot it and knock it down."

The unexpected continued in the second semifinal, in which Gonzaga beat second-ranked North Carolina 82–74. Tyler Hansbrough and Ty Lawson, who two years hence would lead the Tar Heels to a national championship, were limited to nine and 11 points, respectively.

So there it was, a mid-major match-up deluxe: Butler vs. Gonzaga.

"Butler and Gonzaga in the finals, I think it's good," Tar Heels coach Roy Williams said. "It's not good for North Carolina right now. But I have no problems with that. I think it's what makes our game the best game there is."

• • •

The day in between the semifinals and final fell on Thanksgiving Day. Rather than practice, the Bulldogs went sightseeing in the rain. They visited the Statue of Liberty at the invitation of Stephen Briganti, a Butler alum who was president and CEO of the Ellis Island Foundation. Earlier they watched the Macy's parade from their Times Square hotel overlooking Broadway.

It was a deviation in routine, but it also underscored a Lickliter mantra: don't get into a routine. He reasoned that a team dependant on that would unravel if something went wrong.

Lickliter wanted players to concentrate on what's important—the opponent—and not worry about uncontrollable things such as bus breakdowns. The best teams are those that know when it's business and when it's not, he said.

"Trips are pretty long, and you cannot be on edge the whole time," Lickliter said.

If the off-day was intended to relax the Bulldogs, it had the desired effect. In three previous NIT games, Butler fell behind Notre Dame by seven, Indiana by 12, and Tennessee by 13. This time, Betko scored the game's first points on a 3-pointer . . . and then the Bulldogs turned it on.

In one stretch of the half, they were 8-of-12 from the arc, getting 3s from five different players in building a 37–20 lead.

Gonzaga had an advantage inside with 6-foot-11 sophomore Josh Heytvelt, but foul trouble limited him to eight minutes in the half. Butler led by 14 points at the half, and that margin grew to 18 in the second half. Butler made 17-of-19 free throws over the final 7½ minutes and defeated Gonzaga, 79–71.

Green and Graves were a collective 14-of-14 on free throws in the final 3½ minutes and 18-of-18 for the game. Graves scored 26 points, Green 16, and Betko 13. Graves was voted the NIT's most outstanding player and was joined on the all-tournament team by Betko.

"They outplayed us in any facet and every facet that I can possibly think of involved in basketball," Gonzaga coach Mark Few said.

Butler players gathered at midcourt afterward and danced in a huddle. Later, they sang the "Butler War Song," as they always do after big victories:

We'll sing the Butler War Song
We'll give a fighting cry
We'll fight the Butler battle
Bulldogs ever do or die
And in the glow of the victory firelight
History cannot deny
To add a page or two
For Butler's fighting crew
Beneath the Butler sky

"Now ya'll know who Butler is!" yelled Mendee Ligon, mother of Brian, from her seat behind the bench. "I get aggravated because nobody gives them credit. They call them Cinderella, and they're no Cinderella. They're a good team with a good coach."

Butler won four successive NIT games in which it was an underdog and did it over four teams that were nationally ranked at the time or would be later.

New York media loved the underdog theme, especially in the case of Graves, a small-town kid epitomizing the spirit of *Hoosiers*.

"Maybe a small part of me is excited about it, but mainly I'm indifferent to it," Graves said.

They were loving the Bulldogs back in Indianapolis, too. Moe & Johnny's Bar & Grill, an unofficial campus hangout, was full for the NIT games, and students weren't even on campus.

"It was like a Colts crowd in here," a waitress said.

The Bulldogs' euphoria was necessarily muted. They had another game in a few hours.

Butler had not prepared for the contingency of winning the NIT. The championship was November 24, and Butler had scheduled a home game on November 25 against Kent State.

Butler had a charter flight to return to Indianapolis, but as with its flight to New York, there was a delay. The Bulldogs didn't arrive home until about 3:00 a.m. Lickliter never went home, sleeping for a few hours on his office couch.

There was little time for the ticket office to capitalize on success, and only 3,657 attended the next night at Hinkle Fieldhouse. Fortunately for the Bulldogs, the fans made the sound of many more.

"They just kept fueling us," Graves said.

The weary Bulldogs needed that, for their tank had emptied. They were up against a Kent State team that had been to the NCAA Tournament the season before and would win 21 games.

Butler shot 20 percent in the first half and fell behind 25–20. After the Flashes expanded their lead to eight, it appeared as if the fictional nature of Butler's season had been replaced by the hard facts. This was mortal Butler returned from New York, not Superman from Metropolis.

The Bulldogs would not let go, and briefly they surged ahead 52–50. With the shot clock expiring and 19 seconds to play, Omni Smith's 3-pointer sent Kent State ahead 57–55. The Bulldogs needed another miracle from Graves, and his shot missed. But Ligon was underneath, and he tapped in the ball with seven seconds on the clock to tie it at 57.

On to overtime. After three 40-minute games in four days, what's another five minutes?

The Bulldogs couldn't hold onto a four-point lead, and they trailed 67–64 as the clock dipped under 10 seconds. When Graves should have been fading, he kept firing. His 3-pointer swished with five seconds left, and Kent State's missed layup on the other end allowed the score to stay tied at 67.

On to a second overtime.

Graves twice stole the ball and drove in for layups. He made two free throws with seven seconds left to push the Bulldogs ahead 83–80, and that secured the outcome. On a night in which he began shooting 2-of-17, Graves scored 22 of his 26 points after halftime.

"He's a hard guy to stop for 40 minutes," Kent State coach Jim Christian said.

Or for 50 minutes.

Graves said it was the toughest thing he had ever done. Yet this had been a collective comeback. Green scored 16 points, Crone 15, and Ligon a career-high 13. The evening capped an extraordinary 75-hour period of Butler basketball.

"I'm about half amazed that these guys could do what they've done," Lickliter said.

On Monday morning, the Associated Press poll was released. Butler was 19th, its highest national ranking since 1949, the first year the poll was introduced. Butler was as high as No. 4 on the sportsillustrated.cnn.com Web site.

Sports information director Jim McGrath was besieged with interview requests from New York to Los Angeles, exceeding the media storm that followed the 2003 run to the Sweet Sixteen. Instead of one week of media attention, the Bulldogs would have to cope with this for an entire season.

Campus buzzed all day Monday. Students were back from Thanksgiving break, and basketball talk dominated conversations around Jordan Hall, Atherton Union, and the Greek houses.

The Bulldogs were 7–0. As they kept reminding everyone, it was early. They knew their anonymity had vanished.

"I think as a group, as a team, we'll have to realize that we are not going to be overlooked anymore," Betko said.

● ● ●

Brian Ligon was a representative figure of Butler's program. He was a top student with a team-first approach. He merited the success

Butler was enjoying as much as anyone, considering what he had endured while waiting for it to happen.

In the 21st game of both his freshman and sophomore seasons, he tore an anterior cruciate ligament. Both knee injuries came without collisions. Once, he was running at a shooter. The other time, he landed awkwardly after blocking a shot. As a junior, he wondered if he should just sit out the 21st game.

He used time away from basketball to reflect on his career path. He originally majored in finance, but the more afternoons he observed his parents, both dentists, the more he realized that's what he wanted to do.

"I think it's a great way to help people," he said.

Besides pre-dentistry, Ligon studied music production at Butler. He played piano and saxophone growing up and started keyboard while in high school. He and best friend Mike Brown created a ministudio in Ligon's bedroom, producing one CD.

In his junior year at Lakewood High School, Ligon helped his team to a 33–2 record and Florida's Class 4A state championship. He was a 15-point scorer for a 26–6 team as a senior and was voted Lakewood's outstanding male student.

At Butler, "Big Lig" never scored as many as 10 points in a game until he was a senior, but that was an inadequate measure of his contributions. He supplied post defense, toughness, and leadership. While going to college 1,000 miles from his Florida home, his teammates became an extended family.

"It's a team sport, and that's what I love about basketball," Ligon said. "You have a bunch of guys that you come to love, and they become like brothers to you."

• • •

After beating Valparaiso 60–47 to complete an 8–0 November, the Bulldogs returned home and twice won blowouts. They opened Horizon League play with a 70–45 victory over Cleveland State and won more emphatically over Ball State, taking a 30-point lead in a 65–41 victory. It was Ball State's lowest output since 1957. The Cardinals had previously lost to heavyweights such as Kansas, Western Kentucky, and Georgetown, but none dispatched them as the Bulldogs did.

"They're quick, but they don't hurry," Ball State coach Ronny Thompson said. "They're deliberate, but they attack."

Green scored 21 points and drew praise from Thompson as "the real deal." Green credited the Bulldogs' play with the fact that they actually had time to practice. During November, they played eight games in 20 days around travel to New Orleans, New York, and northern Indiana.

Butler climbed to 15th in the AP poll, and a top 10 ranking was possible ahead of its December 9 visit to Indiana State. The Bulldogs were already No. 1 in two computer rankings, RPI and Sagarin. Moreover, there was speculation that Butler could go undefeated—31–0—before the NCAA Tournament. No mid-major had done something like that since, coincidentally, Indiana State. The Sycamores were 34–0 until losing to Michigan State in the Larry Bird/Magic Johnson duel climaxing the 1979 NCAA Tournament.

Butler was the highest-ranked team to visit Indiana State in more than 20 years. The Bulldogs had often floundered there, as evidenced by their 5–16 record in the past 21 trips to Hulman Center.

It became a night in which anything that could go wrong for Butler, did go wrong. Typifying that was a sequence in which Graves, a 98 percent foul shooter, was poked in the right eye late in the first half, requiring him to leave the game. Green came off the bench to shoot two free throws and missed both. Graves sat out eight minutes of the second half and didn't score again until 45 seconds remained in Indiana State's 72–64 victory.

"I would not be honest if I didn't say they did struggle a little bit more offensively with him not in there," Indiana State coach Royce Waltman said.

Gabe Moore scored a career-high 24 points for the Sycamores and wasn't as magnanimous as his coach. "Not to disrespect their team," he said, "but their team is not very quick."

Crone said the Bulldogs were looking for officiating calls early, didn't get them, and allowed Indiana State to take control. Graves seemed almost relieved when he conceded there would be "no more buzz," and they could get back to business.

"I think they've handled the prosperity maturely and with as great a character as anybody I've been around," Lickliter said. "Now we've got some adversity. We'll see how we handle that."

•••

Butler's players had an irregular week because practices had to be held around final exams. That was of concern because the Bulldogs had rarely been sharp in their first game after finals. Of more concern was that the next opponent was 8–1 Purdue, revived under coach Matt Painter and on the verge of breaking into the Top 25.

Butler was meeting Purdue at Conseco Fieldhouse in the Wooden Tradition, a doubleheader honoring John Wooden, the most revered figure in college basketball and certainly in his home state of Indiana.

It was another chance for the Bulldogs to perform on a big stage. As they had done previously, that brought out their best. They defeated Purdue 68–65, completing a sweep of the state's giants—Notre Dame, Indiana, and Purdue—for the first time since the 1948–49 season.

As usual, the Bulldogs downplayed their achievements. Crone, whose hometown of Frankfort was close to the Purdue campus, conceded: "I really wanted this one."

He played like it, despite missing his first nine shots. His 3-pointer midway through the second half stalled the Boilermakers' surge. After future NBA forward Carl Landry dunked to put Purdue ahead 64–63, Crone converted a three-point play to restore Butler's lead to 66–64 with 58 seconds left. Seconds later, he slapped the ball away from a Purdue player to help secure the outcome.

"He made probably the two or three most important plays in the game," Graves said. "Even if he's not doing things you see in the stat sheet, he's the leader of this team."

Graves continued to lead by example. Of the record 130 games he played for Butler, this was as efficiently as he ever shot: 8-of-14 from the field, 4-of-7 on 3s, and 5-of-5 on free throws. He scored 18 of his 25 points in the first 14 minutes of the second half, including one dazzling basket that he arched in from balcony height.

The Bulldogs had one more pre-Christmas date, and 8,027 fans showed up December 22 to watch them defeat Evansville 76–65 and extend their home streak to 15.

Bulldog fever was contagious. Hinkle Fieldhouse's Gate 4 area was crowded with intersecting lines for tickets, concessions, and merchandise. Fans' devotion was tested with an initial offering of $50 courtside seats, and all 24 sold. Butler's online store had page after page of "currently out of stock" items.

The Bulldogs made the Evansville game more suspenseful than desired. Butler came in with the nation's best free throw percentage (.808), then proceeded to be a shaky 21-of-31. Jason Holsinger, from nearby New Palestine, Ind., sank five 3-pointers for the Purple Aces, who were within six points with two minutes left.

"We've got a strong team, and it takes a strong team to be able to do what these guys are doing," Lickliter said.

•••

This Christmas was an especially joyous holiday for Julian Betko. Mom was in town.

Eva Betkova prepared traditional Slovakian cuisine: krupica, a sweet appetizer resembling grits, cabbage soup, and pork chops. Local stores didn't stock farm-grown carp, a Slovakian favorite, but home cooking is always good. It's good even if home is not Slovakia, as Betko's Hoosier housemates, Brandon Crone and Drew Streicher, could attest.

"My teammates are leaving nothing on their plates," Betko said.

His mother had seen him play

Pete Campbell shoots against Old Dominion in the first round of the NCAA Tournament. Campbell, who set a Horizon League record with .581 accuracy on 3-pointers in 2006–07, made a flurry of 3s to help Butler beat Old Dominion 57–46 (Butler University Arhive).

in America for the first time in wins over Purdue and Evansville. The festive nature of her visit contrasted sharply to Betko's introduction to the United States. He arrived on August 30, 2001. Twelve days later, terrorist attacks resulted in downed planes in New York, Washington, D.C., and Pennsylvania. Would Eva Betkova's son be okay?

"She wanted me to come home," Betko said. "It was really tough. Is war going to happen?"

Betko didn't know English well enough to understand the news coverage. He called home for an explanation of September 11. He stayed in America and flourished in basketball, averaging 23 points a game for the high school in Sharon, Pa. He kept in contact with family through telephone and e-mail. Eva, with her son translating, said anxieties diminished after her husband came to the high school's graduation and met her son's host family.

Betko earned a scholarship to Clemson and played all 28 games there as a freshman in 2002–03. He played in one game the next season, injured his right knee, and transferred to Butler at midyear. Then he needed another surgery and sat out for one and a half years, prompting Butler to petition the NCAA for eligibility in 2007–08. Betko already had a degree in international management and was studying for a master's in finance. He was in no hurry to leave.

"I love it here. I love the place," he said.

Hockey was his first love, but after his hometown built a basketball arena when he was 10, his sports allegiance changed. His mother said he was fulfilling the sports dream of her husband, Ludovit, a former pro volleyball player.

Betko's transformation from those early days in America was so complete that he forgot Slovakian expressions. He asked his mother to translate.

"Almost every day, she's my dictionary," he said.

He could always look up the words. There was no substitute for Mom's cooking.

•••

The Bulldogs resumed Horizon League play December 30 at Milwaukee, which had the worst record in the league, at 3–11. The game brought out the Bulldogs' worst. Maybe it was because after so many games so early, this was their third game in 21 days.

Butler trailed by eight points in the first half, never led by more than two until the closing three minutes, and had uncharacteristically bad ball handling (15 turnovers) and 3-point shooting (1-of-10). Graves and Green combined for 27 second-half points in a 55–50 victory.

In the week leading up to a home game vs. Wright State, the Bulldogs made amends for Milwaukee. Scrimmages between the first and second teams were as contentious as family fights.

"We really went after each other, both teams," Streicher acknowledged.

Streicher made the plays of the day in Butler's 73–42 trampling of Wright State. He sprawled on the floor to wrest the ball from DaShaun Wood, calling timeout to keep possession. Seconds later, Streicher took Crone's pass, laid it in, and sank a free throw to finish a three-point play highlighting a 14–0 run. In running their home winning streak to 16, the Bulldogs had 19 assists on 23 field goals and equaled a season high with 12 3-pointers.

It was as crisply as Butler had played. That made the next outing inexplicable.

Somewhere on Interstate 65 between Indianapolis and Chicago, the Bulldogs lost their way. They never rediscovered it in time, and time ran out. No. 12 Butler became the highest-ranked team ever beaten by Illinois-Chicago, 73–67, in overtime.

The outcome spoiled a memorable 25 minutes by Graves. In the second half and overtime, he scored 29 of his career-high 31 points. His 3-pointer trimmed UIC's lead to 58–56 with 20 seconds left, and he followed with two free throws to tie the score at 58. As the clock ran out, he missed a long 3-point attempt that would have won the game in regulation.

Graves' seventh 3-pointer pushed Butler ahead 67–66 in OT, but the Flames scored the last seven points. Butler was 13-of-42 on 3-pointers, breaking the school record of 39 attempts set at Detroit 10 months before.

Graves declined to confirm a report that he might have wisdom teeth extracted. But before the Bulldogs' next game, at home vs. South Dakota State, the university announced that he had had the surgery and would sit out. The Bulldogs built a 26-point lead and won 62–47 on an afternoon in which they were especially attentive to defense. Through 35 minutes, South Dakota State was limited to two two-point baskets. Crone said the Bulldogs were eager to atone for the loss at UIC.

"As badly as we played there, we really wanted to come out and show that's not the team we were and that's not the team we want to be," he said.

The team they wanted to be was the one that conducted a 3-point shooting clinic and dominated Youngstown State 67–39 and Green Bay 80–59. The Bulldogs were 14-of-24 from the arc against Youngstown and 14-of-23 against Green Bay—a cumulative 60 percent. Green Bay coach Tod Kowalczyk called these Bulldogs more skilled than the version reaching the 2003 Sweet Sixteen.

"Every time they had an open 3," he said, "it seemed like they made it."

Pete Campbell, who played sparingly early in the season because of a stress fracture, was a collective 8-of-12 from the arc in the two home games. Bare-chested fans calling themselves "Campbell's Crew" had *P-E-T-E* painted on their chests.

Graves, feeling depleted after oral surgery, played 13 minutes of the first half against Youngstown and sat out the second half. He was fully recovered for Green Bay, scoring 21 of his 28 points in the first half. In the half in which he had last played healthy—the second half at UIC—he scored 29. Counting halves 10 days apart, that would be a 50-point game. Graves was 9-of-9 on free throws, extending his streak to 63 in a row and season total to 91-of-92 (98.9 percent).

• • •

Butler waded into a stretch of four league games in seven days, with three on the road. First up on January 25 was Loyola, which was 4–3 in the league but had been the preseason favorite. Loyola coach Jim Whitesell was generous in praise of the Bulldogs, calling Crone "a matchup nightmare" and Graves an All-America candidate. Loyola featured a difficult matchup in Blake Schilb, a 6-foot-7 senior.

The Bulldogs led by 10 points early in the second half but were overtaken by Loyola, which went ahead 59–57 on Schilb's basket with 24 seconds left. He was fouled but missed his free throw. Graves was fouled with 13 seconds left, and he made two to even the score at 59 and send the game into overtime.

The OT was all A.J. He scored 10 points thereafter, giving Butler the lead on each of his three overtime 3-pointers in a 70–66 victory. He finished with 26 points and had five taken away—a 3-pointer on which Butler was called for a foul away from the ball and a layup disallowed because Butler had signaled timeout.

Graves more than made up for a missed free throw that ended his streak at 63. He later missed another.

"I'm just glad that those two didn't cost us the game," he said. "I put the two in that needed to go in to put (us) into overtime."

Butler was 18–2, the best 20-game record in school history.

The Bulldogs then overcame a Calihan Hall jinx—they had lost six of seven there—in beating Detroit 68–58. Not since 1996 had Butler won at Loyola and Detroit in the same year.

The Bulldogs finished the month with a January 31 victory at Youngstown State that represented another milestone—best record in the nation. Their 71–58 victory, coupled with Indiana's 71–66 upset of second-ranked Wisconsin, left Butler and Wisconsin both at 21–2.

"We probably won't be able to fit on that plane. Big heads," Lickliter joked afterward.

The victory at Youngstown was Butler's fourth in seven days in four states. Green equaled his high from Towson, scoring 23 points, and roommate Campbell added 20 on 8-of-10 shooting.

Butler extended its home winning streak to 21 by beating Milwaukee 66–47 before a season-high crowd of 9,086. Graves ended a mini downturn with 20 points, equaling his total from the previous two and a half games.

At 22–2, the Bulldogs remained tied with Wisconsin for the nation's best record. In February's first polls, they climbed into the top 10 for the first time in school history—No. 9 by AP, No. 10 by ESPN/*USA Today* coaches' rankings—or one spot above their No. 11 from 1949.

● ● ●

One day the previous season, when Pete Campbell was on the scout team, Butler moved a practice because of a conflict at Hinkle Fieldhouse. The Bulldogs worked on zone defense at nearby Marian College.

Campbell made the Bulldogs wish they had called off the whole thing. He made so many 3-point shots that he ruined the zone. He ruined the whole practice.

"He didn't miss," assistant coach LaVall Jordan said. "It was unbelievable."

In 3-point workouts, Campbell made as many as 46-of-50. He couldn't shoot effectively early in the season, playing with a leg brace while recovering from a stress fracture. He continued to come off the bench but earned more minutes as his defense improved.

At Yorktown High School, he played goalkeeper in soccer and first base in baseball. Basketball came first, though. At age three, he accompanied his father, David, to the gym. By 12, Pete was playing pickup games against adults. Considering his lineage, it was inevitable he would play sports. Virtually all of his male relatives were athletes.

Campbell's uncles, John and Joe Sutter, were Marion High School basketball stars who became pros in Europe. John was an All-American at Tulane, and Joe, an Indiana All-Star, played at Davidson. The uncles were tennis players, as was Pete's maternal grandfather, Jack Sutter.

The grandfather played college tennis in his 40s for Indiana Wesleyan University, which named its facility after him.

By high school, Campbell's summers were devoted to basketball for an AAU team coached by Butler great Billy Shepherd. Campbell averaged 21 points as a Yorktown senior, wearing jersey No. 33 in honor of his hero, Larry Bird. He was recruited by the military academies, Wright State, and Davidson. He signed with IPFW—too early, he conceded—so he would be close to home.

He redshirted one season and played the next. He was put off by new IPFW coach Dane Fife and started looking for another school. Shepherd directed him toward Butler. Transferring meant Campbell had to sit out again, thus confining him to three college seasons inside the five-year window allowed by the NCAA.

"The way it happened is the only way it could have happened, so I don't regret any of the decisions I've made," he said.

Opponents became wary of Campbell not because he could make a 3-pointer. It was his multiple 3s. Throughout a two-year Butler career, his play featured the "Campbell Cluster," or 3-pointers in short succession.

Mike Green said that if Campbell made one 3, he immediately passed to him again. Another make, another pass. Go to Pete, then re-Pete. And re-Pete again.

"Pete's a game-changer," Green said. "I like to call him a hired hit man."

At 6-foot-7, Campbell could shoot over most defenders, as Bird could. Campbell would end this season shooting an astonishing 58 percent from the arc in Horizon League play, a record. At the end of the 2007–08 season, he ranked 21st in Division I history at 45.1 percent, based on a minimum of 200 made and an average of two per game (248 in 94 games, including one IPFW season).

•••

The Bulldogs, in their first outing as a top 10 team, visited Cleveland State in what was not so much a contest as it was a performance. This is what it was like:

Nick Rodgers, a freshman walk-on, had never taken a shot in college. He launched a 3-pointer with 80 seconds left. Swish. It was the Bulldogs' *20th* 3-pointer, punctuating a 92–50 victory with an exclamation point.

Butler was 20-of-33 from the arc, or 60.6 percent. Six Bulldogs made 3s, led by Campbell's 8-of-11 accuracy.

"One guy can get in a zone. But a whole team in a zone?" Cleveland State coach Gary Waters said.

Butler broke the league's 3-point record of 18, set on three occasions. The NCAA record, 28, was set on December 10, 1994, by Troy—but in 74 attempts against George Mason.

The Campbell Cluster was at its most potent. Campbell didn't enter until five minutes into the game, then sank his first 3-pointer a couple of minutes later. He was 5-of-5 in a span of less than five minutes as Butler stretched the lead to 29–10. He finished with 28 points in 22 minutes played, adding a couple of two-pointers from barely inside the arc. The Bulldogs ended with 27 assists on 33 field goals, both season highs. Lickliter attributed their shooting to moving and sharing the ball.

"It's easy to talk about, but it doesn't always happen," he said. "These guys are not only willing, but eager, to do it."

Butler took a nine-game winning streak to Wright State two days later. As impressive as the Bulldogs had been, their 11–1 league record was only a half game ahead of Wright State, at 11–2. The Raiders could not only climb past Butler in the standings, they could challenge for the No. 1 seed in the league tournament.

The Raiders' only defeat in the previous 10 games had been the 31-point drubbing at Butler, and the rematch in no way resembled that. Wright State trailed by four late in the first half, then scored the final 12 points of the half to go ahead by eight. The Raiders expanded that to 11 to begin the second half and went on to upset the Bulldogs 75–63. Students in the record crowd of 10,827 swarmed onto the court.

In contrast to the game before, the Bulldogs shot 5-of-26 on 3-pointers. Lickliter suggested that they might have become flustered when shots didn't fall as they had previously.

If you thought the success of the Butler Bulldogs over the last decade was something, wait until you see the next 10 years...The Bulldogs have added more and more talent to their roster and in the next few years are preparing to make a leap to being a legitimate player on the national stage. And when I say national stage, I mean national championship.

— Joe Dlugosz, blogger for Ramblermania.com

"Maybe we're a little bit a victim of our own success," the coach said. "It hasn't been easy, but there's been some fairly smooth sailing. You can get anxious."

A subplot was the duel between Wright State guard DaShaun Wood and Graves for league player of the year. Wood scored 23 of his 30 points in the second half, including 21 of the Raiders' final 31. Graves scored 10 in his worst shooting game of the season, going 3-of-16. He conceded that it was a strain to be every opponent's biggest game.

"Every time we roll into a new town, they show up. Their crowd comes ready, their team comes ready to play," he said. "It really is difficult trying to have to come in with that concentration every night. Tonight, we just couldn't get it done."

• • •

The Bulldogs fell three spots, to 13th, when the next AP poll was released. The buildup for the week was all about their Saturday game against No. 16 Southern Illinois in a BracketBuster pairing. The BracketBuster was introduced in 2003 as a partnership between mid-major conferences and the ESPN networks. The concept was intended to promote the leagues and allow teams in contention for the NCAA Tournament to enhance resumes.

Before SIU's Salukis came to Indianapolis, the Bulldogs had a midweek game against Florida Gulf Coast, a Division II team from Fort Myers, Fla. A winter storm shut down most of the city, and hazardous driving conditions limited the crowd to about 1,000. Gulf Coast had six Division I transfers, a 22–5 record, and a 14-game winning streak—and proved to be as capable as any Horizon League opponent.

Butler's lead, which was 17 in the first half, was trimmed to nine with less than two minutes left. The Bulldogs made eight successive free throws, six by Green, to complete a 79–65 victory and extend their home winning streak to 21. Green scored a career-high 24 points, and Graves' 22 were the most he had scored in seven games.

"We're the hunted now," Green said.

That was underscored by the ferocity with which Southern Illinois played Butler. For the first time in the fieldhouse's storied history, both Butler and its opponent were nationally ranked.

The crowd of 10,827, boosted by a contingent from Carbondale, Ill., represented the first sellout since the March 1, 2003, game against Milwaukee. The Salukis emphasized defense as much as the Bulldogs, and each possession was as close to combat as rules permit. Southern

Illinois proceeded to build a 10-point lead in the second half and beat Butler 68–64.

"I just can't imagine there's been a harder fought, better game throughout the course of this season," Lickliter said.

Some fans were incensed by the officiating crew from the Missouri Valley Conference, although Butler coaches and players made no complaints publicly. Under provisions of the BracketBuster, officials came from the visitors' league. Southern Illinois' victory margin came via a 27–19 edge in free throws made.

The Salukis raised their record to 23–5 and won on the road over a ranked opponent for the first time since 1975. Guard Jamaal Tatum scored 10 of their last 15 points and finished with 20. Graves vomited during one stoppage of play and was obviously in an impaired state. He scored a season-low five points.

It was an outcome that reinforced doubts about Butler. Yet Lickliter allowed that the "incredible" atmosphere contributed to a special afternoon.

"When you saw this crowd, when you saw the environment, when you felt it, you got to feel Hinkle Fieldhouse the way Hinkle should be," he said. "And you got to see it on national TV. If that's what it takes, OK, we'll deal with the conference stuff afterwards."

• • •

The regular-season league title was within reach of the Bulldogs, who finished with another demanding stretch—three games in six days, beginning at Green Bay. Butler's athletic department, far from affluent, eased the burden by chartering a jetliner at a cost of about $10,000. Players gathered for Sunday evening dinner at the Milano Inn, an Italian restaurant that has been an Indianapolis fixture since 1934, and watched the NBA All-Star Game on television.

The team was bused to the airport for the short flight, checked into the motel in Green Bay, and reconvened the next day for a shootaround at the Resch Center. As with all such practices, players couldn't adjourn until someone made a half-court shot—a contest involving student managers, assistant coaches, and volunteers.

Lickliter shouted "Let it rain!" to lighten the mood, repeating a line from a character who delivered absurd commentary on the basketball court in the movie *Along Came Polly*. The team once watched the movie on a bus trip, and Lickliter thought it was hilarious.

"He just loved it," Crone said. "That's the only time I really heard him laugh like that. 'Iceman!' Let it rain!'"

The tone turned serious against the Phoenix, which turned a seven-point deficit into a 30–28 halftime lead. It was an ominous sign for the Bulldogs, who had trailed at the half in all four defeats. Another Campbell Cluster eliminated concern.

He sank three 3-pointers in less than two minutes—the first two coming 33 seconds apart—in a personal 9–1 run that built Butler's lead to 47–40. Those were the only field goals he made in 17 minutes. Green Bay coach Tod Kowalczyk said that short sequence determined the outcome.

"Fortunately, I was able to start hitting because in the first half my shot didn't feel real good," Campbell said.

Nearly 10 minutes remained, but the Graves/Green backcourt knew how to protect a lead. Graves scored 10 of Butler's last 16 points and finished with 20 in a 68–58 victory.

Butler could wrap up a share of the league title by closing out the week, and regular season, with two home victories. The Bulldogs had won six home games in the Horizon by an average of 25 points, and none was closer than 19. Beyond that, they had won 16 straight in the league at home, and visiting Loyola had lost 17 in a row at Hinkle Fieldhouse.

"Our goal is to win the conference tournament and then the championship," Crone stated. "Any slip-ups now, and we're done."

Tony Dungy, coach of the Indianapolis Colts, and team president Bill Polian were at the fieldhouse and received an ovation when they stood at center court with the Lombardi Trophy won at the Super Bowl over the Chicago Bears. This Indianapolis/Chicago meeting would not end as favorably.

Loyola overtook Butler at the end of the first half and led by 12 points early in the second. The Bulldogs reclaimed the lead but couldn't hold it. Loyola shot 53 percent and persevered for a 75–71 victory behind Blake Schilb's 28 points. Graves scored 24 but couldn't repeat his earlier heroics at Loyola.

It was the third loss in five games for Butler, which had fallen from 23–2 to 25–5. Oddly, Butler had been 25–4 three times in six years and each time lost its 30th game.

Compounding the Bulldogs' distress was that they could have taken the No. 1 seed in the Horizon tourney and thus home-court advantage. Instead, the semifinals would be at Wright State, which secured the No. 1 seed despite a 72–57 loss at Youngstown.

Dungy addressed Butler's players afterward, reminding them that the Colts' season paralleled theirs. The Colts, too, had floundered late. Butler's run to the championship of the NIT Season Tipoff inspired the Colts, Dungy told them.

"It was incredibly thoughtful of coach Dungy to come in and speak to our players," Lickliter said. "And we were very appreciative of his time with us."

Time as a college player was ticking away for Brandon Crone, Brian Ligon, and Marcus Nellems. The senior day game against Detroit would be their last at Hinkle Fieldhouse, and their task was incomplete. Butler, once considered a probable No. 4 or 5 seed in the NCAA Tournament, was sliding toward No. 8 or 9. At minimum, Butler needed a league co-title.

The Bulldogs accomplished that mission by smothering Detroit 56–36—the fewest points allowed by Butler in 181 games. Crone scored 17 points in 21 minutes before leaving to an ovation.

"Coach kind of got on us a little bit, like he should have, after Loyola," Crone said. "We didn't want to leave Hinkle like that."

When league honors were announced two days later, Lickliter was coach of the year and Green newcomer of the year. Graves joined Schilb and Wood, the player of the year, as a unanimous all-league selection.

•••

After the 2002 snub year, Butler never again entered the league tournament with assurance. The snub remained a conversational topic—and motivation—for the 2007 team. All projections placed the Bulldogs in the NCAA Tournament, but the lesson they learned was that nothing was sure.

One difference was that Butler was 36th in RPI, compared with 77th after the 2002 league tournament. Joel Cornette, the coordinator of basketball operations who was a junior on that 2002 team, often told players the story of that season.

"I think they can tell, when I still talk about it, how much it hurts and bothers me," Cornette said. "They don't want that to happen to them."

Under the tourney format, No. 2-seeded Butler and No. 3 seed Loyola advanced directly to a semifinal at Dayton. After two meetings decided by four points each, one in overtime, this one played out similarly.

In the closing 14 minutes of regulation, Butler and Loyola were never separated by more than three points. The score was tied at 43, 45, 50, 52, and finally 54. Graves missed a one-hander with three seconds on the clock—he finished 0-of-9—and Loyola called timeout. Schilb's 42-foot attempt also missed, and the teams went to overtime.

Although Schilb pierced the Bulldogs as usual—his 29 points gave him 84 in three games against them—he missed two of three shots in overtime while defended by Ligon.

"I wanted to make sure I didn't give up anything easy," Ligon said. "Because this is my last year, and you've got to go all-out."

Ligon, a poor free throw shooter, made two to tie the score at 61 with 1:11 left. Butler was 10-of-10 on free throws in the overtime, the final six by Graves.

Butler survived 67–66, setting up a rematch against Wright State for the championship. Wood scored 25 points in the Raiders' 67–51 semifinal victory over Green Bay. Talk radio in Dayton was that a Raider victory over Butler was a foregone conclusion, with the only question being NCAA seed. The Raiders were 13–1 at home.

"Our motivation is to go there and prove they didn't see the real Butler team last time and to show them that," Crone said.

The game created a stir around Wright State. Students stood outside the Nutter Center in the cold starting at 11 a.m. The administration purchased about 2,000 available tickets, then gave them away free on a first-come, first-served basis, leading to a near-sellout of 10,686.

Butler began purposefully, bolting ahead 10–0. Wood kept chopping away, too quick to be guarded by Graves. Lickliter delayed assigning the 6-foot-7 Streicher to Wood, who scored 21 points in the opening 22 minutes and six thereafter. Also, as the Bulldogs struggled to score, Campbell sat on the bench for all but 11 minutes and had two points.

With Butler trailing by three and time expiring, Graves sidestepped Wood, who brushed him. Graves missed a 3-point attempt on an up-and-under move, and Wright State's Will Graham was fouled on the rebound. Graham had just made two free throws, and he made two more with 1.3 seconds left, completing Wright State's 60–55 victory. For the second time in 25 days, Wright State fans washed over the court, exulting in the school's first NCAA Tournament berth since 1993.

Graves said the final play was not a foul. Crone, despite 18 points, said he failed the team. Lickliter said nothing was wrong, despite a fourth loss in eight games. Considering the Bulldogs' resume, there was no reason to believe they would be snubbed as they were in 2002.

"That's something I have some peace with," Lickliter said. "Because if this were the last game, I'd be crushed. Because I don't want it to end."

• • •

Brandon Crone, as much as anyone, was playing as if he did not want the season to end. In eight games preceding the NCAA Tournament, he averaged 15.5 points, seven more than his career mark. Not that scoring defined his game, but it was one measure of the urgency he felt. He and Brian Ligon took their roles as captains seriously. Crone and Ligon rebuked teammates more harshly than a coach would have.

"That's just the way we were," Crone said. "I'm not spending four years here and not getting to the (NCAA) tournament. It's not going to happen.

"Guys had no problem with it. We were hungry to win. We were hungry for success. And it showed."

Crone's parents divorced when he was two, and he lived with his mother, Wanda Mitchell, in Frankfort, Ind. His father, Barry Crone, remarried and lived in Indianapolis. Brandon has seven siblings.

Brothers and sisters attended Pike High School, a basketball power on Indy's Northwest side. In 2002–03, when Crone was a senior, Pike assembled one of the best teams in Indiana history and won a state championship with a 29–0 record. Crone considered moving in with his father and transferring from Frankfort to Pike.

"I knew I would get a state title, but I didn't know if I would get to be an Indiana All-Star," Crone said. "It felt a little wrong just to hop on that squad."

He said his biggest regret from high school was not winning a sectional. Frustration was compounded when Butler couldn't sustain success after Crone arrived on campus. So it was gratifying when the Bulldogs resumed winning.

Team chemistry was enhanced by the fact that the players were such friends. The Bulldogs bowled together, hung out together, and played games together.

"Out of all the seasons we played together," Crone said, "that was by far the closest team."

• • •

The Bulldogs spent the days leading up to Selection Sunday listening to fans and media speculate about their seeding and defending themselves against accusations that the long season had fatigued them.

Butler's players just wanted to play in the NCAA Tournament, something none of them had done. To do so was unimaginable after Butler was forecast to be sixth in the Horizon League.

"I don't think it was ever the case that we wore out," Crone said. "Sometimes you hit a slump."

On a Web site of 27 projected brackets, Butler had an average seed of No. 8. Only one forecast had the Bulldogs better than a No. 7. Campbell bet his father that Butler would be a No. 5, but that was a minority view.

To watch the selection show, players gathered at Lickliter's home.

As Butler's players scattered to different rooms to watch the announcement, CBS didn't keep them in suspense long. In the third pairing, there it was: Butler, next to the number 5.

"We earned a 5 seed. They didn't give us nothing," Mike Green said emphatically.

Butler (27–6) was assigned to play 12th-seeded Old Dominion (24–8) in a Midwest Regional game in Buffalo, N.Y. It was the highest Butler had ever been seeded since the tournament expanded to 64 teams in 1985. The selection committee minimized late-season losses and credited the Bulldogs for a 6–3 record against the NCAA Tournament field and a 14–4 mark away from home.

"I believe in this team," Lickliter said, "and I'm glad that other people did, too."

Many others didn't. In fact, in a quarter century of the tournament, it would be hard to find a No. 5 seed generating so much skepticism. Much of that came down to history: A No. 5 seed had lost to a No. 12 in all but two tournaments since 1983. ESPN analyst Jay Bilas called Butler "the darling" of the selection committee in scoffing at the seed. Print and broadcast journalists picked Old Dominion to win. Oddsmakers showed little confidence in the Bulldogs, who were 1 ½-point favorites.

Old Dominion and 21st-ranked Butler were two of six teams outside the six power conferences to make the field as an at-large invitee. The

Indianapolis Colts coach Tony Dungy, right, speaks to Butler coach Todd Lickliter. Dungy addressed the Bulldogs after a dispiriting home loss to Loyola, telling the players that the Super Bowl champion Colts recovered from similar setbacks (Butler University Archives).

Monarchs saw a 12-game winning streak end in a 79–63 loss to George Mason in the final of the Colonial Athletic Association Tournament.

Lickliter defended Butler's late-season performance and said that all the losses were to good teams. Old Dominion coach Blaine Taylor was not going to be swept into that discussion.

"You don't go around the country and find many people who play basketball better than Butler," Taylor said.

The Bulldogs endured travel problems similar to those delaying their flights to and from New York City. Their charter to Buffalo left Indianapolis 4½ hours late. The day before the game, they practiced at Daemen College in suburban Amherst, N.Y., before their assigned workout at HSBC Arena, home of the National Hockey League's Buffalo Sabres.

In a cold-shooting first half, Butler (29 percent) fell behind 20–19 against Old Dominion (32 percent). Lithuanian forward Valdas Vasylius, one of the Monarchs' four foreign players, scored his first field goal—a 3-pointer—to push Old Dominion ahead 32–29. This one was evolving like so many recent Butler games, back and forth. Abruptly, that changed.

Graves tied the score with a 3-pointer, followed by one from the arc by Campbell. Campbell sank a second 3-pointer less than a minute later, and Old Dominion called timeout. By now, it was raining 3s. Campbell sank yet *another* from the arc, pushing the Bulldogs' lead to 41–32.

Green's 3-pointer and driving layup completed a 17–0 run. Butler led 46–32. Campbell's three 3s came in a 92-second span, and they were his only points in 14 minutes off the bench.

"He was the game-changer. Campbell was the difference," Old Dominion's Taylor said afterward.

The Bulldogs' 57–46 victory forestalled a 12-over-5 upset and advanced them into the second round against No. 4-seeded Maryland. The Terrapins overcame 30 points by Davidson freshman Stephen Curry for an 82–70 victory.

Ligon and Streicher combined to limit Vasylius, an all-Colonial forward, to 10 points, or six under his average. Without a game for nine days, the Bulldogs were fresher and defended better, Lickliter said. He compared their play at the beginning to the fog shrouding nearby Niagara Falls as they ate dinner the night before.

"When we came back out, it was clear and beautiful," Lickliter said. "Much like the first half and second half of today's game."

The Maryland game allowed Butler to revert to a more familiar role: the small school, the lower seed, the outsized mid-major going against one of college basketball's powers. For months the Bulldogs had been the target of every opponent.

Not that Maryland was without burdens. The Terps (25–8) were trying to reach the Sweet Sixteen for the first time since 2003.

In an era in which it was hard to retain players for four years, Maryland had three seniors who had scored more than 1,000 points: D.J. Strawberry, Mike Jones, and Ekene Ibekwe.

"This is why we came to the University of Maryland, to make our mark," said Strawberry, son of former baseball slugger Darryl Strawberry.

Maryland coach Gary Williams wasn't supporting the theory that the Bulldogs were underdogs. Maryland players said the right things—

you can't underestimate anyone—but it was impossible to determine whether they meant it.

Certainly, the teams' styles were opposites. Maryland was 16–1 when scoring 80 or more points and 2–5 when scoring fewer than 70. Butler was 20–0 when holding opponents under 60.

Buffalo, without a local team to cheer, nevertheless nearly filled the hockey arena with 18,801 fans. Maryland began by exploiting its superior size, retrieving three missed shots before Ibekwe dunked on the fourth. However, the tempo and scoreboard favored Butler after that. The Bulldogs led by 11 late in the first half, fell behind briefly, then never trailed in the closing 15 minutes.

Betko injured his shoulder in a collision against Old Dominion but played 29 minutes against Maryland. He made two driving layups in the first half, and his 3-pointer in the second half extended Butler's lead to 51–46.

With little more than two minutes to play, Graves drove to the hoop and missed. Green snared the ball and passed out to Graves, who had run around to the corner. Graves hit a 3-pointer—the last of his 19 points—to extend Butler's lead to 61–56.

After Maryland trimmed that to 61–59 and stole an inbounds pass, Strawberry was called for charging with 41 seconds left. Butler ran time off the clock until Betko missed a 3-pointer that was rebounded by Green. Green was fouled and sank one free throw with 3.6 seconds on the clock for the final points of a 62–59 victory. Butler scored 36 points on 12 3-pointers, including four by Graves and three each by Crone and Campbell.

The Bulldogs validated—if it was needed—that early run in New York City with additional achievement in New York state. A collection of small-town Hoosiers, city kids, and transfer students had made it to the Sweet Sixteen.

"We've shown all year that when 12 players play together, anything can be done," Crone said. "It's exciting for me, but I just love sharing it with these guys. I don't want it to end."

• • •

The Bulldogs waited a day to learn the identity of the Midwest Regional semifinal opponent they would play in St. Louis, a four-hour drive from Butler's campus. Moments after Florida beat Purdue 74–67, Ligon's cell phone rang. Calling from Florida was his father, Reggie.

"Gotta go get those Gators," he told his son.

So it would be Florida vs. Butler. Florida conjured up many images: defending national champion, top seed, roster of future NBA players, memories of heartbreak. Florida defeated Butler 69–68 in overtime in the first round in 2000, when assistant coaches LaVall Jordan and Joel Cornette were players.

"It still hurts," Jordan said.

The Bulldogs needed no additional incentive in a bid to advance further in the NCAA Tournament than ever before. What was directly ahead was daunting enough without looking behind. Florida's 6-foot-11 Joakim Noah, 6-foot-10 Al Horford, and 6-foot-9 Corey Brewer were all taller than Butler's center, the 6-foot-7 Ligon. The Gators were first in the nation with 53 percent shooting and fourth in rebounding. If that weren't enough, they had two 3-point shooters in Lee Humphrey and Taurean Green.

"The beauty of our system is it applies to every style of play," Streicher said. "We just need to apply our same principles that we started working on in October and keep working on those."

Florida coach Billy Donovan had more time to devote to the Bulldogs than Maryland did and was grateful for a Friday game. More time to prepare, Donovan said.

In a year in which no double-digit seed made it to the Sweet Sixteen for the first time in 12 years, the tournament's underdogs had become Butler and Southern Illinois. Other teams were from the power conferences, except Memphis and UNLV, which had been strong so long that they didn't fit the mid-major label.

The national media, as usual, obsessed over Butler as a giant-killer. It was the post-NIT aftermath all over again. Sports information director Jim McGrath was buried under about 300 e-mails, mostly from reporters. Butler originally printed 1,200 media guides, and they were all scooped up by the day before the Florida game.

Predictably, Donovan denied that Butler was an underdog. TV analysts agreed, up to a point.

"They just play the game the way it should be played," said Len Elmore of CBS. "If you can do that, many times you can overcome what people perceive as a lack of talent by comparison."

Butler's players were seemingly unshaken by all the sideshows: fans watching practice inside the Edward Jones Dome, media inquiries, and speculation that Lickliter would be hired away by a higher-paying university.

Crone felt loose enough to be teased about his hairstyle, a "Brian Evans buzz cut" modeled after a former Indiana University player. The woman who cut his hair was supposed to be experienced, Crone said. Even worse was that Campbell was in the stylist's chair when Crone walked in.

"But he didn't warn me," Crone said.

Florida, on the other hand, had been warned about Butler.

• • •

Governor Mitch Daniels declared Friday, March 23, as Butler Bulldogs Day in Indiana. There was a pregame rally for fans in St. Louis at a downtown Hilton. Back in Indianapolis, admission was free to a viewing party at Clowes Hall, and about 400 fans showed up at Moe & Johnny's on College Avenue to cheer the Dawgs.

Early, everyone had plenty to cheer. Crone went on a personal 10–0 run, featuring successive 3-pointers, and shot Butler into a 14–6 lead. The Bulldogs expanded that to nine points. As they concentrated on defending taller Gators, Taurean Green hit them with four first-half 3s. Florida closed the half on a 13–0 spurt to go ahead 35–29.

Graves, after a scoreless first half, converted a three-point play early in the second. Campbell twice scored to push the Bulldogs ahead, once when he shot from nearly behind the backboard and again on a 3-pointer. When Streicher made both ends of a one-and-one, Butler led 54–53 with 3:33 on the clock. A dome crowd of 26,307, along with a national TV audience, sensed the improbable was becoming possible.

That's when the Gators reclaimed control, outscoring Butler 10–1. Horford converted a three-point play, backing down and inducing Crone's fifth foul, to push Florida ahead 57–54. Mike Green missed two free throws with 2:13 left—making both would have cut Florida's lead to one—and Butler couldn't recover. Florida scored its final six points on free throws in a 65–57 victory.

It was over. Except for grief and regret.

"We didn't come here to give them a scare, man," Mike Green said. "We came here to win."

Butler finished one victory short of 30; one short of the Elite Eight.

Crone, Ligon, and Nellems would never again play in a Butler jersey. Betko had a reprieve—he had been awarded another season—but kept thinking his time as a teammate with those three seniors was past. His tears were as eloquent as words.

"That's what happens when you're so close, when you care about each other so much, and you know it's coming to an end," Betko said. "There's a lot of love we share at Butler. We just wish it wasn't over yet."

Lickliter felt the aftermath, too. He had no way of knowing he soon would leave for Iowa, taking the job one day after being honored by the National Association of Basketball Coaches as coach of the year. His Iowa contract called for $8.4 million over seven years. At Butler, it would take nearly 40 years to earn that much. At Butler, he had lived the coaching year of a lifetime.

"Every game once the tournament started, I knew it could be the last game I get to coach these guys," Lickliter said. "But I just wouldn't allow myself to think about it because it's seldom—and I've been coaching a long time—that you get a group of guys who are selfless, that pay attention to detail, that compete at an incredibly high level."

Florida went on to repeat, beating Thad Matta's Ohio State Buckeyes 84–75 for the NCAA championship in Atlanta. The Gators led by margins of six to 15 points in the second half and were not challenged, as they were by Butler.

The Bulldogs wouldn't stay down long. The spirit of St. Louis endured. Despair gave way to renewed ambition for the next season.

The 2007-08 Team (30-4):
The Best Ever?

Butler began the 2007–08 season with a new head coach who wasn't new at all. Throughout the decade, the university went through changes in coaches, players, athletic directors, opponents, and the league's name. There was one constant throughout the changes: Brad Stevens.

Less than three days after Todd Lickliter resigned, Stevens was promoted on April 4, 2007. Stevens, 30, became the third-youngest head coach in major college basketball. He had been on the staff since 2000, when he left a marketing job at the pharmaceutical giant Eli Lilly and Co. to take an unpaid position. Stevens was an assistant coach under Thad Matta and Lickliter.

There was speculation that athletic director Barry Collier would return to his former job, but he didn't want that. Collier received more than 100 contacts from prospective candidates via phone calls, text messages, and faxes, but none of that correspondence was as influential as what he heard from players. They wanted a Butler man.

Three Butler assistants—Stevens, LaVall Jordan, and Matthew Graves—were interviewed. Resolution came quickly, and the job remained in the family, as it did with Matta and Lickliter before. Graves stayed on as Stevens' top assistant, and Jordan joined Lickliter's Iowa coaching staff.

"I've been able to watch Brad work with this team in practice and, speaking with him, it became clear he's ready for this job," Collier said. "To have the right man come from under your own roof should make for a smooth transition."

Stevens credited Collier, Lickliter, and Matta for being mentors and said he would continue to emphasize team play. No major changes. That's why players wanted an internal hire, Stevens said.

"They love the way we play, and, as much as anything, you have guys that are on the same page and believe in each other and believe in the system a lot," he said.

Stevens' methods so resembled Lickliter's that veteran players nicknamed him "Little T," as in Little Todd. Don't mess with success.

• • •

Unlike the previous season, when the Bulldogs were forecast to finish sixth in the Horizon League, they would not surprise anyone. They were picked first, and A.J. Graves was the preseason player of the year.

Butler's players prepared purposefully in the off-season. Pete Campbell reported back in better condition so he wouldn't break down as he had the previous fall. Mike Green worked out against NBA players in Indianapolis and Philadelphia. No matter what any of the players did all day, summer nights were devoted to open gym.

Stevens fed Green a diet of positive reinforcement so he wouldn't dwell on moments like the two missed free throws late in the 2007 NCAA Tournament loss to Florida.

"As far as haunting me, I came back and worked as hard as ever," Green said. "That's all you can do. I'm getting better at learning I can't control every single thing."

Butler's senior-laden team might once have been the rule, but no more. With so many players leaving early in an attempt to enter the NBA, the sport's powers rarely relied on such experience. Basketball had changed so much that by November 2007, Butler's lineup was nearly as old as that of the NBA's youngest. Here's how Butler players compared to those of the NBA's Atlanta Hawks:

Butler	Atlanta Hawks
Pete Campbell, 23	Al Horford, 21
Drew Streicher, 22	Marvin Williams, 21
Julian Betko, 24	Joe Johnson, 26
A.J. Graves, 22	Josh Smith, 21
Mike Green, 22	Mike Bibby, 29

The only peculiarity was that veteran Butler—coming off a 29–7 record, Sweet Sixteen appearance, and No. 13 ranking in the final *USA Today*/ESPN coaches' poll—did not crack a preseason Top 25. If it had not been Butler boasting those credentials, and instead was Duke, North Carolina, or UCLA, such an oversight could not have happened.

"It doesn't mean much to me," Graves said. "We weren't in the Top 25 starting last year, either."

• • •

Butler's November 9 opener represented a homecoming for Pete Campbell. Ball State is located in Muncie, Ind., his hometown. He often attended games at Ball State's Worthen Arena. Ball State was regrouping under new coach Billy Taylor following a tumultuous off-season that included the resignation of coach Ronny Thompson, NCAA violations, and a continuing investigation.

Fans supported the Cardinals with a turnout of 7,331—more than attended any home game the year before—and grew louder after Ball State trimmed Butler's 17-point lead to eight midway through the first half. Streicher and Betko were on the bench with four fouls each, so the Bulldogs were ailing. The cure? A Campbell Cluster.

Campbell sank three 3-pointers in less than three minutes, and the lead lengthened to 50–33. He finished with five 3s and 17 points in a 61–45 victory. Freshman center Matt Howard made an auspicious debut, scoring 14 points in 26 minutes.

The Bulldogs' absence from the Top 25 lasted one week. They were 25th the following Monday, then reinforced their ranking by beating Indiana State 76–48 and Evansville 60–47. Butler's 28-point victory over Indiana State at Hinkle Fieldhouse was its largest in the series since 1960 and broke a three-game losing streak to the Sycamores. Graves scored 26 points, and Butler featured one 10–0 burst that lasted just 94 seconds.

At Evansville's Roberts Stadium, Graves scored 22 in what was otherwise a feeble output by Butler. The Bulldogs fell behind by seven early, but after allowing 15 points in the first six minutes, they limited the Purple Aces to 32 over 34 minutes.

"They don't give you anything easy," Evansville coach Marty Simmons said.

• • •

Of college basketball's early-season institutions, the Great Alaska Shootout had the most colorful and unusual history. It was the brainchild of Bob Rachal, former coach of the University of Alaska-Anchorage. When he arrived in 1977, he had an idea for luring teams to a new tournament because of an NCAA rule stating that games outside the contiguous states don't count against the normal limit of 28. Skeptics thought he was nuts, and they told him so.

Nonetheless, seven teams joined Alaska-Anchorage in the inaugural Sea Wolf Classic in November 1978 at 4,000-seat Buckner Field House in Fort Richardson, near Anchorage. The tournament was so well received—by visiting coaches who liked the hospitality and by fans watching on regional television—that it returned in 1979. Except by then it was known as the Great Alaska Shootout, a phrase credited to TV broadcaster Billy Packer.

ESPN began televising the tournament in 1985, and the champions would come to include the kings of college basketball: Kentucky, North Carolina, Louisville, UCLA, Duke, and Kansas. That was big, especially for remote Alaska, whose 586,400 square miles make it twice the size of Texas.

When the Bulldogs arrived at the Anchorage airport on a Monday after a 3,000-mile trip, they didn't make a splashy entrance. All the players filed by on the way to baggage claim, and Stevens was last in line. He was asked if he was with Butler.

"Where's your team?" someone asked.

"That gives you an idea of what we look like," Stevens said.

The next night, players from Butler and five other teams visited the Alaska Native Heritage Center to sample local cuisine such as reindeer sausage, fried halibut, and salmon chowder. They watched a film about the people and places of Alaska, listened to a lecture about tribes of the state, and were entertained by the Yup'ik dance group Kicaput. Players were invited onstage to participate, and one did: Mike Green. If you're a take-charge point guard, that's what you do. Green loved it, except the dance moves were "tiring," he said. It wouldn't be the last time he stood out in Anchorage.

At the next afternoon's luncheon, Stevens and Texas Tech coach Bob Knight sat at adjacent tables. They were separated by three feet . . . and 889 victories. The 67-year-old Knight, the winningest coach in the sport's history, had brought his Red Raiders to Alaska after twice taking the Indiana Hoosiers. He entertained a packed banquet hall with stories and jokes and didn't spare himself. After saying he enjoyed previous trips, he added:

"The disappointing part of that is, my fishing over the years has been a hell of a lot better than my coaching."

Indiana was 1–2 in the inaugural Shootout in 1978 and 1–2 again in 1995.

Every dignitary who preceded Knight, including Governor Sarah Palin, mentioned Knight. This was some nine months before Palin emerged from relative obscurity to be the running mate for Republican candidate John McCain in the 2008 presidential race. Palin had a journalism background. Knight, a longtime adversary of the media, didn't hold that against her. He called Palin intelligent and "the best-looking governor" in the country.

The Bulldogs have so few alumni and such a small fan base, compared with the megaschools, that they rarely draw supporters on the road. Moreover, they were thousands of miles from campus.

However, four members of the Dawg Pound, the student fan section, traveled to Alaska to cheer: sophomore Kevin Swanson, junior Danny Engelhardt, and seniors Loren Snyder and Abe Mulvihill. Snyder, the Dawg Pound president, purchased cloth moose antlers and asserted that for this tournament, the Bulldogs would be the "Bull Mooses." The antler-wearing students were a hit on TV.

The Shootout had long since outgrown its original site and was played at 8,000-seat Sullivan Arena. The 22nd-ranked Bulldogs opened against Michigan, entertaining an ESPN2 audience with marksmanship from the 3-point line. Coincidentally, Michigan relied on 3s under new coach John Beilein, who successfully developed such a system at West Virginia. The upshot? Don't engage Butler in a shooting contest.

The Bulldogs set a tournament record by sinking 17 from the arc—eight in a row in the second half—during a 79–65 victory. Virginia Tech coach Seth Greenberg, whose Hokies were up next in the semifinals, got an up-close look at the Bulldogs when he entered the locker room to use the bathroom.

"By the way," he asked, "do you guys always make every shot? I've never seen a display like that."

The victory was Butler's first over the Wolverines in 42 years of an irregular series. The Bulldogs beat then-No. 3 Michigan 79–64 on December 22, 1965, at Indianapolis.

Campbell, playing with a wrap on an injured right thumb, was 6-of-11 from the arc and scored 18 points. Graves was 5-of-10 on 3s, adding 17. Voted player of the game was Green, who had this stat line: 14 points, eight assists, five rebounds, one turnover.

"The way they're playing right now, I told my team that's what we should envision ourselves playing like in the future," Beilein said.

On Thanksgiving Day, the Bulldogs prepared for Virginia Tech by practicing at Alaska Club West, a fitness center, before relaxing at Center Bowl. It was obvious that the players spent more time in a gym than in a bowling alley. Strikes were less frequent than 3-pointers. The Bulldogs dined that evening at Simon & Seafort's, a downtown restaurant on L Street overlooking the Cook Inlet and featuring a panoramic view of Mount Susitna.

These players couldn't abide being away from the gym for more than a few hours, so they returned to the arena in time to watch No. 14 Gonzaga, the tourney's highest-ranked team, defeat Western Kentucky 74–71. Texas Tech dispatched the host Seawolves 74–47.

Virginia Tech's roster included 6-foot-7 Deron Washington, a high-flying dunker who was drafted by the NBA's Detroit Pistons. However, he wasn't the threat that 6-foot-7, 258-pound freshman Jeff Allen proved to be. Five Bulldogs took turns guarding Allen. Betko took the assignment at the end and played 37 minutes, despite a sore knee.

Butler appeared to be headed to the championship game after leading by 11 points with less than nine minutes to play. With Butler ahead 68–66, Campbell's long baseball pass intended for Green on an inbounds play was intercepted by the Hokies. With 15 seconds left, Allen tied the score at 68 with a layup—the last of his 21 points—but he missed a free throw that would have put Virginia Tech ahead. Graves' shot to win for Butler rimmed off.

Overtime.

That's when Green and Campbell—teammates, roommates, and complements—foiled Virginia Tech. All those old practices as redshirts on the scout team reaped new dividends. Green scored the first four points of overtime, then passed to Campbell for a 3-pointer that expanded Butler's lead to 75–70. Green followed with a 3-pointer in what became an 84–78 victory.

Of Butler's 16 overtime points, Green scored 12 and Campbell four. Campbell finished with seven 3-pointers, one off the Shootout record, and scored 26 points. Green scored 23.

"From the first time we ever got together in a 5-on-5 situation and Mike and I were on the same team, we just clicked pretty well," Campbell said.

The tournament was called a shootout, and Butler was making it that. With 14 more, its two-game total of 3-pointers reached 31—three less than the three-game record of 34 set by UC-Irvine in 1990. Allen acknowledged that it was hard to defend against Butler's long-range shooting.

"You had to run off so many screens," Allen said. "It was confusing."

A Butler/Gonzaga rematch from the 2006 NIT Season Tipoff was in the making, except for one impediment: Texas Tech. Knight's Red Raiders beat the Zags 73–63 in the other semifinal.

The championship matched Stevens, who grew up cheering the Indiana Hoosiers, against Knight, who coached them. Stevens was born about seven months after Knight won his first NCAA championship in Indiana's 32–0 season of 1976, perfection that has not been equaled.

Before a sellout of 8,700, Butler's hot shooting continued in building a 12-point lead against Texas Tech. The Raiders cut that to 34–32 by halftime. Butler's second half was effectively an instructional DVD. The Bulldogs shot 65 percent from the field (15-of-23)—including 75 percent from the arc (9-of-12)—and didn't commit a turnover in the half until two minutes remained.

Butler won 81–71 and did so with the greatest 3-point shooting in the Shootout's 30-year history. Butler was 16-of-24 from the arc against Texas Tech, setting championship game records for 3s made and percentage (.667). Graves tied the title game record with six 3-pointers, and Campbell and Green added four each. Butler's three-game total of 47 obliterated the tourney record, and its cumulative percentage (.528) on 3s was .005 off the record. Knight was not a proponent of the 3-point shot, but that didn't influence his evaluation of the Bulldogs.

"If I were just a fan," he said, "I'd love watching them play."

Green had 23 points and seven assists. His three-game totals of 60 points and 20 assists ranked second and third, respectively, in the tournament. He was voted the most outstanding player and was joined on the 10-man all-tournament team by Graves and Campbell. Green joined elite membership. Previous winners included NBA stars Sean Elliott (1987), Glenn Robinson (1993), Ray Allen (1995), and Dwayne Wade (2001).

"That Butler team really deserves to be complimented, and the best compliment that I could give them is I wish that we played as smart as they do," Knight said.

Although Gonzaga coach Mark Few said that Butler was in March form, Stevens contended that there was room to improve. Certainly, the Bulldogs could defend better—Texas Tech shot 60 percent—and perhaps keep Howard out of foul trouble.

But as it had done the year before in New York, Butler positioned itself to climb the rankings and enhance its resume. Over the past two Novembers, Butler was 14–0. Alaska, the Last Frontier, was a first step toward another season manifesting the Butler Way.

● ● ●

The Bulldogs returned to Indianapolis to prepare for a rare occasion—a game against a Big Ten opponent at Hinkle Fieldhouse. Because of his relationship with Butler, Ohio State coach Thad Matta agreed to a four-game home-and-home series. Matta was a player, assistant, and head coach for the Bulldogs, and he hired both Butler assistant coach Brandon Miller and Stevens. Miller was on Matta's staff at Xavier and later at Ohio State.

"Like I've said before, I'm indebted to him for allowing me to be in this business at all," Stevens said.

Throughout Tony Hinkle's tenure and afterward, from the 1920s to 1970s, visits by Big Ten opponents to Butler were commonplace. That era had long since passed. No Big Ten team had played at Hinkle Fieldhouse since Indiana on November 27, 1993, and the Buckeyes hadn't visited since November 25, 1978.

Butler/Ohio State had been approaching a sellout anyway, and the Bulldogs' Alaska triumph heightened anticipation. Such a large crowd was expected, and so few parking spaces were available that the university arranged for a free shuttle service from the nearby Riviera Club.

It was to be a homecoming for Indianapolis heroes Greg Oden and Mike Conley, who led Lawrence North High School to three state championships before enrolling at Ohio State. Instead, they left for the NBA after their freshman seasons, and Matta had to piece together a new team. The Buckeyes had talent—they always would under Matta, a top recruiter—but little college experience. Their new star was 7-foot Kosta Koufos, a freshman from Greece and MVP of the under-18 European Championships. Ohio State was coming off a 66–55 loss to top-ranked North Carolina.

Butler students stood in line as early as 8 a.m. for a December 1 game that wouldn't start for nearly 12 hours. The sellout crowd of 10,000 was deflated, though, because Ohio State couldn't miss a shot. And Butler couldn't make one.

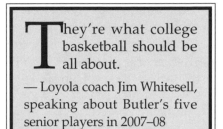

They're what college basketball should be all about.

— Loyola coach Jim Whitesell, speaking about Butler's five senior players in 2007–08

Koufos scored nine points in the first 10 minutes, and the Buckeyes built a 14-point lead. While the Bulldogs started 0-of-15 from the 3-point line—a stark contrast to the Alaska accuracy— Howard prevented a blowout by scoring 13 of Butler's first 15 points. Graves ended the drought from the arc by hitting as the first-half clock expired, cutting Ohio State's lead to 30–20. Considering Ohio State shot 65 percent, Butler was fortunate to be that close.

During halftime, Stevens gave each of the Bulldogs a wad of paper and had them toss it into a trash container. That's how easy shooting is going to be in the second half, the coach said. That lightened the mood, and the Bulldogs began lighting up the scoreboard.

The crowd grew so loud that Stevens couldn't make himself heard to a player standing 10 feet away. Graves' 3-pointer pulled the Bulldogs into a tie at 38, and Green scored from the arc to put them ahead for good, 43–40. Stunningly, Butler outscored Ohio State 45–16 in the second half and won 65–46. Fans rushed the court to celebrate another milestone.

"Once we got going," Green said, "it was hard to stop us."

Howard's breakout game resulted in 23 points, seven more than his freshman counterpart, Koufos. Green scored all of his 15 in the second half, and Graves added 14. One measure of how much travel can affect teams is that the seven visitors to Alaska were 3–4 in their first game after the trip. If the Bulldogs were weary or flat, they overcame that.

"This team has a chance to do something. You just don't see five seniors in a starting lineup any more in college basketball," Matta said.

The downside to Butler's victory was an injury to Campbell, who slipped on a wet spot in front of the bench. He sat out the closing 12 minutes with what was diagnosed as a sprained right knee and was placed on crutches. Although Butler was achieving inside/outside balance with Howard's emergence, and featured multiple shooters, Campbell's absence affected spacing and caused the offense to flounder.

The Bulldogs opened Horizon League play with a weekend trip to Detroit and Wright State, two opponents accustomed to their style and certainly not intimidated by the nation's 13th-ranked team. Butler needed another big night from Howard, whose 20 points contributed to a 53–46 victory at Detroit.

Graves and Green were a collective 0-of-8 on 3-pointers and combined for 17 points, or half their average. Detroit guard Jon Goode said the Titans' plan against Butler's guards was to "stay in their footsteps," and the strategy succeeded. Yet Goode said the Bulldogs never became rattled.

"You could see it in their faces," Goode said.

Wright State lost its league opener to Valparaiso 71–66, ending a 14-game home winning streak, before facing Butler. Yet the Nutter Center jinx continued to grip the Bulldogs, who lost there for the seventh time in succession. Wright State held them to two points over the final nine minutes and handed them their first defeat, 43–42. Graves' potentially winning 3-point attempt at the end missed.

Graves and Green were limited to six points each. In their first 43 games together, they had never both been held under 10 points. Now, that had happened in successive games.

Green was visibly frustrated on those occasions in which he drove to the basket, missed the shot, and did not draw a foul. On similar forays in Alaska, he at least shot free throws. If Graves was not the object of opponents' attention elsewhere, he certainly was in this league. At Detroit and Dayton, he was 0-of-11 from the arc.

"Part of our game plan is to guard him as hard as humanly possible," Wright State coach Brad Brownell said. "We, probably more than teams in the BCS conferences, know how good that guy is. If you guard him like a regular guy, he's going to kill you."

Brownell conceded that Butler was easier to defend without Campbell, whose activity was restricted to riding a stationary bike. If the Bulldogs had grown weary from playing seven of nine games away from home, they addressed that by taking three days off from practice. Green and Graves said the Bulldogs would push through the adversity.

"One good game or one bad game is not going to define us," Graves said.

If there was one way to define the Bulldogs, it was their success against BCS teams. They had another such opponent, Florida State, coming up in the Wooden Tradition. The Seminoles' 9–2 record included a 65–51 victory over Florida's defending national champions.

Despite heavy snowfall, 17,170 fans showed up at Conseco Fieldhouse for the first half of the basketball doubleheader, many of them red-clad Louisville supporters. After Purdue upset No. 22 Louisville 67–59, most of them disappeared. A smaller audience watched to see whether Butler's offense would reappear.

It did.

Graves and Green combined for 45 points—scoring 22 of the team's final 28—as the 18th-ranked Bulldogs beat Florida State 79–68. Graves scored 25 and set a Wooden Tradition record by making seven 3-pointers, several in key moments. Florida State coach Leonard Hamilton said Graves was the best he had ever seen in coming off ball screens, in which a teammate sets a screen for the player who has the ball.

"He was certainly clever with how he used those screens," Hamilton said.

In their final home game of 2007, the Bulldogs built a 15-point halftime lead and beat Bradley 83–64. The Bulldogs shot 57 percent in a 49-point second half.

Campbell, after missing three games, sank one 3-pointer in a nine-minute stint.

● ● ●

For the most successful high school and college sports programs, it is never all about the sport. It is about sport as a microcosm of life. No Butler coach will ever deliver, nor any Butler player ever hear, a more meaningful message than the one delivered by Matt White in Fort Myers, Fla., on December 21, 2007.

The Bulldogs were there to play Florida Gulf Coast, which was in its first Division I season. White, a former Butler runner who was diagnosed with amyotrophic lateral sclerosis, commonly known as Lou Gehrig's disease, addressed the team the night before the game. If White were confined to three words, this is what he would tell others: live life fearlessly.

He said that's what he had done ever since he was told, in 2000, that he had four years to live. That was eight years ago.

In his address, White stated:

Knowing what I faced after my diagnosis, I had to decide what to do with the time I had left. Living fearlessly, I decided to control as much *of my future as I could and to make the most of this negative. The first four years I did what most would call "lived with ALS." I worked as long as I could at a job that I loved, trying to make a valuable contribution. I traveled and spent time with family and friends, doing my favorite things, including playing golf at each of the top 10 golf courses in the United States. I created a charitable foundation, and with the generous support of so many colleagues and friends, helped raise more than $300,000 for ALS research.*

I spent time reading and praying, seeking greater faith, peace of mind, and courage to face the day when I would stop breathing and die. I lived life like the end was nearing. Ultimately, I gave up driving, golfing, walking, eating, and the independence of bathing and dressing myself. I left Chicago and moved to Florida to be near my parents in my final months. I felt good about my life and what I had done in the recent years. After my life was extended with the ventilator, I have continued to live a life without fear. A life on life support that most would think impossible. . . .

I read and hear about the Butler Way. I cannot define what it means, but I know for sure that it includes playing fearlessly. The way this team and this program have developed into one of the best in the nation is a testament to the power of courage. To approach new and scary opportunities fearlessly is an absolute requirement if you want to achieve greatness.

People will tell you that you can accomplish anything if you put your mind to it. Well, that is just not true. What is true is that you can try anything, and your chances improve dramatically if you try it fearlessly. I think that is one of the reasons that those I became closest to and people I barely know tell me I am an inspiration, and hopefully that is why I am here tonight. To show you how a life lived without fear can be a very successful life and can overcome almost anything.

I find inspiration in this program, in this team, and in the way each of you plays. Keep playing fearlessly, keep winning fearlessly, and when you are done, live fearlessly.

The next night, the Bulldogs added perspiration to inspiration. After trailing by nine in the first half, they pulled away to defeat Gulf Coast 78–66 before a near-capacity crowd of 3,843, including about 100 fans and alumni.

Afterward, Butler players filed up the stairs at Alico Arena to where White was seated in a wheelchair. They thanked him and awarded him the game ball on his 41st birthday. Think he wasn't an optimist? Through his wife, Shartrina, who speaks for him, White asked for a Final Four game ball.

"If the NCAA would let me, I'd have flown our team down here just for that," Stevens said. "What an unbelievable story of courage and fearlessness and toughness."

Betko, who had chronic knee pain, said White's story influenced him.

"I tend to complain a lot and ask, 'Why me?' And to meet somebody like that and to hear what his life is like, that was very inspirational to me," Betko said.

• • •

As Butler's players separated for the Christmas holiday, the one with the shortest distance to travel was Shawn Vanzant, a freshman from Tampa, Fla. It was just as well. He had come so far already.

There was once a time when Vanzant was asked what he wanted for Christmas. He was thankful for what he had. So he returned a blank sheet of paper.

Personal hardships had resulted in Vanzant moving in with another family. Vanzant, then 17, revealed to the mother that he hadn't received Christmas gifts since he was in the seventh grade.

"I thought, 'Well, buddy, I've got news for you. You're about to have a Litton Christmas,'" Lisa Litton said.

Jeff and Lisa Litton, their three sons, and Vanzant took turns opening packages. Saved for last was a box containing a designer watch with two rows of diamonds. To Vanzant, it was as exciting as a buzzer-beating basket.

"It was the very first time that Shawn and I exchanged an emotional connection. Because he was so overwhelmed he couldn't look at me," Lisa Litton said. "He got up and hugged and would not let go."

Vanzant's story was more complex than one of triumph over tragedy. If not for the love of his own family, he would not have been allowed to live with what became a second family. If not for heartbreak endured by his second "mother," he might not have been so readily embraced as another son.

Vanzant's mother, Effie, died October 9, 1990, or 10 days before his second birthday. She was 39. He carried a photo of her in his gym bag. His father, James, moved his sons, Wesley and Shawn, from Cleveland to Omaha, Neb., in 1992, and to Tampa in 1997. After Vanzant's father was diagnosed with diabetes and ran into financial stress, Shawn moved in with his brother, who is seven years older but looks like a twin. Wesley ran afoul of the law but made sure little brother did not.

Vanzant called Wesley his other half. *Wes* is tattooed on Vanzant's right arm.

Finally, there came a crossroads. Vanzant's father, whose illness prevented him from continuing as a welder, and brother, who was arrested, couldn't do anything for him. The then-sophomore told Wharton High School coach Tommy Tonelli that he would return to Cleveland and live with a grandmother.

That's where the Littons came in. One son, Zach, also a basketball player, was Vanzant's best friend. They were inseparable. The Littons offered to let Vanzant move in, if his father approved.

"I took a deep breath, closed my eyes, and said, 'OK,'" James Vanzant said.

The arrangement was supposed to be for a few weeks. Vanzant stayed through the end of high school. The culture clash was not one of a black teenager going to live with a white family. It was going from a family of males to one with a mother.

"She was coming at me like I was her own," Vanzant recalled.

That was Lisa Litton. Tough and tender. Tough, as in a survivor of uterine and cervical cancer. Tender, as the team mom, cooking pregame meals and transporting players to games. One more boy in the house wasn't going to crimp her style. There were chores and a curfew and a few bumpy patches. But mothering was her mission.

When Lisa was 8, she and her 6-year-old sister were left by their mother at the Miami airport. The girls never saw her again. That experience influenced her in situations like that confronting Vanzant.

"I didn't want him to feel like he had no place to go," Lisa said, "because I've been there."

To Vanzant, she was Mrs. Litton no more. She was Mom.

Basketball was Vanzant's refuge. From age 12, he was coached by David Bastian with the New Tampa Wildcats on the summer circuit. Bastian played at North Central High School in Indianapolis under Arlan Lickliter, father of former Butler coach Todd Lickliter. The Lickliter link led to Butler's recruitment. As a high school senior, Vanzant averaged 16.4 points for a 29–2 team.

After Lickliter left for Iowa, Vanzant honored his commitment to Butler. He became a valuable player off the bench, adjusting from star player to role player.

"I can adjust to anything," Vanzant said.

Christmas was glorious.

● ● ●

After Butler players reconvened the day after Christmas, they headed back on the road. This was the downside of the BracketBuster series, in which teams that host a game one season must visit that opponent the next. It is awkward finding dates for a reciprocal game, and the Bulldogs were dispatched December 28 to Carbondale, Ill.

Not only was Southern Illinois one of Butler's most difficult opponents the previous season, but the Salukis were 82–4 at home since the start of the 2001–02 season. Moreover, Butler couldn't participate in its customary shootaround the day before the game because there was a high school tournament at SIU Arena.

Happy New Year, Dawgs.

The Salukis didn't feature the scorers from the previous season but continued to play belly-to-belly, baseline-to-baseline defense. Butler went nearly 14 minutes of the second half without a field goal, until Campbell's 3-pointer forged a 50–47 lead with three minutes left. Southern Illinois reclaimed the lead but twice missed free throws in the final 23 seconds, clinging to a 55–54 edge.

With six seconds left in the game, Graves took an inbounds pass and dribbled. He stopped left of the top of the key and shot from behind the 3-point line. The ball curled around the rim, off glass, and dropped through as time ran out. Graves, who had shot 2-of-10 up to then, gave Butler a 57–55 victory.

"It did feel good, but I couldn't really see it," Graves said. "I think two guys were jumping in my way. I seen it go down, and I heard the horn sound, so I guess that's all that matters on that play."

After that, all that mattered was the league standings—and Butler was looking up at Valparaiso and Cleveland State. The Crusaders were 2–0 in the league when they visited Butler, and their only losses had been to No. 15 Vanderbilt, No. 25 Wisconsin, and No. 1 North Carolina— teams with an aggregate 54–3 record.

Valparaiso led by as many as nine points in the first half. Vanzant and Willie Veasley supplied energy off the bench, and Green supplied everything else. Butler's playmaker scored 17 of his career-high 24 points in the second half, making three 3s in a 73–65 victory. Graves was limited to a season-low five points and missed a free throw, ending a streak of 26 in a row.

"I get caught up in playing the perfect game sometimes, and I won't do certain things," Green said. "It all comes down to picking your spots."

In a Monday/Thursday/Saturday week, the Bulldogs won at Loyola and returned home to defeat both Wisconsin schools, Green Bay and Milwaukee.

At Chicago, with students gone for winter break, there were more fans in Butler blue than those cheering for Loyola. The Bulldogs won their 10th game away from home, the most in the nation, and never trailed in a 66–55 victory. Howard scored 19 points in 20 minutes.

Green Bay, too, was fed a steady diet of Howard. On a night in which the Bulldogs missed their last nine 3-point attempts, Howard scored 22 points in a 74–65 victory. Three Green Bay players fouled out in an attempt to guard the freshman. Howard scored 17 in a 72–56 victory over Milwaukee, giving him 58 points in a three-win week.

At 16–1, Butler had achieved the best 17-game start in school history.

Butler needed to keep winning because, at 5–1, it still trailed 5–0 Cleveland State in the standings.

• • •

Cleveland State had been, unequivocally, one of the nation's most dreadful college basketball programs. It had lost 103 games in five seasons and was 17–63 in the league in that period. In the previous 15 games against Butler, Cleveland State was 2–13. It's not like anyone in Cleveland, a pro sports town with a commuter campus, was eager to see the Vikings, either. Under Gary Waters, all that was changing and faster even than the 55-year-old coach expected. Cleveland State was in the process of becoming one of the few in NCAA history to go from 20 losses in one year to 20 victories the next.

Waters not only changed the roster—10 new players—but also the culture. He required the Vikings to work hard and work together. He was fired after five years at Rutgers, but he knew how to build a winner. He took Kent State to the NCAA Tournament in 1999 and 2001.

Butler was in much the same position as in the previous season at Wright State. Win, and the Bulldogs would move closer to earning home-court advantage for the tournament that decides the league's automatic NCAA berth. Lose, and the advantage would shift to Cleveland State.

An animated crowd of 5,352 showed up at the Wolstein Center to watch the Vikings face 12th-ranked Butler. Only once in school history—an 83–79 upset of No. 16 Indiana in the 1986 NCAA Tournament—had Cleveland State beaten a ranked team.

Graves missed a practice early in the week because of a sore toe, continuing a pattern of foot injuries that would plague his career. He would never acknowledge impairment, nor would Butler's coaches and trainer elaborate on his condition.

Cleveland State led by as many as eight points in the first half but could never pull away from the Bulldogs, who endured 6-of-23 shooting from the arc. That contrasted hugely to the previous year's 20-of-33 exhibition. Campbell was hot, and other Bulldogs were not. And Campbell was held without a 3-pointer over the final 14 minutes.

Green, who sat out 12 minutes of the first half with two fouls, went end to end for a layup to put the Bulldogs ahead 44–42. They couldn't sustain it. With Cleveland State holding a 55–52 lead, Butler missed three 3-pointers in the final 25 seconds. J'Nathan Bullock sank the first of two free throws with 2.6 seconds left, and the Vikings celebrated a 56–52 victory. Stevens didn't have to chide Butler players afterward because they were more publicly critical than their coach ever was.

"You just have to go out there and be man enough to play," Graves said. "And half of our team wasn't man enough to play, and we got beat."

The Bulldogs have a slogan: the toughest team sets the rules. On this night, they said, that was Cleveland State—from the first play. Green took personal responsibility for defeat, asserting that he did not lead the team.

"Everybody's not in tune. Everybody is not doing their jobs," Green said.

Underscoring the difficulty of league play was Butler's record in the previous seven Horizon road games—3–4, all while nationally ranked.

• • •

The Bulldogs closed January with three league victories, starting with a 78–69 win at Youngstown State.

Green nearly had a triple double: 16 points, eight rebounds, and 10 assists. As usual, Butler's traveling road show attracted an audience: 6,198, the largest crowd at the Beeghly Center since 2001.

The drama before the Bulldogs' next game—home against Loyola—came during the day. The night was no problem, ending with a 63–50 victory. Green, Campbell, and Betko were first declared ineligible because they accepted tickets to sit behind the Iowa bench for a game at Indiana. Iowa assistant coach LaVall Jordan left tickets for the players. Campbell said they would not have accepted them if they thought it was a rules violation.

"I thought it was pretty harmless, to be honest," Campbell said.

The NCAA agreed. But not before compliance officer Julie Arnold called the Horizon League office for clarification. Just in case, the players delivered $29 checks to cover the cost of the tickets.

Loyola coach Jim Whitesell found no fault in the Bulldogs. After the game, he spoke to each of Butler's five seniors, and it was more than "good game." Green said he had never seen a coach do that, and Campbell called it a classy gesture.

"They're what college basketball should be all about," Whitesell said.

Butler finished the month by beating Illinois-Chicago 73–57, and Graves showed signs of pulling out of his slump. He made his first four shots, ending with 16 points and four 3-pointers, his highest totals in more than a month. He had shot 27 percent in seven previous January games, so the Hinkle Fieldhouse crowd of 4,952 cheered his every basket. They were waiting for him to start hitting, Campbell said, "like he always does."

At 19–2, the Bulldogs headed into a nine-day layoff.

• • •

Eight league games remained in the Bulldogs' season. Effectively, their title ambitions would be determined in the next three, all on the road—Valparaiso, Green Bay, and Milwaukee. Inactivity not only gave the Bulldogs a needed respite, but a boost in the polls and the standings. They climbed to No. 10 in the rankings, and an 8–2 record put them two ahead in the loss column because 7–4 Cleveland State lost four in a row.

Little could have prepared the Bulldogs for what they faced next. A deafening, standing-room-only crowd of 5,432 was the largest in Valparaiso history, exceeding a 2002 home game against Purdue. ESPN2 analyst Doug Gottlieb told the TV audience it was necessary to be there to understand how difficult such an environment was for visitors.

Making it worse for the Bulldogs was that they fell behind 12–0. Clearly, they weren't ready, a rarity for such an experienced team.

Butler pulled even at 19–19, but the Crusaders shot 65 percent in the first half and built a 10-point lead by early in the second half. Howard picked up his fourth foul with 16 minutes left and sat down. Every time the Bulldogs crept closer, Valparaiso pushed back.

Then Graves, guarded closely on the perimeter to protect against the 3-pointer, started going toward the hoop. In the closing three minutes, he scored on three short-range jumpers, tying the score each time—at 60, 62, and 65. The Crusaders went ahead 68–65 on Jarryd Loyd's 3-pointer with 38 seconds left, and their lead finally looked secure.

Green drove for a field goal, trimming the margin to 68–67, and then fouled out. Loyd went to the foul line . . . and air-balled the first of a one-and-one. The shot did not reach the rim. The ball went back to Butler and into Graves' hands. Except this time, as he moved toward the goal, he didn't shoot. He passed into the right corner, where Campbell was unguarded behind the 3-point line. The ball splashed through the net like a rock into a rain puddle. After 39 minutes and 45 seconds, Butler had its first lead, 70–68.

Butler escaped with a 71–68 victory. Graves protested that he did not put the team on his back, but Butler needed all of his 20 points.

Four days later at Green Bay, the Bulldogs again went to the end. Again, they were a big attraction. The crowd of 6,984 represented the sixth time in seven games the Bulldogs drew a season high to a league venue. When they arrived, they were as big as rock stars, though not as popular.

"With a rock group, there's no way they can lose," Green said. "We have to battle."

At Green Bay, Butler relied on a mini Campbell Cluster—two 3-pointers 30 seconds apart—to expand a two-point lead to eight. Graves sank six successive free throws in the final 87 seconds, and Butler won 62–57 to raise its record to 21–2.

The Bulldogs had two days off before playing at Milwaukee, which had been preparing for this game for nine days. It showed. Although a late-afternoon snowstorm limited attendance to 4,055, the Panthers rewarded their fans by pouncing early. They led by 12 and would have been ahead by more if not for Butler freshman Zach Hahn, who came off the bench for three first-half 3-pointers. He hadn't scored in a more than a month.

The second half was painted Green. He got cute. He got hurt. He got going. He was called for what he said was the first technical of his career. Two technical free throws expanded Milwaukee's lead to four with 14 minutes left. For the third successive road game, Butler trailed in the second half.

"I didn't cuss or nothing. I guess he didn't like my sarcasm," Green said, referring to the referee.

He reinjured his right ankle with less than five minutes left but soon returned. His two free throws sent Butler ahead 67–64 with five seconds left, and Butler chose not to foul. Milwaukee's Ricky Franklin hit a 3-pointer with less than a second on the clock, tying the score at 67 and forcing overtime.

Campbell opened the OT with a 3-pointer, and Butler never trailed again in an 83–75 victory. Green scored 10 points in the overtime, four on two nifty left-handed layups. He scored 22 of his career-high 24 after halftime, and he nearly achieved Butler's first triple-double since 1984: 24 points, 13 rebounds, and eight assists.

The newly ninth-ranked Bulldogs returned home for two victories, but the games couldn't have been more contrasting. The Bulldogs shot 62 percent against Youngstown State, 65 percent on 3-pointers. After the 89–73 victory, Green noticed that some fieldhouse lamps had gone dark.

"Our guys pretty much shoot lights out in here, and that's what we did tonight," he said.

Butler led Cleveland State by 11 in the first half of their rematch, then grasped a 51–46 victory. The Bulldogs were limited to three points over the closing nine minutes but were so stout on defense that Cleveland State never overtook them. It was a bumpy afternoon for Green, who scored a season-low six points and had as many turnovers (three) as assists. Defenders clung to Campbell, whose lone basket extended his streak to 26 straight games with

> We're challenged a little bit physically. But as far as thinking, we might be one of the best-thinking teams in America.
>
> — Butler guard Mike Green

at least one 3-pointer. Howard led Butler with 17 points, and Graves added 15 on 5-of-9 shooting.

The twin wins elevated the Bulldogs to No. 8, for their highest ranking in history. They didn't live up to that at Illinois-Chicago. Graves came through again in a 51–46 victory, identical to the Cleveland State score. With a defender in his face, he sank a 3-pointer with 45 seconds left to break a 46–46 tie. His two free throws secured the outcome and assured Butler of a share of a sixth regular-season league title in nine years.

The Bulldogs were repeatedly left open against UIC's zone and responded poorly by shooting 35 percent (13-of-37) from the 3-point arc. Their five two-point field goals were a season low. Howard's two points were a season low. Green's three points were a season low, and his six turnovers a season high.

Yet it was the Bulldogs' ninth straight win—their longest streak of the season—and it inflated their record to 25–2, second in the nation behind No. 1 Memphis (26–0).

•••

For a BracketBuster opponent, Butler drew the Missouri Valley Conference leader, as it did the year before in Southern Illinois. No. 16-ranked Drake, at 23–3, was one of the unlikeliest stories in college basketball. Drake, also nicknamed the Bulldogs, was picked to finish ninth in the Valley. Drake point guard Adam Emmenecker, the Valley's player of the year, arrived on campus as a walk-on.

Butler and Drake so closely resembled each other—both featured seniors, played team basketball, averaged nine 3-pointers a game, and shot 38 percent from the arc—that one journalist suggested they were actually the *same* team. "After all," he wrote, "have you ever seen the teams on the floor at the same time?"

For Butler and Drake, this matchup was no joke. It had consequences for NCAA Tournament seeding because neither had played so-called elite teams. Each had played one opponent from the RPI top 50.

Butler's Bulldogs had the measurable pluses: a home court in which they had won 11 in a row—including 10 this season by an average of 15 points—and their highest ranking ever. They had won nine in a row, and Drake had lost two of three.

Mysteriously, Butler never seized control. Uncharacteristically, Butler was plagued by turnovers, poor decisions, and missed free throws. Butler sank eight consecutive field-goal attempts in the first half to go ahead 34–31, but Drake reclaimed the lead and extended it to 41–34 to begin the second half. After Butler took its biggest lead, 58–54, it was limited to six points over the final six minutes.

During Drake's closing surge, Streicher and Green missed the front end of one-and-ones. With 56 seconds left and Butler trailing 64–62, Green was called for charging. Then, with the shot clock expiring, Green fouled Drake guard Josh Young behind the 3-point line with 20 seconds left. Young sank all three free throws in what became Drake's 71–64 victory, disappointing most of the 10,000 fans in sold-out Hinkle Fieldhouse.

One fan tossed a water bottle onto the court, and the Valley officiating crew exited to loud booing. That vexed Stevens more than defeat. He later submitted a letter to the Butler community, stating that profanity and throwing objects are unacceptable.

Although some Butler failings were unfamiliar, there were two common threads. Butler trailed at halftime, as it had in all 10 losses over two seasons. Also, 3-point accuracy deserted the Bulldogs, who were 1-of-8 in the second half and 6-of-24 overall. Young scored 25 points for Drake and Graves 18 for Butler.

Damage of the Drake defeat can't be overestimated. It harmed Butler's seeding and probably caused a premature ending to an NCAA Tournament stay.

•••

It's not as if Butler could bounce back against a pushover. Visiting Indianapolis next was Wright State, which had won the past three meetings in the series, albeit all at Dayton. Moreover, Wright State had recently won 11 straight.

The Bulldogs went ahead for good late in the first half and won 66–61, securing a second straight regular-season title and No. 1 seed for the Horizon tournament. Fittingly, two seniors, Betko and Green, made sure they could play more games at Hinkle Fieldhouse. Betko scored all of his career-high 17 points in the first half, sinking his first five 3-point attempts. It was one of those rare occasions in which his aching knees felt spry.

"It was not very sore," Betko said. "I'm just happy we won."

So was Green, who committed another late foul on a 3-point attempt. Wright State's Vaughn Duggins, from nearby Pendleton, Ind., sank the three resultant free throws and trimmed Butler's lead to 57–53. Then Green, with the shot clock running out, responded with his lone 3-pointer. He finished with 15 points, scoring nine over the closing six minutes. Afterward, Green hugged his mother, who traveled from Philadelphia along with about a dozen friends and family.

"Timely shots, man," Green said. "When the game's on the line, I like to step it up and take our team to another level."

Afterward, before Stevens could intervene to stop them, Butler players cut down the nets. The coach didn't want them celebrating before a more important task—winning the Horizon tourney—could be completed.

The regular season finished with a senior day lovefest before 7,880 at the fieldhouse. Campbell tied a career high with eight 3-pointers, and roommate Green narrowly missed a triple-double in a 65–31 blowout of Detroit. At one point, Detroit had barely outscored Campbell, 27–24. The Titans' 31 points were the fewest by a Butler opponent since 1947.

Butler players wore *Dawg Pound* shirts in warm-ups to honor student fans. It was such a special occasion that Graves stooped to pet Blue, the bulldog mascot, after he was introduced. Petting the dog is a ritual at home games, but he had never done so because he is "not a dog person." Graves scored a career-low two points.

Butler's seniors sat out the last 10 minutes, except for a curtain call in which Stevens took timeout to insert all five. The seniors left to an ovation.

"All the wins, all the accolades don't compare to the type of people they are," Stevens told the crowd during a ceremony afterward.

Green had 11 points, 12 rebounds, and nine assists, again falling short of a triple-double. He said he would have more chances. That's what his coach wanted to hear.

"I don't want them to think this is the most memorable part of their career," Stevens said. "We've talked a lot about that. We want to maximize the next month and a half."

• • •

Perhaps no one in the 2000s came to epitomize the Butler Way more than Drew Streicher. His story was certainly among the most unusual in college basketball.

Here is the abridged version:

Not recruited out of high school. Invited to walk on. Earned a scholarship. Started for a top 10 team and became an Academic All-

American. Finished school with a master's of business administration and acceptance to medical school.

"He's so smart. It's ridiculous, man," Mike Green said.

Obviously, Streicher knew how to take tests. That's how he earned a 3.95 grade-point average in chemistry and a perfect 4.0 in the MBA program, in which he enrolled in his fifth year. When tested on the court, results were similar. Brad Stevens once watched film of a game to rate players on each possession. The coach was not checking to see if they made every shot but if they went to the right place at the right time. Streicher did.

"And he did it 100 percent of the time," Stevens said.

Streicher once considered himself more of a soccer player in Washington, Ind., where he was a defensive midfielder. Butler coaches noticed him in basketball while trying to recruit Luke Zeller, who became a Mr. Basketball before heading to Notre Dame. Streicher was going to Butler anyway to study pharmacy.

Not only did Streicher get better at Butler, he got bigger. From 6-foot-5 and 175 pounds, he grew to 6-foot-8 and 205. He was never an offensive force—he didn't average 10 points a game in high school—but discovered defense was "my ticket to the court," he said.

He was long and deceptively athletic, and he dunked more easily than anyone else on Butler's team. His lateral mobility was exceptional, a trait attributed to years of soccer. He guarded players as short as 5-foot-10 and as tall as 7 feet. In practice scrimmages, he was usually on the winning side.

"Drew does a lot of things for us that don't show up in the box score," Green said.

Academic achievements were easier to measure. John Esteb, an associate professor, said Streicher was among the top 3 or 4 percent of approximately 1,000 students he has taught in organic chemistry.

"He's one of those very, very special people who excels at everything he does," Esteb said. "He has natural intuition and intellect. He works hard, on top of that. You put those together, and there's nothing he can't do."

Streicher spent one summer working at a pharmacy but didn't like it. Esteb was influential in guiding him toward medicine, as was Streicher's girlfriend, a med student. Moreover, after having injuries treated in each of his first three years at Butler, he became familiar with what a doctor does.

Drew Streicher cuts the net to celebrate Butler's 2008 Horizon League Tournament championship. Streicher, who arrived at Butler as a walk-on, made the all-tournament team (Butler University Archives).

Seemed perfect. Nothing less than perfect would have been appropriate.

● ● ●

While awaiting its Horizon semifinal, Butler collected league honors: Green as player of the year and Howard as newcomer of the year. (Howard was the first true freshman to win since 1996.) Green and Graves were on the all-league first team and Howard on the second team. Green and Streicher made the all-defensive team.

Stevens, despite a 27–3 debut, was not coach of the year. That honor was shared by Wright State's Brad Brownell and Cleveland State's Gary Waters.

The quarterfinal round marked the 80th anniversary of the first game ever played at what was then Butler Fieldhouse, on March 7, 1928. No. 4-seeded UIC earned a shot at the top-seeded Bulldogs by beating Loyola 60–49. In the other game, No. 6 seed Valparaiso won 72–67 to eliminate No. 3 Wright State, the defending champion.

The two top seeds, Butler and Cleveland State, won semifinal games to set up the league's fifth 1-vs.-2 championship in six years.

The Bulldogs sank 12 3-pointers to beat UIC 66–50—and would have won by more if they had kept the Flames off the offensive boards. Without 25 second-chance points and 12 free throws, UIC scored only 13 points. No. 2 seed Cleveland State built an 18-point lead and held off Valparaiso 78–73.

For all Butler had achieved in recent seasons, it had not won the league tournament since 2001. Butler had gone 0–3 in subsequent title games, although none of the three was in Indianapolis.

Now, the Bulldogs had no mitigating circumstances. They had a No. 12-ranked team that was 28–3, featured five seniors, and were playing at home. The 9:00 p.m. start, ESPN television, and students' spring break limited attendance to 5,021, but Butler would have been motivated if this had been played in private. For good luck, Stevens kept in his pocket a piece of net the Bulldogs cut down in 2001 after winning what was then the Midwestern Collegiate Conference.

The Bulldogs didn't need luck. They could have used practice on their celebratory moves but saved stylish performance for the game. Green tied career highs with 24 points and 13 rebounds, and Butler pulled away from Cleveland State 70–55. The Bulldogs' balance was underscored by the fact that Graves and Campbell were held to one 3-pointer each and a collective eight points.

Surrounded by fans who rushed the court, Butler players did cartwheels at midcourt, continuing a long tradition at the university. Former football coach and athletic director Bill Sylvester had his teams clap and sing the "Butler War Song" after big victories. Barry Collier, after becoming basketball coach in 1989, had such admiration for Sylvester that the practice was extended to basketball. Cartwheels are reserved for *huge* victories, and this qualified as one. A photograph of A.J. Graves' awkward-looking cartwheel ended up in the pages of *Sports Illustrated*.

"I've never been on a team like this," Green said. "This is the epitome of team. There's no loose ends. Everybody's happy for each other. We have no jealousy on this team. You won't find many teams like this, so it's a special thing."

Backing him were Howard with 16 points and Streicher with 11. The crowd intoned "Droooh" in appreciation of his uncharacteristic three 3-pointers.

Selection of Streicher to the all-tournament team completed an unusual sweep. All five seniors—Green, Graves, Campbell, Betko, and Streicher—made at least one all-tournament team during their careers.

•••

In every category except one, Butler's 2007–08 résumé exceeded that of the previous season. In 2006–07, Butler was 27–6 with a No. 21 ranking, No. 27 RPI, 4–1 against the RPI top 50, 7–3 against the top 100, and an 11–4 record away from home. This time the corresponding figures were 29–3, No. 11 ranking, No. 16 RPI, 1–1, 10–3, and 15–2.

Projections had placed Butler in the No. 4–6 range. Its solitary shortcoming—1–1 against the top 50—caused the committee to give Butler a No. 7 seed in the NCAA Tournament. When Butler players gathered at Stevens' home to watch the CBS selection show, their response to seeing a 7 on the TV screen was silence.

Publicly, Butler players didn't complain. Privately, they must have been bewildered. Especially vexing was that the committee chairman, Tom O'Connor, was from George Mason, which shockingly reached the Final Four in 2006.

"Scheduling for the non-BCS schools is difficult. I can tell you that, being from a non-BCS school," O'Connor said. "Butler did as good a job as they could. And we feel they're right where they should be seeded."

Of Butler's five BCS opponents—Michigan, Virginia Tech, Texas Tech, Ohio State, and Florida State—only Ohio State was in the top 50. Worse was the home loss to Drake, which could not be offset by everything else.

For the second straight year, Butler was paired against another mid-major. South Alabama (26–6) earned a No. 10 seed as an at-large from the Sun Belt Conference. Looming in the East Regional's second round was No. 2 seed Tennessee, which a few weeks earlier ranked No. 1 in the nation.

What Butler had that none of the 64 other teams did were two 1,500-point scorers in the backcourt, Graves and Green. Its biggest concern was the health of Campbell, who injured his left ankle two days before the game.

For 14 minutes, Butler and South Alabama played evenly. Domonic Tilford dribbled baseline to baseline for a layup, pushing the Jaguars ahead 23–22. It was their last lead. Campbell, playing with a heavily taped ankle, scored a rare two-pointer that restored Butler's lead. That was the start of a Campbell Clusterfest.

In the closing six-plus minutes of the half, he scored 14 points and turned a one-point deficit into a 17-point lead. The Bulldogs sank 15 3-pointers and led by as many as 27 in the second half of an 81–61 rout. In one stretch, they were 11-of-12 on 3s.

Five of Campbell's seven first-half baskets came on assists from Graves, who took over the point after Green sat with two fouls. Campbell finished 8-of-10 from the arc—making his final six in succession—and equaled a career high of 26 points in just 20 minutes. Coincidentally, it was five years before in the same arena where Darnell Archey's 8-of-9 shooting from the arc propelled Butler past Louisville. Friendly Birmingham rims?

"I don't think Pete's shots hit the rim, actually," Graves deadpanned.

As hot as Campbell, on the other end of the floor, was Streicher. He held South Alabama's 6-foot-4 Demetric Bennett to six points, or 14 below his average. Butler more than compensated for Green's five point, four turnover off-day.

The Bulldogs achieved multiple milestones:

- Their most lopsided victory ever in the NCAA Tournament
- A 30th victory, breaking the school record set the year before.
- A fourth straight first-round victory (After two NCAA tourney wins in the 20th century, they had six in the decade.)
- The 31-year-old Stevens becoming the youngest coach since 1950 to win 30 games in major college basketball

Butler, at 30–3, advanced to play Tennessee, 30–4. Here they were, ranked 11th and fifth, respectively, in the final AP poll, meeting already. It was the first time ever that two 30-game winners were matched as early as the second round.

Months later, Betko conceded that the athletic Vols were the worst possible matchup for Butler in the entire tournament. Vols coach Bruce Pearl, who is customarily outspoken, conceded there was reason not to award them a No. 1 seed. But based on the math, he added, Tennessee and Butler "did everything we possibly could" to avoid having to face such an opponent so early in the tournament.

Pearl, who coached against the Bulldogs while at Milwaukee, gushed over them. He didn't have to remind his Vols that they had been thumped by Butler 56–44 in the previous season's NIT Season

---

Tipoff. Perceptively, Pearl added that Butler's system is built to beat the power teams.

"In fact, I would say that what they do works against more traditional size than it does even in their own league sometimes," Pearl said, "where they see smaller players that are able to match up with what they do."

On game day, an Easter Sunday, the Bulldogs went through a morning walkthrough at a high school in Hoover, Ala., before returning to the Wynfrey Hotel. The young sons of Stevens and director of basketball operations Micah Shrewsberry had been promised an Easter egg hunt outside a ballroom, so Green helped the boys scoop up plastic eggs while teammates watched the fun.

Tennessee opened the game not by collecting eggs, but 3-pointers. The Vols sank three in the opening six minutes and surged ahead of Butler 13–2. The lead grew to 12 points before the Bulldogs countered with their own 3-pointers—three each by Graves and Campbell—and trimmed the halftime deficit to 38–34.

Howard was enduring a forgettable 1-of-7 game and later acknowledged that the Vols "got in my head a little bit." He sat down after picking up his third foul early in the second half, but Butler persevered even after falling behind by 10.

Graves converted a one-and-one to tie it at 60. Butler pulled even again at 63 on Veasley's tip-in with 37 seconds to play. A Tennessee traveling violation returned the ball to Butler with four seconds remaining, but Green lost control as time expired. On to overtime.

Graves supplied Butler its only lead, 68–66, on a drive with 1:46 left. The Vols outscored Butler 10–3 thereafter and pulled away to a 76–71 victory. Graves finished with 21 points. Campbell scored 12, only two in the second half.

Green, so spectacular in overtime against Virginia Tech and Milwaukee, was a bundle of frustration against Tennessee. Time after time, he maneuvered to the goal with the intent of scoring, drawing a foul, or both. Time after time, he came away with neither. He had typical totals—15 points, seven rebounds, five assists—but shot 4-of-17 and committed six turnovers, several in crucial situations. That he set a Butler season assists record of 172 was of no consolation.

"Those shots that I've been making all year long, for some reason, they didn't go," Green said.

Butler would go no further in this NCAA Tournament.

During the 2008 Horizon League title game against Cleveland State, coach Brad Stevens kept a piece of net from Butler's 2001 league championship in his pocket (Butler Univeristy Archives).

● ● ●

Was this the best team in Butler basketball history?

It's a question that must be asked, even if it cannot be answered definitively. With a 30–4 record, these Bulldogs belong in the discussion. If not for a missed free throw here, or a botched layup there, they would have moved on to play opponents arguably no better than Tennessee.

Butler players didn't go on record stating long-term ambitions, but they believed they could reach a Final Four. Or win a national championship, even though odds against that were listed at 100-to-1.

"I have no reservation saying that," Pete Campbell said. "We definitely did."

Yet they did not make it. The Bulldogs played two top 20 opponents, Drake and Tennessee, and lost to both. They lacked a marquee victory, although winning the Great Alaska Shootout was consequential, as was a 16–2 Horizon League record. They did not make the Sweet Sixteen, as Butler did in 1962, 2003, and 2007.

Yet should that be the only measurement? Butler had no so-called bad losses. The Bulldogs lost by one, four, seven, and five (OT) to teams that won 21 or more games. They achieved the program's highest ranking ever: No. 8. If they had reached the Sweet Sixteen—and they were an overtime away from doing so—then 2008 would go down as Butler's best season ever.

Butler's five seniors came together more by serendipity than design. Only A.J. Graves arrived as a scholarship freshman. Drew Streicher was a walk-on. Julian Betko (Clemson), Mike Green (Towson), and Pete Campbell (IPFW) transferred. Matt Howard, a freshman, ended up at Butler because Purdue ran out of scholarships.

Among the seniors, only Green and Campbell continued playing basketball the next year, both in European leagues. Graves went to an Indianapolis lab science firm, Streicher to med school, and Betko to coaching.

This Butler team did not have the chip-on-the-shoulder edginess of 2003. Joel Cornette, the 2003 center, said his Bulldogs had "nasty guys." When he visited a practice before the 2008 NCAA Tournament, he was struck by the Bulldogs' businesslike manner. They played a "calculating style of basketball," Cornette said. There was no denying their simmering fire, however.

"They're a lot more like snipers," Cornette said. "My teams in 2002 and 2003 were more like front-line soldiers."

Tennessee's Bruce Pearl called this the best Butler team he had seen, and he coached against Butler's best: 2002, 2003, 2007, and 2008. The trouble is, many others never saw this team.

In that respect, the 2008 team resembles the 2002 Snubbed Team. Neither season finished satisfactorily. Both sets of Bulldogs embodied the Butler Way, seeking improvement every day. The best was yet to come . . . and then the days ended.

The 2008–09 Team (26–6):
Never Too Young

At college basketball programs such as North Carolina, Duke, Kansas, or UCLA, there is never a dearth of talent. Even if players leave early for the NBA, there are high school All-Americans ready to succeed them. Such is not the case at Butler.

The Butlers of the world spend years recruiting players overlooked by bigger schools, developing them, and molding them into a team. When those players become juniors and seniors, they are prepared to compete with, and sometimes defeat, opponents with more talent and resources.

Throughout the 2000s, experience had been the foundation of Butler's winning teams. But in the fall of 2008, the Bulldogs were confronted with an unfamiliar challenge. According to one statistical ranking, Butler was the fourth-youngest out of 344 major-college teams. There was not a senior on the roster. Just two juniors, Willie Veasley and Avery Jukes, were on scholarship. There were five freshmen and four sophomores. The oldest player, Veasley, had only recently turned 21. And with the exception of sophomore Matt Howard, none of the players had been regarded as an elite recruit coming out of high school.

The outlook was so unfavorable that a panel of media and coaches picked Butler to finish fifth in the Horizon League. An employee in Butler's athletic administration told colleagues he wasn't expecting more than 12 wins, which would be the worst season since 1992–93. Butler's 32-year-old coach, Brad Stevens, joked about the team's youth during a preseason gathering right before Halloween. He said the Bulldogs were so young that

- "I don't get asked how old I am anymore,"
- "every practice we have nap time *and* recess," and
- "on Friday we have to cut practice short to end at 5:00 because

trick-or-treating starts at 6:00."

Despite all that, there was no gloom within the team. Nor among an excited fan base. It was apparent that Butler had attracted an exceptional freshman class, even if the players weren't highly rated. Three freshmen —Gordon Hayward, Garrett Butcher, and Chase Stigall —had been chosen to the Indiana All-Star team. That team annually plays the Kentucky All-Stars, whose roster featured another Butler recruit, Shelvin Mack.

In the first game of June's all-star doubleheader, played in Indianapolis, Hayward had 11 points and eight rebounds as Indiana erased an 11-point deficit to beat Kentucky 83–82. Mack was even more productive for Kentucky, scoring 24 points. Two days later, in Louisville, Ky., Mack scored 16 as Kentucky ended a streak of eight straight losses in the series, 95–78.

The Indiana/Kentucky tally was even at 1–1, but there was one clear winner: Butler.

•••

There was one incoming freshman, Ronald Nored Jr., who didn't have to be taught the Butler Way of selflessness and servanthood. He learned that from his late father.

Ronald Nored Sr. was an African Methodist Episcopal pastor who helped a church and community change a Birmingham, Ala., neighborhood plagued by unemployment, substandard housing, drugs, and crime. Over a period of eight years, the decay was replaced by single-family homes, parks, sidewalks, street lights, and youth and jobs programs. It was "a complete 360," Ronald Jr. said.

The pastor's book about the transformation, *Reweaving the Fabric*, was published in 1999 and features a photograph of 7-year-old Ronald Jr. on the cover. The book is dedicated to the pastor's three sons.

Ronald Nored Sr. died of pancreatic cancer on October 11, 2003. He was 43.

That was a painful period for young Nored, who was in eighth grade and enduring all the issues of adolescence. In the South, football is king, and he was a star running back in middle school. Ronald Jr. created an uproar when he abandoned football to concentrate on basketball. His mother, Linda Williams Nored, said it was an especially difficult time because her husband was so close to his sons.

"He instilled a lot of values in them and about the kind of people they should aspire to be," she said. "I think it really did stick with them."

Ronald Jr. accompanied his father when he went into the decrepit Ensley section of the city to help build homes. Every Christmas morning, the boys didn't awaken and begin opening presents under the tree. First, they went with their father to distribute gifts to children who otherwise would not receive any. If people needed a meal, they could eat at the Nored's home. If someone wandered into the church and asked for money, Ronald Sr. would reach into his own pocket and hand over cash.

"He was an awesome person to be around," Ronald Jr. said. "If you really, really got to know him and listen to him and hear him talk and hear what he was about, it was a wonder."

Ronald Sr. was once honored as the Birmingham Citizen of the Year and posthumously with the Martin Luther King Jr. American Dream Award.

Ronald Jr.'s mother is an Indianapolis native. She once worked at Methodist Hospital in the city, and when it came time to give birth to Ronald Jr., she traveled to Indy so she could deliver her first child at that hospital. Her parents, Leonard and Delores Kennedy Williams, live on 40th Street, or a few blocks from Hinkle Fieldhouse.

Ronald Jr. often visited his grandparents' home and rode his bicycle around the Butler campus and Holcomb Gardens. There was never a thought of him becoming a student there one day. He became a standout high school player in the suburb of Homewood, Ala., and signed with Western Kentucky.

But when Western Kentucky's coach, Darrin Horn, left to take the job at South Carolina, Nored received a release from that commitment. Stevens had seen Nored play and acted swiftly. The coach drove directly to Nored's home, only a few miles from where the Bulldogs played in the NCAA Tournament weeks before. Nored promptly committed to Butler.

He said it was "kind of weird" that he ended up on the campus where he had played as child.

Years after his father's death, Nored can speak about him without sadness. He said his father's life was something to celebrate, learn from, and live by.

"I'm just trying to do half as well as he did," Nored said. "I think if I do that, I will have accomplished a lot."

• • •

Nored was a winner, a characteristic common to all the newcomers. The five scholarship freshmen had all been to a high-school state championship game or played for a No. 1-ranked team:

- Gordon Hayward capped Brownsburg's improbable run to an Indiana state championship by sinking the winning basket as time expired in a 40–39 victory over Marion. Brownsburg, also nicknamed Bulldogs, was not ranked in Class 4A at the end of the regular season before finishing 22–5.

- Shelvin Mack was playing varsity basketball as early as eighth grade at Bryan Station in Lexington, Ky. As a senior, he averaged 23.7 points for a 30–3 team that climbed to No. 1 in the state.

- Ronald Nored averaged 15.3 points for a 31–5 team that reached Alabama's Class 6A championship game.

- Garrett Butcher, as a junior, led Edgewood High School of Ellettsville to Indiana's No. 1 ranking in Class 3A. Edgewood was 45–4 in his last two seasons there, and he was sixth in the state in scoring as a senior with a 25.2 average. Butcher became Monroe County's all-time leading scorer, surpassing Sean May, who helped North Carolina win a 2005 NCAA championship before heading to the NBA.

- Chase Stigall became the fifth guard from New Castle in this decade to choose Butler, following Darnell Archey, Brandon Miller, Bruce Horan, and teammate Zach Hahn. Stigall and Hahn helped New Castle win a 3A state championship in 2007.

Recruiting ratings are so subjective that analysts themselves caution against an overemphasis. Dave Telep, of scout.com, said Butler's coaches know what they're looking for and how to identify players who fit the system.

"That is the only thing that's important to them," Telep said. "And that's why they're successful. Not because of where their guys are rated.

"They know their program better than anyone else. I think that is the brilliance of Butler basketball."

Serendipity can influence recruiting, too. Hayward and Mack performed spectacularly as high-school seniors, after player ratings are finished and most college commitments made.

During the off-season, Butler players didn't need to compare résumés to discover that the dim forecast might be unwarranted. While taking summer classes, returnees and newcomers played informal games and began forming bonds—and expectations—that would carry over into fall and winter. The freshmen all lived in Ross Hall and came to feel like a band of brothers.

• • •

The November 15 opener was at Drake, which had come into Hinkle Fieldhouse and beaten Butler 71–64 nine months before. This Drake team was missing key pieces from those Missouri Valley Conference champions, notably coach Keno Davis. He left after one season to coach at Providence of the Big East.

Ideally, Butler's young team would have opened at home. But provisions of the BracketBuster require teams that host one season to play at the opponent's arena the next. This was the only date available, so Butler's players found themselves on a flight to Des Moines, Iowa. If Stevens had misgivings about taking the Bulldogs on the road, he didn't say so publicly. New Drake coach Scott Phelps said he didn't think inexperience would matter, either.

"Butler has a certain culture about their program," Phelps said. "They play the same way."

Phelps proved to be more accurate in his statement than his players were in their shooting. Drake's Bulldogs seemed nervous and unsure of themselves, despite support of a Knapp Center crowd of 6,012, the largest for a home opener since 2000. Butler played as if it had been together for years rather than weeks.

Butler built a 14-point lead in the first half, held Drake to 31 percent shooting, and won 58–48. Zach Hahn came off the bench to lead the Bulldogs with 13 points. For the second consecutive year, Butler had beaten a Valley team on the road after losing to that opponent at home. The previous year, Butler traveled to Southern Illinois to win a rematch.

"Butler is Butler," Phelps said afterward. "They have a way about them."

The Bulldogs returned to Indianapolis for four successive home games, beginning with the 100th meeting against instate rival Ball State. The Cardinals were 1–7 in the previous eight meetings but were reviving under second-year coach Billy Taylor.

The home opener also marked the debut of a new bulldog mascot. Four arrests had been made in connection with an August theft of two mascot costumes from Hinkle Fieldhouse. Four men, none of them Butler students, were eventually sentenced to a year of probation and ordered to pay $14,000 for the cost of replacing the costumes.

Thefts were kept to a minimum on the hardcourt. Butler committed six turnovers in beating Ball State 64–55. The Bulldogs were guilty of 16 at Drake, and in a program long among the nation's leaders in fewest turnovers, that was an unacceptable figure.

"You know you've got a good team when you can focus on something, and everything else stays at a high level," Stevens said. "You're going to be what you emphasize sometimes."

Butler's next game against Indiana University-South Bend figured to be a mismatch, and it was.

Ronald Nored learned about servanthood from his late father, an Alabama pastor (Photo by John Fetcho).

The Bulldogs won 87–33, featuring a 15½-minute stretch in which they went on a 45–3 run. The 54-point margin was the second-largest in school history, behind an 82–14 victory over Indiana Law School in November 1921. Mack (19 points) and Hayward (17 points) were exceptionally efficient in 17 minutes played each.

A Thanksgiving eve game against Northwestern promised to be anything but a blowout. This was a Wildcats team that later would end Michigan State's 28-game home winning streak. Northwestern featured a Princeton-style offense of back-door cuts. Its coach, former Princeton coach Bill Carmody, is considered among the sport's top offensive minds.

The Wildcats asserted control during a 14–1 spurt that resulted in a 33–21 lead. They shot 68 percent (15-of-22) in the first half, scoring on five back-door cuts. Butler went the final 12 minutes of the half without a field goal. Northwestern's halftime lead was 36–27, and it could have been bigger. It should have been bigger, Carmody said. The Bulldogs depended on their defense for a 57–53 comeback victory.

"I think we were fortunate to win this one, personally," Stevens said. "But I'll take it."

Northwestern guard Craig Moore, coming off a career-high 31 points, was limited to 11. Forward Kevin Coble, who would score 31 in that upset of Michigan State, was limited to three by Veasley. The Wildcats shot 27 percent in the second half.

"I would say that we let one get away," Carmody said. "But I think that they took it away from us."

● ● ●

Thanksgiving break was a short one for the players, with an upcoming Saturday game. The holiday allowed time for introspection, though, especially for Avery Jukes. The 6-foot-8 junior from Snellville, Ga., didn't hesitate to identify a Thanksgiving blessing.

"Just the simple fact of being born in the U.S. is a blessing in itself," he said.

Jukes' academic major is mechanical engineering, and his interests include travel and humanitarian issues. He was among the Butler students who made a June trip to Uganda, in east central Africa, as part of Ambassadors for Children. The organization serves children around the world. Except for a cruise to Mexico, Jukes had never been out of the country.

"It opens your eyes to a lot of different things," he said. "It makes you well-rounded."

Outside the Ugandan capital of Kampala, the students chopped down small trees and tall grass to clear the way for a primary school serving 325 children. The group also visited clinics and other volunteer organizations. Northern Uganda has been embroiled in civil strife for years, but Jukes said the southern part of the country they visited was safe.

Jukes wasn't adventurous with local cuisine—he declined to eat grasshoppers—but enjoyed a safari in which he saw a lioness, hippopotamus, water buffalo, and elephants. Besides the Ugandan people's ready smiles, what he most remembered was the dirt huts in which they lived.

Jukes turned the short-term service project into a long-term commitment. He started the Jukes Foundation for Kids (www.jukesfoundationforkids.org) in an attempt to improve the quality of life for children in the United States and Uganda. The not-for-profit group collected children's books and organized a fund-raising gala at the NCAA Hall of Champions in Indianapolis. Jukes' contribution to the Butler Way will last for years and be felt 7,700 miles away from campus.

● ● ●

Butler ended the month by beating Evansville 75–59 and extending three long winning streaks: 20 straight November victories, 10 over instate opponents, and eight at home.

"They're obviously a fun team to watch. Not to play against," Evansville coach Marty Simmons said.

Stevens called the second half the best the Bulldogs had played so far. Hayward began the half by dunking on a lob from Howard, and then Mack took over. Mack scored 13 of his 18 points in the second half, including nine in a five-minute flurry right after halftime.

At 5–0, Butler began December with seemingly its most difficult Horizon League test—at Cleveland State, the preseason favorite. Butler had lost four starters from the previous year, and Cleveland State returned four. Cleveland State featured two tough-minded seniors: Cedric Jackson, a point guard who transferred from Rutgers, and J'Nathan Bullock, a 6-foot-5 dreadlocks-topped forward who later signed with the New York Jets as a tight-end.

The Vikings led 27–20 at the half, and each time Butler crept closer, Cleveland State pulled away. Cleveland State led 41–33 with less than six minutes left and 43–36 at under the four-minute mark.

Then Butler put the ball, and the game, in Hayward's hands. Of Butler's 14 points over the closing four minutes, he had a hand in 12. He sank a 3-pointer and three free throws and assisted on 3s by Shawn Vanzant and Hahn.

Bullock's layup put Cleveland State ahead 48–47 with 5.4 seconds left, and Butler called timeout. The Bulldogs wanted Hayward to take the inbounds pass because he was tall enough to see over defenders. Late-game plays rarely work as designed, but this one did. Hayward dribbled once and threw across the court. Hahn caught the ball and then paused to let Bullock fly by. Then Hahn let the ball fly from beyond the arc. Swish. Ballgame.

"Guys never conceded defeat. That was the bottom line," Stevens said.

Hahn celebrated by sliding across the floor on his belly. In their 50–48 victory, the Bulldogs achieved something even the veteran 30-win team had not—a victory at Cleveland State. Hahn said he had never made a winning shot like that at any level of basketball. And he did so coming in cold off the bench.

"It was a little difficult, but you know, when coach calls your number, it gives you confidence that coach wants you in the game at that point," Hahn said.

Made baskets were a rare occurrence. After starting 6-of-9, the Bulldogs were 7-of-41 (17 percent) over the subsequent 30 minutes. They missed 10 in a row from the arc before making their final three. Cleveland State shot 26 percent for the game and 14 percent (4-of-28) in the second half.

The Bulldogs' errant shooting didn't carry over into the Youngstown State contest. Mack sank four 3-pointers, all in the first half, and four teammates added 3s. The Bulldogs built an 11-point halftime lead and were ahead by as many as 19 in a 79–71 victory.

Howard scored 23 points, sinking 13-of-15 free throws, and Mack 22.

● ● ●

The Bulldogs were 7–0 for the third successive season and halfway through a four-game stretch of road games in which one win would have been welcome. Already, they had two.

Next was a midweek trip to Peoria, Ill., to play the Bradley Braves of the Missouri Valley Conference. Although Butler fans often advocate that the university abandon its league for the Valley—to which Butler briefly belonged in the 1930s—there is no disputing the fact that the Valley would be harder to dominate. Heading into this meeting, over the previous two years, the Valley was 3–6 against Butler and the Horizon 5–31.

The young Bulldogs were oblivious to history but not to the task at hand. Hayward scored 17 points in the opening 16 minutes—with 5-of-8 shooting from the 3-point arc—in Butler's 87–75 victory before a near-capacity crowd of 9,366.

The Bulldogs shot 54 percent and sank 13 from the arc, equaling the most 3s ever allowed by Bradley at Carver Arena. Butler led by 15 points in the first half and by 14 midway through the second. When Bradley trimmed that to 62–57, Butler scored the next 11 points.

"Going into the season, the question mark for me was: 'What are we going to be like when those moments occur?'" Stevens said. "You're worried about when you're on the road, you have a lead, it gets cut, the crowd gets into it. Do you step up and handle that situation? And thus far, they have."

The Braves' defeat was only their third in 35 nonconference home games. Sitting courtside was Kirk Wessler, executive sports editor of the *Peoria Journal Star*, whose column published the next day summed up what witnesses were thinking:

"If that was a rebuilding project that ripped through the Bradley Braves on Wednesday night at Carver Arena, I'll make this prediction right now. Butler is going to be one scary team for the next few college basketball seasons."

Butler took an 8–0 record to Ohio State, which was ranked No. 21 and led by former Butler coach Thad Matta. It was the Bulldogs' third game in Ohio in 10 days and certainly their most difficult. Butler had a 10-game winning streak in the regular season over BCS (power conference) opponents but a three-game losing streak against the Top 25.

Butler, an 11-point underdog, was tentative and fell behind 13–5. Hayward found openings against Ohio State's zone, and his 14 points (including four 3s) allowed the Bulldogs to pull even at 19–19. Ohio State pushed ahead 29–23 by halftime and soon extended that to 43–30. But these Bulldogs were more athletic than previous editions, and they applied so much defensive pressure that Ohio State was limited to one field goal over the closing 12 minutes.

Hayward's seventh 3 tied the score at 51, and Nored stole the ball and went in for what would have been a go-ahead layup. Instead, Jeremie Simmons blocked Nored's shot. Evan Turner's jumper restored the Buckeyes' lead to 53–51 with 3:08 left, and that would be enough. The Buckeyes were 1-of-6 on free throws down the stretch but held on for a 54–51 victory.

"I told our guys we beat an NCAA Tournament team today," Matta said.

Hayward was nudged by defender David Lighty on a 3-point attempt as time expired. It wasn't a flagrant collision, though, and no foul was called. Hayward would have gone to the free-throw line with a chance to shoot three and send the game into overtime.

"It could have been a foul," Turner conceded afterward. "We'll take it."

Hayward's seven 3s set a Butler freshman record, and he finished with a career-high 25 points. The Bradley and Ohio State games introduced a pattern that would persist—his biggest outputs came on the road, not at home. Hayward acknowledged he was hit in the shooting arm at the end, but he said referees were not going to call a foul in such a situation.

"It was a nice defensive play," Hayward said.

Butler had a week off before extending its home winning streak to nine in a 73–53 victory over Florida Gulf Coast. The Bulldogs sank 12 more 3-pointers, by seven different players. They did so without Hahn, who was so ill he didn't attend the game.

• • •

Late-December games shouldn't mean so much. Yet for a team like Butler, more recognition would accrue from a single victory over a Top-25 team than an 18–0 run through the Horizon League.

So the Bulldogs' visit to No. 14 Xavier, before a national television audience on ESPNU, was momentous. It would be Butler's last game against a Top-25 opponent until the NCAA Tournament, offering a chance to end a four-game losing streak against ranked teams. Win at Xavier and finish first in the league, and Butler would almost certainly get another NCAA at-large bid. Lose at Xavier, and a victory in the Horizon tourney might be required. Xavier was No. 7, its highest ranking ever, until losing to No. 5 Duke, 82–64, at East Rutherford, N.J., days before. That didn't diminish the game's importance to Butler, an eight-point underdog.

Xavier advanced to the 2008 Elite Eight, and its program had grown to such a stature that it refused to be classified as a mid-major. Xavier once dominated the Midwestern Collegiate Conference, winning a record six MCC Tournaments between 1981 and 1995. Xavier was 14–2 in the previous 16 meetings with Butler, although the teams hadn't played since 1998.

The Bulldogs made the two-hour bus trip east before freezing rain around Cincinnati made travel hazardous and shut down several highways. Despite the storm, an announced sellout of 10,250 had most seats occupied at the gleaming $46 million Cintas Center, where the Musketeers had won 15 in a row.

Xavier fell behind 12–4 before forging ahead 26–24 late in the first half, and it seemed inevitable that the bigger Musketeers would prevail. Their lineup averaged 6-foot-7, and 7-foot freshman Kenny Frease came off the bench to score three baskets in the first half. However, a rare 3-pointer by Nored and Vanzant's basket allowed the Bulldogs to go ahead 29–26 at halftime. They never relinquished the lead in a second half that exasperated Xavier.

Butler was 26-of-30 on free throws in the second half, making the last 10 in a row, and protected that lead all the way to a 74–65 upset.

Howard (19 points, 14 rebounds) and Hayward (19 points, 10 rebounds) both had double-doubles and scored 13 points each in the second half. Veasley scored 12 on a career-high four 3s.

"The fact their freshmen and sophomores executed the way they did in our arena is really phenomenal," Xavier coach Sean Miller said.

Miller was visibly incensed with the officiating and was called for one technical foul. He said he couldn't say what he was thinking or he would be suspended. Witnesses said he chased one referee afterward, seeking an explanation. Miller said the game was "called differently" in the second half and that he would ask the Atlantic 10 to review videotape.

Nored played his finest game so far, collecting 10 points, three assists, and just two turnovers in 26 minutes. The Musketeers' length and quickness could have rattled him, but he thrived in the environment.

"He lives for these moments," Howard said.

Butler's players separated to go home and spend Christmas with families, but they had another marquee opponent to prepare for upon returning to campus. They returned with a new national ranking, moving into the AP poll at No. 25.

Butler had contracted for a series against Alabama-Birmingham, coached by Mike Davis, who succeeded Bob Knight at Indiana University in 2000. Hoosiers fans forgot that Davis had taken them to an NCAA championship game in 2002, and it was a relief to them and to Davis when he resigned in 2006.

Now, Davis was bringing his UAB Blazers to Indianapolis so Robert Vaden could play in his hometown. Vaden transferred from Indiana to UAB, continuing under the same coach. As a high school junior, Vaden played for 29–0 Pike, which won the Class 4A state championship and was No. 2 in *USA Today*'s national rankings. If he hadn't transferred to

Bridgton (Maine) Academy, he likely would have been Indiana's Mr. Basketball in 2004. Anticipation was so great that attendance was 8,141, the most for a midweek game at Butler in nearly seven years.

The Blazers had more than Vaden, and in the first half, they had more than Butler. Vaden scored 10 points in the opening 15 minutes, and UAB built a 13-point lead. Yet as they did in falling behind Northwestern by 12 and Ohio State by 13, the Bulldogs erased that deficit. This time, it was strictly a Mack attack. Mack scored 17 points in a six-minute segment, including five 3s, and Butler opened the first 5½ minutes of the second half on a 20–4 run to go ahead 45–42.

"I was wide open," said Mack, who equaled his career high with 22 points. "I was just making shots."

Davis was assessed a technical foul with 6:44 left, and Hayward made two free throws, followed by Howard's two for a UAB foul. The four-point possession sent Butler ahead 62–52.

The Bulldogs made enough free throws to secure a 72–68 victory. They survived 19 turnovers and ended December at 11–1. Butler completed the 2008 calendar year at 29–4, trailing only the 30–4 record of 2001.

• • •

Outside the Horizon League, there was speculation that Butler could go through the rest of the season without a league loss. Butler was not subscribing to that theory. In fact, after a relatively poor start, teams in the league had performed so well that 2009 began with the Horizon 10th out of 31 conferences in computer rankings.

"By far, to me, this is the best I've seen our league in the nine years that I've been here," Stevens said.

When the Bulldogs resumed league play with three games in a week, they did so as the pursued—a familiar position for Butler, if not for this team. In a third straight league road game, Butler was victimized by Valparaiso's 14–0 run in falling behind 27–20. The Crusaders were fueled by Indianapolis native Brandon McPherson, whose off-season knee surgery left him limping and grimacing during 23 minutes played.

Yet McPherson's 22 points weren't enough to offset Butler's inside/outside combination of Howard and Hayward. During a 19–4 run to open the second half, Hayward scored nine points on three 3s and Howard added 10. Howard finished with 16 points, and Hayward and Veasley had 15 each in a 75–62 victory.

The Bulldogs returned home to face nemesis Wright State, which was 9–3 against Butler in the previous 12 meetings. Wright State had begun 0–6 but recovered from that and had won six in a row. The Raiders couldn't recover from what Butler did to them. The Bulldogs started 5-of-8 from the arc—3-of-3 by Hayward—and bolted ahead 34–14 en route to a 64–48 victory.

As impressive as they were, the Bulldogs had a short 40-hour turnaround before playing Detroit on a Saturday afternoon. Stevens sounded like a worrywart when he suggested Butler would face a "scary" opponent. After all, Detroit was 4–10 and a 20-point underdog. The Titans hadn't won a league game on the road in nearly two years.

Instead, Stevens' anxiety was warranted. The Titans built an eight-point lead in the first half. Even after falling behind 46–40 with less than six minutes left, they stormed back to go ahead 50–49. The Bulldogs finished with two 3-pointers, the fewest they had made in 71 games. Howard was limited to 26 minutes by foul trouble, but ultimately, he was the difference in a 54–50 victory. He scored 15 points, passed for the go-ahead basket, pulled down the last rebound, and made two free throws to wrap it up.

"He's just a relentless worker," said Detroit coach Ray McCallum, a native Hoosier who was formerly the head coach at Ball State and an assistant at IU.

At 14–1, Butler tied five others for the best 15-game start in school history. Five of those six were in the 2000s. The Bulldogs extended their league winning streak to 16, nearing the record of 21 set by Green Bay from 1995 to 1997.

• • •

The vagaries of league scheduling hadn't always allowed Butler the convenience of playing two Chicago opponents, Loyola and Illinois-Chicago, on the same weekend. Still, not since 2001 had the Bulldogs beaten both on the same trip, and only once (in 2008) had they beaten both on the road.

The front half of the assignment couldn't have been easier. Butler spurted at the start of each half and handed Loyola its worst home defeat in more than eight years, 78–55. Mack sank three 3s in a 67-second span of the first half to highlight a 22–0 run that created a 24–4 lead. The Horizon's No. 2 scorer, Loyola guard J.R. Blount, scored two points, or 13 under his average.

"They guard their man," Loyola coach Jim Whitesell said, "and they also guard well together."

For the game at UIC, Butler coaches went barefoot in support of Samaritan's Feet, a nonprofit group that collects shoes to distribute worldwide. At the forefront of the cause was another Indianapolis college coach, Ron Hunter of IUPUI. Hunter was the first Division I coach to go barefoot on the sideline, and more than 300 coaches across the country pledged to do the same. Stevens said coaches, collectively, are a giving group.

"They're talking about team all the time," he said. "It's kind of what our livelihood is. The chance to serve somebody else is certainly meaningful."

While their coaches shed shoes, the Bulldogs abandoned their shooting accuracy. In a quick turnaround like the one preceding Detroit, the Bulldogs struggled before an afternoon audience on ESPN2. Butler started 0-of-10 from the arc and was fortunate that the halftime deficit was no greater than 28–17. The Flames later expanded that margin to 13 points.

"We just had to figure out a way to stay in it until the shots started falling," Stevens said.

As he had done repeatedly, Hayward prospered on the road in leading Butler to a 59–52 comeback win. He scored 16 of his 25 points in the second half, finishing with seven 3s. Mack nearly had a triple-double (18 points, eight rebounds, eight assists). Veasley locked down another opponent, limiting league scoring-leader Josh Mayo of UIC to seven points.

Butler's players remained in the moment, as they had been coached to do. Mack conceded that they were probably "clueless" about their record. There were clues that another historic season was evolving. Butler was

- 16–1, equaling its best start ever;
- 7–0 in the league, equaling its best league start since 1991;
- winner of 18 straight in the league, three off Green Bay's record; and
- 8–1 on the road, leading Division I in road wins.

"Butler just seems to get over the hump when they need to get over the hump," Collins said. "Some of the rest of us don't."

The Bulldogs weren't running away in the league standings. They had a chance to do so by completing January with three successive home games. First up were their two closest pursuers: Green Bay (6–1) and Wisconsin-Milwaukee (7–1).

Another poor shooting half left the Bulldogs behind Green Bay 25–22 at halftime. It marked the eighth time Butler had trailed or been tied at the half, but its only loss in those games was at Ohio State. The Bulldogs closed with 13-of-16 shooting from the field, and their 46-point second half buried the Phoenix 68–59.

Butler, up to No. 16 in the rankings, was capturing Indianapolis' attention. For Milwaukee, attendance was 9,418, representing the largest crowd at Hinkle Fieldhouse for a Horizon League game in almost six years.

The Bulldogs effectively ended this one in 56 seconds. That's how long it took for Mack to sink two 3-pointers, sending Butler to a 6–0 lead en route to a 78–48 blowout. (The outcome contrasted to the one on March 1, 2003, when a sellout of 11,043 watched Butler beat Milwaukee 76–74.)

The Bulldogs held Milwaukee to 12.5 percent shooting in the first half, and Vanzant came off the bench to score a career-high 20 points.

"There's not one person on our team that's selfish," Vanzant said. "That's the main reason I came here when Brad (Stevens) was recruiting me, because I loved the way they play."

It seemed inevitable that Butler would complete an 8–0 January by beating Valparaiso in a rare Friday night game. Colleges usually don't play that night to avoid conflicts with high school games, but the Horizon League had an ESPNU agreement for a game of the week.

The TV audience saw a more suspenseful game than predicted. A wacky college basketball season had already seen long winning streaks end at Brigham Young (53 games), Notre Dame (45), and Tennessee (37). Would it be Butler's turn?

Here were the 13th-ranked Bulldogs trailing Valpo, a 17-point underdog, with six minutes left and clinging to a two-point lead with 66 seconds on the clock. Butler stopped sputtering long enough to win 59–51, extending its home streak to 11.

"I don't think all of us were here tonight, and that's kind of a bad thing for us," reasoned Hayward, whose 18 points were the most he had ever scored at Hinkle Fieldhouse.

Butler became 19–1 for the first time in the program's 117-year history. Its 21-game Horizon streak tied Green Bay's record. It was one of four once-beaten teams in the country.

It had been a smooth ride. Were there to be no potholes? The Bulldogs went on the road again to find out.

• • •

Green Bay was the Bulldogs' first stop on a six-day, three-game tour that more closely resembled an NBA itinerary than that of a college team. With Butler at 10–0 in the league and Green Bay 9–2, the outcome would determine whether the race was effectively over. The Bulldogs had won nine in a row in the series but barely pulled out victories in 2007 and 2008 visits to the Resch Center. Green Bay coach Tod Kowalczyk was bitterly disappointed after those defeats, and forward Ryan Tillema was calling this Monday night game the most important of his career.

Troy Cotton's 3-pointer created a 30–28 halftime lead, and Green Bay built a 13-point margin in a 75–66 victory. That ended Butler's 11-game winning streak and 21-game Horizon run. The No. 11 Bulldogs became the highest-ranked team ever beaten by Green Bay, and students in the crowd of 6,978 rushed onto the court in celebration.

It was a peculiar game in that Green Bay was 30-of-33 on second-half free throws, similar to what Butler did at Xavier. On three occasions, Butler players fouled Green Bay on 3-point attempts, resulting in nine points. Tillema scored 21 points, making 10-of-12 at the foul line. Howard blocked five shots but played only 27 minutes because of foul trouble.

The Bulldogs had gone 107 games without losing two in a row, a testament to sustained excellence. That consistency continued when Butler shot 55 percent in a 66–61 victory at Detroit.

Butler again turned to Hayward, who was a perfect 7-of-7 and sank four 3s in a 22-point night. The Bulldogs' 17 turnovers prevented them from securing the victory earlier, but afterward Stevens attempted to put it all in perspective. He had watched a CNN newscast that included the voice of Chesley Sullenberger, a pilot who safely landed a US Airways jet in New York's Hudson River on January 15.

"It was unbelievable, the poise that he kept," Stevens said. "And that was a lot more adversity than turning the ball over a few times in a row. That's a life lesson you take with you."

That would be especially so as the Bulldogs completed the week in Dayton, Ohio. Wright State's Nutter Center had driven them nuts. They were 0–7 there since 2003. The Raiders ranked second nationally in scoring defense (55.2 points per game), and a crowd of 9,735 nearly filled the arena.

Wright State fans never had reason to cheer. The Raiders trailed 27–6 after 9½ minutes, were never closer than 12 points thereafter, and shot 27 percent.

Hahn was 5-of-5 on 3-pointers in the first half and scored a career-high 17 points in a 69–51 victory.

The Bulldogs raised their nation-leading total of road victories to 10, completing a three-game week in which they traveled nearly 1,500 miles.

"That's as tough as any stretch that I've heard of in league play anywhere," Stevens said.

With Vanzant sidelined by a knee injury and five Bulldogs carrying two or more fouls, walk-on Alex Anglin was called upon in the first half. The junior from Kokomo, Ind., an accounting major with a 3.58 grade point average, collected two rebounds in three minutes. At Butler, everyone is expected to contribute.

"Just being a part of this team is one of the best things I've ever been a part of," Anglin said.

• • •

Kevin Kuwik served as coordinator of basketball operations, an administrative post that Stevens first held on Butler's basketball staff. At age 34, Kuwik, a Notre Dame graduate, had fit 13 years of college coaching experience around 10 years of military service. He was twice deployed to Iraq, once taking a leave from Ohio University in 2004. The Army awarded him a Bronze Star for meritorious service before an honorable discharge in April 2006.

He was taking a two-day break from the team to attend the wedding of his brother, Keith, in Buffalo, N.Y. Kuwik was to be joined by girlfriend Lorin Maurer, 30. Maurer, a former college swimmer and an employee of Princeton University, met Kuwik at the previous year's Final Four in San Antonio. The two had sustained a long-distance romance.

Kuwik had dinner with family before leaving for Buffalo Niagara International Airport, where he was to meet Maurer after Continental flight 3407 arrived from Newark, N.J. The airport monitor showed the

> Five players on the floor functioning as a single unit. Team, team, team. No one more important than the other.
>
> — Coach Norman Dale, from *Hoosiers*

plane had landed, and Kuwik expected his girlfriend to text him within minutes, as she always did.

The text never came. The flight was removed from the screen. Kuwik was hearing rumors that a plane had crashed, and he thought it was a small craft—until he saw news cameras rushing to the terminal. Kuwik and his brother hurriedly went back to their car and drove to the crash site, where all they could see was smoke and fire trucks.

"We drove back to the airport, and they made an announcement that no one had survived," he said.

Kuwik started the agonizing process of relaying the news of his girlfriend's death. Stevens received a text at 3:00 a.m., and he knew without looking something bad had happened. He had heard reports of a plane crash near Buffalo. Stevens met that morning with players, explaining that it was important for them to hear from a familiar voice. The players immediately began texting Kuwik, who had become a beloved figure in a short time. The players wanted to do something and decided to wear black armbands on their uniforms for that night's game against UIC. The armbands would remain for the rest of the season.

"What Butler did shocked me, wearing the black armbands," Kuwik said. "That was pretty meaningful."

Kuwik made one request to the Bulldogs: play with passion. They did that and more, leading by 19 points in the first half en route to an 80–61 victory over UIC.

Howard's perfect maneuvering—6-of-6 from the field, 7-of-7 on free throws—coupled with 13 3s supplied an irrepressible inside/outside attack. Hahn came off the bench to make a career-high five 3s for the second game in a row. It had taken him weeks to regain fitness from a virus that had swept the campus.

The victory was a respite, albeit temporary, from the ache that the Butler family felt. Hahn said the victory was for Kuwik.

"We're praying for him, and we're glad he's back with his family," Hahn said. "When he comes back, he'll be with his family here."

It is difficult to measure how grief affects people or influences sports contests, which are inconsequential compared to life-and-death issues. So it is impossible to assert whether the Maurer tragedy had any effect on the Bulldogs when they played Loyola on a Sunday, two days after UIC.

Loyola had lost six in a row, lost to Butler by 23 earlier, lost at Valparaiso by 24 two days before, was 218th in RPI, and an underdog by 19. Yet shockingly, and inexplicably, the Ramblers ended Butler's 16-game home winning streak, 71–67. Even Howard's career-high 30 points weren't enough for Butler, which cut an 18-point deficit to two but couldn't overcome a Loyola team that deservedly won.

"Everything I love about basketball happened tonight," Stevens said. "It just didn't happen on our side."

The surreal nature of the game was underscored by an incident that occurred late. Play was stopped, and the public address announcer asked fans to stay seated while a search was made for a missing child. After about eight minutes, a male cheerleader located the child along the rafters of the fieldhouse.

The upset was the biggest in the league since No. 1-seeded Butler lost to No. 8 seed Green Bay 49–48 in a 2001 quarterfinal of the league tournament. Coincidentally, that loss followed the death of the mother of Butler player Rob Walls, who learned the news in the middle of the night. The defeat cost the snubbed team a spot in the NCAA Tournament. The 2009 Bulldogs could avoid such a fate.

• • •

Losing to Loyola prevented the Bulldogs from earning a share of a third straight regular-season Horizon title, but they could take care of that at Milwaukee three days later. Butler had gone 111 games without back-to-back losses. The only teams with longer active streaks were Kansas (120) and Memphis (147), which met for the NCAA title the previous April.

The funk that enveloped the Bulldogs in Indy persisted in Milwaukee. They began by shooting 3-of-18 from the field, and after 8–7, they never led. Milwaukee built a 13-point lead and handed Butler a third defeat in six games, 63–60.

Stevens dismissed a suggestion that his freshmen had begun to wear down. Hayward and Mack had undeniably declined in production.

Hayward was ineffective against Loyola, and while trying to break in new shoes, he repeatedly slipped on the Milwaukee floor and scored a career-low four points. Mack was shooting 21 percent on 3-pointers over the previous seven games.

Stevens conceded that what he saw, for the first time, was a team that was anxious. There was speculation that Butler, at 22–4, had damaged its résumé enough that an at-large bid to the NCAA Tournament was no longer a given. Maybe Butler would have to win the Horizon's automatic bid.

• • •

Butler's game at Davidson was something of a busted BracketBuster. When ESPN paired Butler and Davidson in its mid-major package, this is not what the network had in mind. Both teams were coming off losses, and Davidson junior Stephen Curry missed a midweek game because of a sprained ankle.

Curry had come to represent the face of college basketball after taking the Wildcats on an improbable run to the 2008 Elite Eight. His 29-point average led the nation.

Davidson and Butler had never met but resembled each other, both as basketball programs and liberal-arts colleges in large metro areas. They actually belonged to the same league, the Pioneer League, in football.

Davidson, located 19 miles north of Charlotte, N.C., was founded in 1837 by Presbyterians and has produced 23 Rhodes Scholars. Its motto, *Alenda Lux Ubi Orta Libertas*, means "Let Learning Be Cherished Where Liberty Has Arisen" and reflects roots in early American history.

With a noon tipoff, fans gathered early in spring-like temperatures on what looked like an idealized version of a college campus. Buildings such as Elm Row, Oak Row, Eumenean Hall, and Carolina Inn dated to the mid-1800s. Fans filled the 5,223-seat Belk Arena, wearing white T-shirts in a "white-out" to support the Wildcats.

Curry wore an ankle brace and after warm-ups, decided he would indeed play. At 22–5, Davidson needed a résumé-boosting victory even more than Butler. Although this was supposed to be Curry's stage, his leading role was usurped by Gordon Hayward.

The Bulldogs' 75–63 victory was fueled by Hayward's career-high 27 points.

After Howard scored eight straight Butler points to build a 17–7 lead, Hayward scored 20 of Butler's next 30—all in a span of 10 minutes.

Remarkably, Hayward spent 3½ of those 10 minutes on the bench with two fouls. He smiled when the announcer mistakenly identified his hometown as Brownsburg, Va., instead of Indiana. As usual, as long as he was away from home, he felt at home.

"It's almost like the team against the world," Hayward said. "It's kind of how it was a little bit today."

It was Ronald Nored against Stephen Curry. That man-vs.-man duel was so central that the *Charlotte Observer* never mentioned Hayward's name in two stories published in the Sunday edition. Curry missed his first eight shots, finished 6-of-23, and scored 20 points in his fourth-lowest output of the season. Nored ran himself dizzy in shadowing Curry everywhere.

"Ron could hardly walk on his way in here," Stevens said in the interview room.

Nored added an exclamation point to his afternoon when he stole the ball in the final minute and dunked. Curry was magnanimous, crediting the Bulldogs.

"They stay between you and the basket and make you make a play," Curry said. "Their help defense was pretty remarkable."

• • •

The Bulldogs headed home with a goal of staying at home. By beating Youngstown State and Cleveland State, they could wrap up the No. 1 seed in the Horizon tourney and not have to leave Hinkle Fieldhouse until the NCAA Tournament.

Mission accomplished, although not without suspense.

On the same day he was honored as an Academic All-American, Howard had 25 points and 10 rebounds to lift Butler past Youngstown, 78–57. The Bulldogs were shooting 60 percent until late and finished at 55 percent.

It had been nearly three months since the earlier Butler/Cleveland State meeting, but little changed in the rematch. Points came grudgingly in a tense, taut, body-banging finale. The Bulldogs led by as many as 11 points in the first half and by 10 midway through the second.

Cleveland State overtook them. With Butler trailing 56–55, the smallest player on the court, the 6-foot Nored, darted in for a rebound basket to put Butler ahead 57–56 with 53 seconds left. The worst free-throw shooter on the court, Nored, made one with 16.7 seconds left and extended the lead to 58–56.

That's the way it ended, bringing the Bulldogs a third straight Horizon championship, the seventh in 10 years.

A third Butler/Cleveland State game was possible in the Horizon tournament. Cleveland State coach Gary Waters used the assembled media as a forum to prophesize:

"Fate's coming, and it may happen in the tournament. Fate comes. Just remember that."

• • •

While awaiting their semifinal opponent in the league tournament—the Bulldogs had a double bye as No. 1 seeds—they reaped the rewards of a 25–4 record. Matt Howard, Gordon Hayward, and Brad Stevens were voted league player, newcomer, and coach of the year, respectively.

Howard was the first sophomore in 17 years to be player of the year, and Hayward the first freshman in 16 years selected to the all-league first team. Although Willie Veasley was the top defender on one of the nation's best defensive teams, he was omitted from the all-league defensive team.

No. 4 seed Wright State beat No. 5 Milwaukee 80–70 to earn the semifinal slot opposite Butler. In the other quarterfinal, No. 7-seed UIC was on the verge of eliminating No. 2- seed Cleveland State. The Flames led by nine with less than five minutes left before crumbling under Cleveland State's pressure. All-league forward J'Nathan Bullock, limited to one point for 34 minutes, scored eight thereafter and Norris Cole scored 26 as the Vikings came from behind to win 67–64.

In the first semifinal, the Bulldogs bolted ahead of Wright State, as they did in two earlier victories. A nine-point lead didn't last long and neither did an 11-point lead in the second half. Not until Howard made two free throws with 5.2 seconds left did Butler clinch a 62–57 victory and advance to the championship game. Howard's 24 points included 14-of-15 shooting on free throws, a statistic that made Raiders coach Brad Brownell cranky.

"You've still got to step up and make it, and he did," Brownell said. "That's why Butler is Butler. They find ways to win."

Butler won despite a season-low two points from Hayward, who took (and missed) one shot from the field. Hahn helped compensate by scoring 11 off the bench.

How difficult had it been for Butler to beat Wright State three times in one year? In the decade, Butler had earned more NCAA Tournament berths (five) and Sweet Sixteens (two) than three-game Raider sweeps (none).

In the other semifinal, the Vikings erased a 12-point deficit and ousted Green Bay 73–67 behind Coles' 23 points. A follow-up dunk by George Tandy, playing in his hometown of Indianapolis, put Cleveland State ahead to stay.

Butler was going to the NCAA Tournament, as an at-large invitee if not as the Horizon champion. Cleveland State, at 24–10, had no such assurance.

In previewing a rematch of the 2008 finalists, Stevens and Howard said the Bulldogs' sense of urgency was as high as it could be. For Cleveland State, which had not been to the NCAA Tournament since 1986, it was obvious how important this was.

"If we want to play with the likes of Butler and the top teams around, we've got to beat one of those teams on a big stage," Waters said. "When you're on a big stage, you send a message."

With a nine o'clock start on ESPN and students away on spring break, a modest 5,107 turned out inside the sultry fieldhouse to see if Butler could cap an improbable season with a second straight Horizon tourney title. The Bulldogs forged ahead by eight in the first half and again early in the second. Then the 3-pointer—long a weapon favored by the Bulldogs—was turned against them.

Cleveland State, ranked ninth in the league with 31 percent shooting on 3s, scored its first 12 points of the second half from the arc. Jackson's 3-pointer put the Vikings ahead to stay, 50–48. His drive increased the margin to 56–50 inside the five-minute mark. The Vikings scored just one more point but held on for a 57–54 victory.

Jackson shot 7-of-12 from the field, scored 19 points, collected eight assists, and was the tourney MVP. Cleveland State was 10-of-19 from the arc, Butler 4-of-19. That's a 30–12 disparity.

"Sometimes I think we overanalyze these things," Stevens said. "Cleveland State is a terrific team."

Fate came.

• • •

Since the snub year of 2002, Butler felt anxiety about the process that determines at-large invitations to the NCAA Tournament. While the Bulldogs made it without winning their league tournament in 2003 or 2007, that didn't negate fears about selection or seeding.

The Bulldogs' résumé in 2009 wasn't as decorated as in 2008, but in one respect, it was better. They had two victories over the Top 50 (Xavier and UAB), and the year before they had none. Also, Butler was 24th in RPI and 11–3 on the road. Yet comparing qualifications of teams like Butler with those from the Big Ten or Big East couldn't be done precisely.

"It's not apples to apples, because they don't have the same starting point. They don't have the same opportunity for scheduling," said ESPN's Joe Lunardi.

Research by CBS Sports' Gary Parrish showed that in 2009, for the fifth straight year, the three best RPIs left out of the NCAA Tournament belonged to non-BCS schools. "Which means a good RPI can save you if you're from a power conference, but it won't do much to help if you're not," Parrish wrote.

Butler's players and coaches gathered on March 15, Selection Sunday, at the Wildman Room inside Hinkle Fieldhouse to watch the pairings announced.

Finally, the name *Butler* emerged on the large TV screen as a No. 9 seed opposite No. 8- seeded LSU in the South Regional. Players cheered, although not vigorously. The winner would almost certainly face No. 1-seed North Carolina in the second round. Besides Butler, the only non-BCS teams to earn at-large spots were Xavier, Dayton, and BYU.

LSU ended the season 21st in the AP poll and Butler 22nd, so neither was awarded a favorable seed. (A No. 8 seed indicates a team was rated 29th to 32nd.) Butler had itself to blame, losing at home to lowly Loyola and to Cleveland State in the Horizon Tournament.

LSU (26–7) had reason to be miffed. It was the regular-season champion of the Southeastern Conference, and coach Trent Johnson acknowledged that the Tigers felt slighted.

But by the time both teams arrived in Greensboro, attention turned from the seeding to the pairing. LSU had ended the season by losing three of four games and Butler by losing three of seven. LSU was a two-point favorite and boasted an overwhelming edge in experience.

Butler was the only team in the tournament starting two freshmen, Mack and Nored, in the backcourt. LSU had two players, Tasmin Mitchell and Garrett Temple, who started on the team that reached the 2006 Final Four. LSU also had the SEC player of the year, 21-point scorer Marcus Thornton.

The No. 8/No. 9 games are among the best of the first round because teams are inevitably closely matched, and in the case of LSU/Butler, of a high quality. CBS likes to open its coverage with such a matchup and assigned its top announcing team, Jim Nantz and Clark Kellogg, to this one.

For Butler, the game could not have started worse. Before two minutes had elapsed, the Bulldogs committed three turnovers and fell behind 9–0. Stevens called timeout, and the Bulldogs stabilized.

Jukes, who had totaled 13 minutes over the past eight games after returning from knee soreness, supplied a lift. With Howard in foul trouble, he came off the bench and delivered two baskets to keep Butler close. LSU responded with another 9–0 run, all by Thornton, and stretched the lead to 31–18.

Willie Veasley dunks against Wright State (Photo by John Fetcho).

Hayward's fallaway 3-pointer with time nearly expired pulled Butler to within 35–29 at the half. Considering how poorly the Bulldogs shot the ball (35 percent) and handled it (11 turnovers), they were fortunate to be within six.

The Bulldogs had overcome deficits of 12 or more against Northwestern, UAB, and UIC, and they were ready to do so against LSU. They went ahead for the first time, 42–41, when Veasley dunked off a lob from Nored. Butler led twice more, at 44–43 and 54–53.

When Howard was fouled with five minutes left, he had to leave because he was bleeding. Hahn came in to shoot the free throws, converting a one-and-one to tie the score at 58. The Tigers then took over, making seven consecutive free throws in the final 47 seconds to close out a 75–71 victory.

Howard, in 25 minutes, delivered 22 points. Mack scored 18 and Hayward 12. Surprisingly, Butler outrebounded LSU 34–30.

Butler had no answer for Thornton. He scored 30 points on 10-of-15 shooting, becoming the first Butler opponent in more than two years to score that many. Stevens said beforehand that Thornton looked like a pro.

"Now, I'm convinced of it," Stevens said.

The Bulldogs had won their previous four first-round games, so the defeat was deflating. It was the fourth time in the decade they had been eliminated by an SEC team, following losses to Florida (2000 and '07) and Tennessee ('08).

There might have been no solace for Butler in what happened thereafter, but it was revealing. Butler (26–6) finished 25th in the post-tournament ESPN/*USA Today* coaches' poll, a sign of respect.

In North Carolina's run to the national championship, the Tar Heels' most difficult of six games was against LSU, which led by five midway through the second half before losing 84–70. Cleveland State, as a 13th seed, upset fourth-seeded Wake Forest 84–69.

Thus the Horizon won a tournament game for the fifth straight year, a feat matched only by the six BCS leagues plus Conference USA (i.e., Memphis). Stevens wondered aloud if the perception—that the Horizon is a lesser league—would ever catch up to the reality.

Of all the Bulldogs, Howard seemed to take the loss the hardest, even after doing the most to prevent it. He had improved dramatically over the 1-of-7 four-point output in an NCAA loss to Tennessee the year before.

"It doesn't help at all," he said. "It doesn't make it feel any better."

The only way to feel better was to get back to work for next season. That is the Butler Way.

Best Players

The following is a list of 21 Butler basketball greats. To be eligible for inclusion, a player had to be on an All-America team, Butler's all-century team (chosen by fan vote in 1998), Butler's team of the sesquicentennial (chosen by committee in 2006), a Midwestern Collegiate Conference/Horizon League player of the year, or be on a U.S. national team. Players are listed chronologically.

Here is the author's choice for an all-time Bulldogs team, featuring three six-man teams and incompletes for players whose careers are in progress:

First Team

Forward: Chad Tucker, 1983–88
Center: Jeff Blue, 1961–64
Guard: A.J. Graves, 2004–08
Guard: Mike Green, 2006–08
Guard: Darrin Fitzgerald, 1983–87
Guard: Billy Shepherd, 1969–72

Second Team

Forward: Darin Archbold, 1988–92
Forward: Tom Bowman, 1960–63
Forward: Ted Guzek, 1954–58
Center: Joel Cornette, 1999–2003
Guard: Thomas Jackson, 1998–2002

Guard: Ralph "Buckshot" O'Brien, 1946–50

Third Team
Forward: Rylan Hainje, 1998–2002

Forward: Jon Neuhouser, 1994–98

Forward: Bobby Plump, 1954–58

Center: Daryl Mason, 1971–74

Center: Brandon Polk, 2004–06

Guard: Brandon Miller, 2000–03

Incomplete
Center: Matt Howard, 2007–

Forward: Gordon Hayward, 2008–

Guard: Shelvin Mack, 2008–

•••

Ralph "Buckshot" O'Brien
Years: 1946–50

Hometown: Indianapolis, Ind.

Career Points: 1,248

Career Highlights: *Look* magazine All-America team, 1950; Mid-American Conference MVP, 1949; All-MAC first team, 1948, 1949, 1950; member of Butler's team of the sesquicentennial and all-century team; inducted into the Indiana Basketball Hall of Fame

The front of the Depression-era grocery store was a gathering place for children on Indianapolis' West side. Winners of boxing matches—yes, kids did that in the 1930s—would be rewarded with an apple or candy bar. Obviously, one kid would never win. Why, he was so small that he was the last one picked for choose-up-sides teams in the backyard. The grocer always recognized him.

"He kept saying that I'd never be bigger than a buckshot," Ralph O'Brien recalled.

His nickname was given. His destiny was of his own making. Suffice it to say that Buckshot O'Brien turned out to be bigger than a quarter-inch piece of lead.

O'Brien, born April 8, 1928, in Henshaw, Ky., as the youngest of 13 children, left behind more than a Butler basketball legacy. He became an NBA player, honored insurance agent, NCAA award winner, youth sports leader, and motivational speaker.

But lest there be any doubt, he'll tell you:

"My great days that I remember that I truly enjoyed were at Butler University."

O'Brien, a 5-foot-9 guard, was a skilled ball-handler and master of the two-hand set shot. He was the first Butler player to exceed 1,000 points, breaking the career record in his junior year. He averaged 18.3 points in his All-America season of 1949–50. Former Butler assistant coach Bob Dietz told him he would have averaged close to 30 if the 3-point line had been used at the time.

O'Brien finished with a flourish, scoring 39 points—a school and arena record—in a 66–65 loss at Ohio State in his final college game on March 9, 1950. Earlier that season, he scored 30 against Ohio State and 33 against Indiana.

During O'Brien's four seasons, Butler was 60–31, including 18–5 in 1948–49. That season the Bulldogs reached 11th in the Associated Press poll—their highest ranking until 2007.

O'Brien was raised in a West New York Street home in an area now occupied by the IUPUI campus and Indiana University's medical complex. He spent much of his time at the Lauder Boys Club. His eight older brothers didn't get to see him play high school basketball because they were away serving in World War II.

O'Brien led the city of Indianapolis in scoring as a senior at Washington High School. Butler coach Tony Hinkle was interested. Hinkle and Dietz went to O'Brien's home, something that constituted aggressive recruiting in the 1940s. When O'Brien visited Hinkle's office, the coach had a baseball game coming up, so the two spoke as Hinkle raked the diamond.

O'Brien became a starter three games into his Butler career, although Hinkle chided him about poor defense.

"I thought he hated me my freshman year," O'Brien said. "He made me work out in the girls' gym playing defense while all the guys were on the big floor playing offense. He told me: 'I know you can shoot. But I couldn't leave you out there if you couldn't guard anybody.'"

O'Brien weighed 140 pounds in his playing days, and to enhance his pro credentials, he started listing himself as 5-foot-9½. No team would want someone so short, he reasoned. He attracted more attention with, ironically, the defense he played against future Hall of Fame player Bob Cousy in a college all-star game.

O'Brien went on to play 119 games for the Indianapolis Olympians in what would become the NBA, averaging 7.1 points from 1951 to 1953. No Butler player has been in the NBA since, although Billy Shepherd played in the ABA in the 1970s.

O'Brien was featured in the book *Playing Tall*, about the 10 players in NBA history shorter than 5-foot-10. He was listed along with modern-era players such as Monte Towe, Spud Webb, and Muggsy Bogues.

As an insurance agent, O'Brien was a member of the Million Dollar Round Table for about 30 consecutive years, requiring $1 million in insurance policy sales each year. He was selected in 1975 as one of five winners of the NCAA Silver Anniversary medal.

"Buckshot came up the hard way and made something out of himself in many ways," Hinkle said in a 1975 interview. "He was a small boy who made it in a big man's game, and he was a poor boy who made himself wealthy. The NCAA honor couldn't have been better placed."

Eligibility for the medal required that an athlete had graduated in the top 10 percent of his class. At a Washington, D.C., banquet, O'Brien sat at the head table with President Gerald Ford, who received the NCAA's Theodore Roosevelt Award. The next day, O'Brien and his wife were the president's guests for a personal tour of the White House.

"It's indescribable," O'Brien said of the event.

As a community leader, he was active in Boys Clubs around Indianapolis. In 1968, he helped launch the athletic program of the First Baptist Church on North College Avenue. That has grown to serve more than 3,000 participants a year.

"It's a nice feeling to know you left something that's still operating," O'Brien said.

After 45 years with Franklin Life Insurance, he retired and moved to Clearwater Beach, Fla. He had quadruple bypass heart surgery on February 17, 2009, but soon resumed playing golf and walking on a treadmill. Even into his 80s, he spoke at a local high school about being what he called a "D" student: desire, drive, determination, direction, discipline, and dedication.

O'Brien had two sons and a daughter, along with 12 grandchildren and four great-grandchildren. His daughter, Kyle O'Brien Stevens, was a member of the first Indiana All-Star girls basketball team in 1976 and an All-American golfer at Southern Methodist University. As a pro, she was LPGA rookie of the year in 1981.

•••

Ted Guzek

Years: 1954–58

Hometown: Hammond, Ind.

Career Points: 1,311

Career Highlights: Helms Foundation All-America team, 1957; All-Indiana Collegiate Conference first team, 1956, 1957

Ted Guzek, nicknamed "Gooze," became the first Butler player with 500 points in one year, scoring 531 in 1956–57 and earning All-America honors. His 21.2 scoring average was a school record that lasted 13 years. His specialty was a one-handed shot, and he was effective driving to the basket.

He was so prolific on the road that coach Tony Hinkle took him aside when he was a sophomore, encouraging Guzek to relax at home games.

"I was too tense," Guzek said. "My shooting was off, and on defense I'd foul unnecessarily. Now all that's straightened out. I think I'll play as well, or even better, at home than on the road from now on."

In his junior year, he continued to be a road sharpshooter, especially in Big Ten venues. He

- scored 23 points in the new St. John Arena in a 98–82 loss at Ohio State in the December 1, 1956, opener,

- scored 37 in a 98–81 loss at Illinois on December 5 in what was labeled one of the greatest one-man performances in Huff Gym history,

- scored 25 in a 73–68 loss at Indiana on December 10, and

- shot 13-of-13 in an 84–77 loss at Michigan on December 15, setting an NCAA record for most field goals without a miss. Through 2008–09, only four players in NCAA history had been perfect in a game with more field goals.

On January 5, 1957, Guzek scored 38 points to lead Butler to an 86–84 upset at Notre Dame, ending a streak of 20 straight losses at South Bend dating back to 1933.

As a senior, Guzek's scoring average declined (11.9) as he fought an illness. But he set a school record with a .540 field-goal percentage and helped Butler reach the NIT for the first time. He is a member of the Hammond Sports Hall of Fame and in 1991 became a charter member of Butler's athletic Hall of Fame.

•••

Bobby Plump

Years: 1954–58

Hometown: Pierceville, Ind.

Career Points: 1,439

Career Highlights: All-Indiana Collegiate Conference first team, 1957, 1958; member of Butler's all-century team and team of the sesquicentennial; Indiana Mr. Basketball, 1954; inducted into Indiana Basketball Hall of Fame

Not many high school basketball players become movie stars. It would be an exaggeration to suggest Bobby Plump was a screen idol. The megahit *Hoosiers* was a movie, not a documentary. But Plump was the inspiration for the character Jimmy Chitwood, and Plump's Milan High School team was the inspiration for the film.

Milan's 32–30 victory over Muncie Central—whose enrollment was 13 times larger—in Indiana's 1954 state tournament seems like a work of fiction. But it really happened, and Plump's game-winning shot changed his life. It didn't end his life.

He was a good college player. So good, in fact, that in fan balloting conducted mostly via e-mail by the *Indianapolis Star* in 2007 to select an all-time Butler five, he came in at No. 1.

"That surprises me. That's very gratifying," Plump said. "I figured people my age would be reluctant to get on the computer."

Plump holds the Butler record for free throws in a career (475) and free-throw percentage in a game (17 of 17). Those free throws contributed to what was then a school-record 41 points against Evansville on January 11, 1958.

In 1958, he helped Butler reach the NIT for the first time.

Does Plump resent the fact that his college career is so obscured by what he did in high school?

"I don't resent that one iota," he said. "The people that followed Butler back then remember."

Plump was born at home in Pierceville, Ind. (pop. 45) and was the youngest of six children. The family had no telephone or indoor plumbing. His mother, Mabel, died when he was five, and his older sister, Dorothea, helped raise him.

At age eight, Plump owned the town's first outdoor basketball goal, a nine-foot hoop attached to a smokehouse. Another family set up a court with a level surface, located in an alley, and kids who played there became known as the "Pierceville Alleycats." They played in all weather conditions, trying to avoid a manure pile on one side of the court.

Pierceville students attended school three miles away in Milan, whose population of 1,150 made it seem like a metropolis. Plump was cut from the sixth-grade basketball team. He kept working on his game and eventually became one of the few players of his era to develop an authentic jump shot.

After high school, Plump chose Butler after turning down larger schools, including Indiana University. That was especially hard.

"Most of the people in Milan at the time, if they went to college, they went to IU," Plump said.

He was sidelined for nine games as a freshman with what was diagnosed as a light case of polio. He left the university as the all-time leader in points with 1,439, and a half-century later he still ranked 11th. For Butler's baseball team, he played shortstop and batted .301.

He played three years for the Phillips 66ers, based in Bartlesville, Okla., in the National Industrial Basketball League. He later became an insurance agent and owner of a restaurant, Plump's Last Shot, located in Indianapolis' popular Broad Ripple district.

Plump lobbied, unsuccessfully, to prevent the Indiana High School Athletic Association from dividing its state tournament into multiple classes. Beginning in 1998, part of a cherished Indiana tradition ended with the introduction of a four-class state tournament.

That assured that there would never be another Hoosier figure like Bobby Plump.

•••

Tom Bowman

Years: 1960–63

Hometown: Martinsville, Ind.

Career Points: 1,334

Career Highlights: Indiana Collegiate Conference player of the year, 1962; All-Conference first team, 1961, 1962; member of Butler's all-century team and team of the sesquicentennial

Tom Bowman, a 6-foot-4 forward and accurate outside shooter, played at Martinsville High School, the alma mater of basketball icon John Wooden. Bowman visited schools such as North Carolina, Purdue, Michigan, and Nebraska. Then he met Butler coach Tony Hinkle.

"I liked the small-school atmosphere, and it was close to home," Bowman said. "I was a small-town boy."

They spoke for an hour or so in his office, and Bowman traveled home . . . and then called Hinkle back to accept a scholarship.

Bowman was the MVP and leading scorer for the first Butler team to play in the NCAA Tournament, in 1962. He averaged 18.4 points a game that season, with highs of 30 against Michigan State and 29 against Bradley. In the 25-team national tournament, Butler was assigned to a first-round game against No. 8 Bowling Green. Bowman compared that game to one 41 years later in which Butler reached the Sweet Sixteen by defeating Louisville 79–71. The Bulldogs upset Bowling Green 56–55, reaching the Sweet Sixteen.

"They were looking past us, as maybe Louisville was looking past Butler," Bowman said.

There was no freshman eligibility when he played. When his career ended, his 1,334 points were the most ever by a three-year Bulldog. Bowman was selected to play for the United States in the first U.S.-Soviet Union game. He was on a U.S. team that toured Poland and Russia in 1964.

Bowman said Lenin's picture was "everywhere" in Moscow and that the city was drab and colorless. He said the department stores had nothing he would want to buy.

"There's only one radio station in Moscow, and it plays a lot of music which sounds a little jazzy, but it's a long way from rock 'n' roll," he said after the tour. "The first night in Moscow I turned on the radio and guess what the first song was I heard? 'Back Home Again in Indiana.'"

Bowman later became a financial planner in Bloomfield Hills, Mich.

• • •

Jeff Blue

Years: 1961–64

Hometown: Bainbridge, Ind.

Career Points: 1,392

Career Highlights: All-Indiana Collegiate Conference first team, 1962, 1963, 1964; member of Butler's all-century team and team of the sesquicentennial; inducted into the Indiana Basketball Hall of Fame

Tony Hinkle never liked to be asked to identify the best players he ever coached at Butler. It's unfair to compare one to another, he said.

But at a banquet honoring the Bulldogs' 1963–64 team, Hinkle acknowledged that Jeff Blue "is one of the finest ballplayers we've ever had at Butler."

Blue left as the school's all-time leader in rebounds, with 953, and top three-year scorer. He was selected in the eighth round of the 1964 NBA draft by the Boston Celtics.

All of Butler's starters returned for the 1961–62 season. Blue, then a sophomore center, turned out to be the piece Butler needed to reach the NCAA Tournament for the first time. (Freshmen weren't eligible for varsity play.) Blue averaged 15.9 points a game and led the Bulldogs in rebounding at 12.0. He set what was then a Butler season record with 336 rebounds and twice broke the single-game record—23 against Michigan on December 9, 1961, and 24 against Valparaiso on January 31, 1962. It's understandable that Hinkle once referred to Blue as "this kangaroo from Bainbridge."

Blue might not have enrolled at Butler at all if his older brother, Mike, had not preceded him there to play basketball. The brothers were close, and Jeff frequently visited the campus. About 90 schools tried to recruit Blue, some with what he called "outlandish" incentives. Hinkle phoned Blue to talk but not to set up a recruiting visit. He proposed that Blue come to see him. Blue said his first thought was, "I think I like this guy's style."

Blue played for Bainbridge, a small high school in northern Putnam County where the town's social activity revolved around the team. In his junior season, Bainbridge won its sectional and then, for the first time ever, a regional. Bainbridge was 26–0, the last remaining unbeaten team in Indiana, before losing in the semi-state at Lafayette. Blue left a year later with 1,798 points, a county record, and was chosen for the Indiana All-Star team that played Kentucky.

• • •

Billy Shepherd

Years: 1969–72

Hometown: Carmel, Ind.

Career Points: 1,733

Career Highlights: *Sport* magazine All-America team, 1971; All-Indiana Collegiate Conference first team, 1970; member of Butler's team of the sesquicentennial and all-century team; Indiana Mr. Basketball, 1968; inducted into the Indiana Basketball Hall of Fame

Billly Shepherd, left, and team MVP Steve Norris made up the backcourt of Tony Hinkle's final team in 1970 (Photo courtesy of Billy Shepherd).

Under different circumstances, or in a different era or environment, Billy Shepherd might have had a different college basketball career. Unquestionably, the 5-foot-10 guard was the most prolific scorer in Butler history. But his penchant for long-range shooting and bullet passes, coupled with an awkward coaching transition, produced as many might-have-beens as actual achievements.

"They were bumpy," Shepherd said of his Butler years. "But they weren't unbearable."

Freshmen weren't eligible for college play at the time, and his best year at Butler was as a sophomore in coach Tony Hinkle's final season. Shepherd's scoring average in 1969–70 was 27.8, a school record, and the Bulldogs were 15–11. Shepherd's averages declined after that, as did Butler's won-loss records—to 10–16 and 6–20. He left Butler with what was then a record 1,773 points, and his career average of 24.1 points remains the record.

Marty Monserez, a college teammate, said Shepherd had "incredible talent," plus shooting range greater than anyone he has seen.

"Unfortunately, that didn't equate to wins for our team," Monserez said.

Granted, it would have been unrealistic to duplicate the storybook high school days Shepherd enjoyed as a member of one of Indiana's first families of basketball. The Shepherds represent three generations of Indiana All-Stars. Billy was coached at Carmel by his father, Bill Sr., a Butler graduate who played for Hinkle. Bill Sr. was an Indiana All-Star in 1945, as was Billy in 1968, brother Dave in 1970, and Billy's son, Scott, in 1992. Billy and Dave were both honored as Mr. Basketball.

Through 2009, Billy was fifth on the state's all-time high school scoring list with 2,495 points, averaging 32 points as a junior and senior. Against Brownsburg on January 6, 1968, he scored 70, a figure surpassed just once in subsequent Indiana high school seasons.

Shepherd was recruited by schools across the country, including UCLA. He chose Butler for three reasons:

- He wanted to be near home so his parents could see him play.

- He wanted to play in a city with an American Basketball Association team, and Indianapolis had the Indiana Pacers. If he was going to play pro ball, he thought, it would be with the ABA's 3-point line.

- He thought his father might succeed Hinkle, who was coaching past age 70.

A Hinkle protégé was the successor, but he was not the elder Shepherd. Former Bulldogs player George Theofanis, then coach at Shortridge High School in Indianapolis, became the new coach.

Billy Shepherd acknowledged that he wanted his father to become Butler's coach and that his father "deserved the job." Making it worse was that Bill Sr. heard the news of Theofanis' appointment on the radio. Theofanis said Hinkle cautioned him about young Shepherd.

"'Kid, he'll drive you crazy,'" Theofanis said, recalling Hinkle's advice. "And he was right. He drove me crazy."

Shepherd said Theofanis tried to make him comfortable, but the relationship was probably doomed from the beginning. In the fourth game of Shepherd's junior season, he scored a school-record 49 points in a 108–92 loss at Arizona on December 5, 1970. Had there been a 3-point arc—Shepherd often shot from nearly 30 feet—he might have exceeded 60 points.

In the Bulldogs' next game, at Northwestern, Shepherd recalled that he sat out half the minutes of a 98–79 loss. The schedule was brutal, with seven road games out of the first 10 and five at Big Ten arenas, and Butler began 2–8.

Shepherd's senior season was impaired by a hamstring injury. He missed six games and said he rushed back into action too soon. Butler's 20 losses were a school record for futility.

Shepherd's best college memories are of that sophomore season. He remembered fans packing Hinkle Fieldhouse for Hinkle's final game, in which Shepherd scored 38 points in Butler's 121–114 loss to Notre Dame.

Shepherd said team MVP Steve Norris, the point guard, made sacrifices and adjusted to Shepherd's strengths. Norris, who later taught math and coached at Carmel High School, said he wasn't bothered by Shepherd's shooting but understood that others were.

"He did so much to make that team 15–11, which was a pretty good season," Norris said.

After his senior year, the little-known Shepherd was surprisingly voted MVP of the East-West college all-star game. He scored 12 points on 6-of-14 shooting, but it was his playmaking that allowed the East to win 96–91.

"I still feel that was the best part of my game," Shepherd said. "It's the only way I was able to play at the pro level."

When Shepherd graduated, he had the top five one-game assist totals in school history, twice with 14. Through 2009, he had four of the top six.

He played three seasons in the ABA, one each for the Virginia Squires, San Diego Conquistadores (under coach Wilt Chamberlain), and Memphis Sounds. In 1974–75, with Memphis, Shepherd led the ABA with a 3-point percentage of .420—the second-best mark in the nine-year history of that league. His career scoring average was 5.7 in 169 games.

Phoenix Suns executive Jerry Colangeo once told him, "If you were 6-4, you'd be worth a million dollars."

Shepherd wasn't, and his pro career was over quickly. He was employed by Converse shoes for eight years before starting his own business and writing a column advising parents on conflicts in youth sports. He coached teams in summer basketball and filled in as interim coach during the 2003–04 season at Muncie Central High School, leading the team to a 20–4 record.

Shepherd and Theofanis eventually made peace. At Hinkle's 1992 funeral, Theofanis approached Shepherd and said he was sorry for way he treated the former player. Shepherd said that offering the apology would have been difficult, and he accepted it.

• • •

Daryl Mason

Years: 1971–74

Hometown: Indianapolis, Ind.

Career Points: 827

Career Highlights: All-Indiana Collegiate Conference first team, 1973, 1974; member of Butler's all-century team and team of the sesquicentennial

Daryl Mason, at 6-foot-7 and 178 pounds, was the most prolific rebounder in Butler history. Coincidentally, his favorite player while growing up was Jeff Blue, whose Butler rebounding records were broken by Mason.

Mason himself has been an inspiration to Andrew Smith, a 6-foot-10 recruit headed to Butler in the fall of 2009. Smith, of Zionsville, Ind., and a graduate of Indianapolis' Covenant Christian High School, led the state in rebounding in 2008–09. He inquired about wearing Mason's jersey No. 22. Perhaps one day Smith can challenge Mason's records.

"I told him, 'Go for it.' Those records have been held too long," Mason said.

Besides Jeff Blue, Mason is the only other Bulldog to average a double-double for a career, with 10.6 points and 12.3 rebounds. Mason holds school records for rebounds in a career (961), season (354), and game (26) and averaged a record 13.6 in 1972–73.

Mason was a late bloomer at Broad Ripple High School. He came to the attention of George Theofanis, formerly the coach at nearby Shortridge and later the Butler coach. Mason said he felt like a "pioneer" because he was one of the few black players or students at Butler in the 1970s.

"In fact, there were times if Coach Theo put more than three African Americans on the floor at one time, our crowd booed us," Mason said. "Coach Theo will never go down in the annals of Butler history as being the best basketball coach. But he deserves a special award for helping lead the diversity at Butler."

Among Mason's most vivid memories was the Bulldogs' near-upset of No. 3-ranked Marquette, which survived, 67–66, at Hinkle Fieldhouse on January 3, 1973. He spoke favorably about his college experience, despite encounters with racial prejudice.

"There's a lot of pain there. Not only with me, but with a lot of players who played during my era," he said. "But after a while you just kind of work through it."

Mason's father, Joe, graduated from Attucks High School, alma mater of basketball icon Oscar Robertson. Joe Mason was once an elite 400-meter sprinter and is a member of Prairie View A&M's sports hall of fame.

After college, Mason became a teacher, a time that included three years at an alternative school in Harlem, and worked for a New York state assemblyman. He helped in the organization of the 1987 Pan American Games in Indianapolis and became a self-employed strategic planning consultant.

•••

Darrin Fitzgerald

Years: 1983–87

Hometown: Indianapolis, Ind.

Career Points: 2,019

Career Highlights: Set NCAA records for 3-pointers made (158), attempted (362), and average made (5.6) in 1986–87; All-Midwestern Collegiate Conference first team, 1987; member of Butler's team of the sesquicentennial and all-century team

He did it first. He did it best.

The 3-point field goal was new to college basketball in 1986–87, so Butler senior Darrin Fitzgerald had no point of reference. The 5-foot-9 guard figured the rule might help the small man.

The rule helped make Fitzgerald the sport's biggest 3-point shooter. He sank 158 that season, for an average of 5.6 a game, leading NCAA Division I in both categories. Although Davidson's Stephen Curry surpassed that total with 162 in 2007–08, Fitzgerald went into the 2009–10 season still holding the record for most 3s per game.

"I couldn't believe at the end of the season that my average was that high or that I had that many," Fitzgerald said.

By comparison, Steve Alford made 107 3-pointers (3.4 a game) in leading Indiana to the NCAA championship in 1987.

Fitzgerald took as many as 1,000 shots a day in the summer. His best friend, Kevin Hendricks, rebounded for him. Fitzgerald continued to shoot 1,000 a day during the season.

Butler coach Joe Sexson designed one drill in which three players rebounded for Fitzgerald and kept passing three balls to him. He'd catch and shoot, catch and shoot, catch and shoot.

"You talk about tiresome," Fitzgerald said.

Sexson never tired of Fitzgerald's gunnery. A season-ending injury to Chad Tucker, who became Butler's all-time scoring leader, left few options. Fitzgerald knew Sexson was serious when the coach benched and scolded him for passing to a teammate near the hoop. The ball went through the player's hands.

"He told me if I ever passed up another shot, I'd be sitting the rest of my career at Butler," Fitzgerald said.

Mike Harper, a 6-foot-8, 220-pound center, became valuable to the Bulldogs as the main screener. When opponents crowded him at the 3-point arc, Fitzgerald backed up and shot from farther away. When he touched the ball within 30 feet of the basket at Hinkle Fieldhouse, there was a buzz of anticipation.

His 3-point percentage was .437, and his average of 26.2 points a game ranked sixth in the nation. His 31.3 average in league games is still the record for the Horizon League (then the Midwestern Collegiate Conference).

Darrin Fitzgerald set the NCAA record of 3-pointers made per game with an average of 5.6 in 1986–87 (Butler University Archives).

"He's amazing," Dayton coach Don Donoher said. "He doesn't even get near the line. I couldn't believe it. He's awesome."

The season produced many thrills but few victories. The Bulldogs were 12–16. Fitzgerald sank 10 3-pointers and scored 40 points in a 90–86 loss at Loyola on January 10, 1987.

Then he set school single-game records for points (54) and 3-pointers (12) in an 88–77 victory over Detroit at Hinkle Fieldhouse on February 9. Fitzgerald was numb afterward and didn't realize what he had done until the next morning.

"It doesn't matter how far out you pick him up, he'll score," Detroit coach Don Sicko said. "His range is just incredible."

Fitzgerald scored 34 in a 104–98 loss to Xavier in the MCC Tournament at Indianapolis' Market Square Arena, nearly rallying the Bulldogs from a 20-point deficit. It was his final college game. He left Butler as the school's all-time leader in points (2,019) and assists (411).

At Washington High School, colleges such as Michigan, Louisville, and Clemson were interested in Fitzgerald—until learning of his size. He showed he could play at that level as early as his sophomore season of college—before the 3-point line—when he scored 22 points against Indiana in a first-round NIT game.

Fitzgerald began learning basketball at age seven from his mother, Alice, a former high school player. His father, Calvin, a baseball and football player in high school, encouraged him to keep shooting, Fitzgerald recalled. Carl Short, his freshman coach at Washington, refined his game and was "the biggest influence on my game, other than my parents," Fitzgerald said.

He played football for three years but gave that up as a senior to concentrate on basketball. Fitzgerald averaged 21.6 points, scoring 39 against Gary Mann. Fitzgerald led the Continentals to a second straight sectional title.

After college, he went to work as a foundry technician at Daimler Chrysler. One of his four sons, Jamarson Fitzgerald, was the MVP of the 2000 city-county all-star game in Indianapolis.

• • •

Chad Tucker

Years: 1983–88

Hometown: Cloverdale, Ind.

Career Points: 2,321

Career Highlights: All-Midwestern Collegiate Conference first team, 1985, 1986, 1988; member of Butler's team of the sesquicentennial and all-century team

During the 1980s, basketball fans in Indiana thrilled to the exploits of Larry Bird and Steve Alford. Fewer saw Chad Tucker. Granted, Tucker never played in an NCAA championship game or the Olympic Games. His pro career was spent in European gyms, not NBA arenas.

Yet Tucker, a 6-foot-7 forward, shared many traits with those Hoosier heroes: Indiana All-Star, small-town roots, lived in the gym, dead-eye shooter, and more clever than athletic.

Because Butler's games were never nationally televised and the Bulldogs had a losing record in his years there, Tucker was scarcely known outside the Midwest. In fact, to promote his All-America candidacy in 1988, the school touted him as "the best player you've never seen."

Tucker was compared to Bird, not only in play, but in appearance and in the drawl that characterized their speech. At age nine, Tucker went to one of coach Bob Knight's summer camps at Indiana University, where he found himself rooming with a skinny kid from New Castle named Alford. For the next seven years, they went to camp the same week.

But if Tucker didn't attain icon status, as Bird and Alford did, he left an imprint on Butler basketball and the lives he touched. Tucker became the Bulldogs' career scoring leader, reaching 2,321 points. Through 2009, he was third on the all-time list for the Horizon League.

"He just had a special sort of shyness about him and always had that special down-home type of attitude," said Ralph Reiff, director of St. Vincent Sports Performance and a former Butler trainer. "There are certain alums that can walk back into Hinkle Fieldhouse, you can shake their hand, and you feel real good about them. He made me feel real good. And, man, could he play basketball."

It all started in Cloverdale, Ind., a town of about 1,000 residents located 47 miles west of Butler's Indianapolis campus. Tucker began attending basketball games before he could walk. His father, Al, was the Cloverdale High School coach. As evidence of the family's priorities, when they built a new home, a hoop was installed before the house was up.

Rather than exploring the tree-covered rolling hills or fishing at the blue lakes of nearby Lieber State Park, virtually all of Tucker's recreational hours were spent at an indoor or outdoor court. He had keys to the high school gym, too, and practically lived there. He perfected the hand/eye coordination that would be manifested in venues around the state, around the country, and around the world.

"Where I grew up, there's not much else to do at night," he said.

During his three years on the varsity at Cloverdale (enrollment: 312), the team was 67–11. When he was a senior, he averaged 24.5 points and led the Clovers to a 1983 regional title—the only one they have won since 1966. Although Tucker was selected to the Indiana All-Stars for the annual game against Kentucky, his recruiting offers were mostly from Division II and III schools. The only other Division I school recruiting him was Murray State, so Butler was an easy choice for someone wanting to stay near home.

What Tucker lacked in quickness and leaping ability was offset by his basketball IQ. In 1983–84, he averaged 13.4 points, and his .623 field-goal percentage was first in the nation among freshman. The next year, encouraged to shoot more, he averaged 19.8 points and led the Bulldogs to a 19–10 record—their best since the 1962 Sweet Sixteen season. The Bulldogs upset Notre Dame 70–69 in overtime, and their season didn't end until they lost to Indiana in the NIT, 79–57. Alford scored 26 in that game and Tucker 21.

As a junior, Tucker led the Midwestern Collegiate Conference in league play at 23.8 points per game and averaged 21.8 in all games. He scored 40 against Loyola on February 8, 1986, and five days later had 29 in only 32 minutes played against Valparaiso.

Chad Tucker set Butler's all-time record by scoring 2,321 points from 1983-88 (Butler University Archives).

"He can get more done with less effort than any player I've ever seen," Valparaiso coach Tom Smith said.

With the combination of Tucker and guard Darrin Fitzgerald, the Bulldogs had the components of a strong team in 1986–87 and started 4–0 for the first time in 56 years. However, in that fourth game—a 72–70 victory at Indiana State—Tucker separated his shoulder in a collision while diving for a loose ball. He was sidelined, and the Bulldogs were 8–16 thereafter.

There was a chance he would return that season, but he announced in February that he would take a medical redshirt and play a full 1987–88 season. It was such a bad injury that it was the type of dislocation usually seen from car collisions.

"I sat, I watched, and I learned a lot," Tucker said at the time. "I discovered some things that should make me better down the line."

When he returned for a fifth year, he began study for a master's degree. Coach Joe Sexson's Bulldogs started boldly again, building a 10–4 record. Tucker scored 29 in a 78–76 upset of 16th-ranked Iowa State at Toledo, Ohio. He hit a career-high 42 against Northern Illinois, 31 at Notre Dame, and 41 at Detroit.

Frustratingly for Tucker, points came more readily than victories. The Bulldogs lost 10 of their final 14 games, evening their record at 14–14. Tucker finished 17th in the NCAA in both scoring (24.1) and free-throw percentage (.870) and was all-conference for a third time.

Tucker wasn't selected in any of the three rounds of the NBA draft in 1988 and was picked in the sixth round of the Continental Basketball Association's draft by Cedar Rapids. He went on to play as a pro for seven years in Europe.

On May 3, 1996, Tucker died in what the Putnam County coroner ruled was a suicide from carbon monoxide poisoning. Tucker's body was discovered on the garage floor between two vehicles at his Cloverdale home. A note written to his family was found on the front seat of the one of the vehicles. The death was linked to depression. Sexson was among the coaches, players, and fans packing Cloverdale United Methodist Church for the funeral.

"Everybody was there, even the team manager," Sexson said. "I've never see anything like it. In the 12 years I was at Butler, he was without a doubt the most outstanding player I ever had. And everybody loved him."

•••

Darin Archbold

Years: 1988–92

Hometown: Markle, Ind.

Career Points: 1,744

Career Highlights: Led the NCAA in free-throw percentage (.912) in 1990–91; Midwestern Collegiate Conference player of the year, 1991; All-MCC first team, 1991, 1992; member of Butler's team of the sesquicentennial and all-century team

Few of Butler's all-time greats had more humble beginnings than Darin Archbold. His hometown is Markle, Ind., with a population of about 1,100. The place is so obscure that his telephone listing was from another town, Zanesville. And the nearest town to his house was Uniondale.

As a Butler freshman, the 6-foot-5 guard played 36 minutes—for the season. When Barry Collier became coach the next season, he reviewed game films from the previous year.

"When I looked at tape, I couldn't find Darin because he didn't play," Collier recalled.

Later, Collier, and everyone else, discovered Archbold could *really* play. Archbold averaged 21.8 points as a junior, becoming the Midwestern Collegiate Conference player of the year, and led the NCAA in free throw percentage at .912. He was such a surprise, that he hadn't been selected to the preseason all-conference first or second teams.

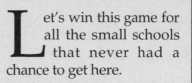

L et's win this game for all the small schools that never had a chance to get here.

— Hickory High School player Merle Webb, from *Hoosiers*

The following summer, Archbold played for a U.S. team that toured Europe, and he averaged 4.9 points in 10 games. He increased his average to 24.8 as a senior, and his 770 points remain a Butler record for one season. Meaningfully, the Bulldogs were 18–11 and 21–10 in his final two seasons, after going 6–22 in his freshman year.

"He had a real gift of body control," Collier recalled. "He wasn't a great leaper, but he was a great shooter. He helped everyone believe we could compete with Dayton and Xavier and Marquette."

When Xavier belonged to the MCC, Butler didn't often beat the Musketeers. In the teams' final 16 meetings, Butler was 2–14. Those two victories came six days apart in 1992.

In the first of those, Archbold scored 42 points, leading Butler to a 96–86 victory at Cincinnati Gardens on March 7. In case he ever wonders if it really happened, he has the videotape as evidence.

"We pull that one out just to watch," Archbold said.

The outcome was a shocking reversal of Xavier's 98–75 victory at Hinkle Fieldhouse a few weeks before. In the rematch, Archold shot 13-of-22—7-of-12 on 3-pointers—and 9-of-11 on free throws.

"Our whole team was just completely on," Archbold said. "It was one of those nights for me as a shooter, everything you threw up, you were pretty sure it was going to go in."

Six days after that upset, he scored 34 as Butler beat Xavier 78–61 in the semifinals of the MCC Tournament at Cincinnati's Riverfront Coliseum. In the championship, No. 1-seeded Evansville beat Butler 95–76.

Collier developed special plays for the moving and cutting Archbold to get open. Even in sideline huddles during crucial situations, the coach received the same message from his players: let's go to Darin.

"So there was never any jealousy," Collier said.

Archbold had been a go-to player at Norwell High School, too. As a senior, he averaged 26.4 points—with a high of 45—in leading his team to a 24–4 record. He left as the all-time leading scorer in Wells County with 1,811 points.

After college, Archbold played two years of pro basketball in Turkey and Germany. He later worked for an investment firm in his native Fort Wayne area.

•••

Jon Neuhouser

Years: 1994–98

Hometown: Grabill, Ind.

Career Points: 1,485

Career Highlights: Midwestern Collegiate Conference player of the year, 1997; All-MCC first team, 1996, 1997; MCC's Cecil Coleman Medal of Honor, 1997

Jon Neuhouser can identify the moment he believed he might be a good basketball player. He beat his sister.

Amy Neuhouser was the top girls scorer in Leo High School history with more than 1,400 points, and she played college basketball at Indiana-Purdue-Fort Wayne (IPFW) and Slippery Rock. She supplied Jon's competition because his two older brothers were teenagers when he was born.

On an outdoor court at a public park in their hometown of Grabill, Ind., Jon beat Amy one-on-one.

"I was just amazed when I was better than her," Neuhouser said. "I thought, 'Wow, I might be pretty good one of these days.' But there was a long stretch when she kicked my butt."

If losing to your sister teaches humility, it was a lesson Neuhouser never forgot. He worked relentlessly to improve himself as a college player—shooting 500 shots a day, lifting weights, climbing stadium steps at the Butler Bowl, and running long distances along the dirt paths of Indianapolis' Central Canal.

The labor paid off in 1997 when Neuhouser became the Midwestern Collegiate Conference player of the year, leading the Bulldogs into the NCAA Tournament for the first time since 1962. He is the only player ever to lead Butler in rebounding for four straight seasons.

"Watching him do layup drills, you'd think he was on fire," said his coach, Barry Collier. "When your best player is your hardest worker, it makes coaching a whole lot easier."

Neuhouser, a 6-foot-6, 220-pound forward, was an Indiana All-Star in high school. He led Leo, located north of Fort Wayne, to a 23–1 record and averaged 22.7 points and 11.2 rebounds a game. He matched his sister's records—he became Leo's all-time boys top scorer—earned 11 varsity letters, and was all-conference in football, basketball, and baseball.

The Bulldogs were projected to finish fourth in the MCC in 1997 but instead were first in the regular season. They won a school-record 23 games (23–11) and beat Illinois-Chicago 69–68 to win the automatic berth in the NCAA Tournament. Neuhouser averaged 15.3 points that season.

Before the following season, he played for Athletes in Action, part of a Christian ministry, in three games in Brazil. His average declined to 12.6 in 1997–98—the Bulldogs ran less and used more set plays—but Butler was 22–11 and returned to the NCAA Tournament.

• • •

Thomas Jackson

Years: 1998–2002

Hometown: East Lansing, Mich.

Career Points: 1,334

Career Highlights: All-Midwestern Collegiate Conference first team, 2001, 2002; Hoosier Classic MVP, 2001; member of Butler's team of the sesquicentennial

Thomas Jackson was not an accomplished college point guard because of his quickness, ball handling, or 3-point shooting.

It was because of his grandmother. Jackson placed her picture on his desk, her initials on one shoulder, and her memory in his soul.

"I think about her probably every day," he said.

Justene Williams knew her grandson was going to be a basketball star when she introduced him to the sport in the third grade. Jackson practiced what she preached: discipline and responsibility.

The 5-foot-9 guard, nicknamed "T.J.," was a steadying influence not only on the Bulldogs. He was a constant in his own family, too.

Jackson helped his mother raise twins—his half-brothers, Marcel and Michael—who were eight years younger than him. Jackson watched them after school, took them to video arcades and movies, and let them stay in his Indianapolis apartment.

There were a few times when big brother gave the twins a "whupping." That's what Jackson's grandmother did to him.

Jackson's parents split when he was a child, and his mother kept her job in Lansing, Mich. Emma Jackson was the secretary to the president of a United Auto Workers local.

Jackson's grandmother didn't believe in day care, so she looked after Thomas at her home in Saginaw, Mich., while his mother commuted on weekends. Grandmother was strict. Jackson had a curfew, even if friends were still outside playing. He was sheltered from mischief.

When Williams became ill, she and her grandson moved into Emma Jackson's home. The grandmother died in 1992. Jackson didn't often speak about that. He was quiet by nature. But his mother said the loss bothered him.

Jackson's grandmother was divorced at the time of her death. His mother and aunt were divorced. His father and the twins' father were in and out—mostly out—of their lives. Thomas was the man of the house.

"He has been the male figure in my family," said his aunt, Wanda Williams Neal. "He's been it."

Jackson's family moved across town before high school, and he attended East Lansing High. He played without flair or fanfare, but his team won, with a record of 21–4 as a junior (reaching the state quarterfinals) and 16–4 as a senior.

His high school coach, Chris Ferguson, called him the best point guard in Michigan, after Jackson averaged 17.2 points and 7.1 assists as a senior. Jackson was third in Michigan's 1998 Mr. Basketball voting, behind winner Dane Fife, who played for Indiana's 2002 NCAA runners-up. Jackson also collected fewer accolades than Marcus Taylor, who went to Michigan State and in 2002 became the second player ever to lead the Big Ten in scoring and assists in conference play.

Because of his size, and perhaps his demeanor, Jackson attracted less attention than his contemporaries. Ferguson said Jackson reminded him of legendary boxer Joe Louis.

"You never knew when Joe Louis was hurt. He had the same expression," Ferguson said. "Thomas—be it a bad call, a good call—he says nothing."

Michigan State coach Tom Izzo eventually regretted that Jackson left town. Jackson knew virtually nothing about Butler when he was recruited by then-assistant coach Thad Matta.

Evidence that Jackson made an impression on Matta is this: Matta remembered the first day they spoke, on August 4, 1997.

"From the first time I talked to him, I knew he was a special kid," Matta said. "As our relationship grew, I knew he was going to be a special player."

Jackson signed in November 1997. Butler needed a point guard, and he needed playing time. He already had the tattoo: a bulldog was on his left shoulder before he had ever heard of the Bulldogs. He became a starter late in his freshman season.

He left Butler with career records in assists (540) and steals (207) and is the only Butler player with more than 1,000 points, 500 assists, and 200 steals. He was the primary ball-handler for a team that in 2001–02 led the nation in fewest turnovers per game (10.1).

"I never thought about breaking records," Jackson said. "It just so happened that it was me that was able to do that."

Butler was 95–32 in his four seasons—22–10, 23–8, 24–8, 26–6—and broke the school record for victories three times under three different coaches, Barry Collier, Matta, and Todd Lickliter.

Yet recognition for Jackson often came grudgingly.

He had such anonymity that those at the Hinkle Fieldhouse gate asked to see his ticket before home games. He never made an all-conference first or second team until his junior season.

Opponents were respectful, however.

After Jackson had 14 points and six assists in a 58–44 upset of No. 10 Wisconsin on January 30, 2001, coach Brad Soderberg said the Badgers simply could not guard him. In the closing minutes of a 2001 conference semifinal at Wright State, Jackson maneuvered along the baseline for two reverse layups to blunt the Raiders' rally in a 66–58 victory.

"He's just fearless," Wright State coach Ed Schilling said. "He's the heart and soul of that team."

Evansville coach Jim Crews said Jackson made everyone else on Butler's team better.

"He doesn't overdo anything," Crews said. "I mean, he knows when to go fast, when to go slow, when to go medium, when to change directions, when to pull it out. I don't know much about football, but he's like a quarterback...No matter what you do, he just makes the adjustment and goes."

Players and coaches at Butler marveled more at Jackson's precision than his data. If he was to run a certain play out of a timeout, he did. If the coach asked him to defend in a certain way, he responded: "I will."

When players gathered for a pregame meal, they piled coats in a chair. Except Jackson. He took a hanger, slipped his coat on it, and took a seat.

Life back home wasn't always so tidy. Emma Jackson was 32 and six-months pregnant upon learning she would deliver twins. She was so shocked that she cried for two months. Thomas shared the care-giving with his mother.

Marcel conceded that Thomas was "sort of tough on us" growing up, but the older brother's influence was obvious. Marcel wrote school papers about Thomas. Michael mimicked his older brother, once styling his hair in an Afro because Thomas did so.

Thomas was a B-student in public relations, and the twins followed his lead. On campus visits, they did homework before anything else. Thomas enjoyed the company of the twins, who teased and told jokes. Marcel interviewed Butler players after games, using a tape recorder.

When it was time for Jackson to leave for college, he said it was hard to go. His mother was worried about Marcel's separation anxiety. His college coaches had the same feeling when Jackson graduated. They never met anyone like him, either.

"He's just made a huge impact on us all," Matta said.

Jackson continued to let his play speak for him in his postcollege basketball career. He completed a seventh European pro season with

Uppsala Basket in 2009, making Sweden's all-league first team and being honored as the guard of the year.

• • •

Rylan Hainje

Years: 1998–2002

Hometown: Indianapolis, Ind.

Career Points: 1,388

Career Highlights: Midwestern Collegiate Conference player of the year, 2002; All-MCC first team, 2002

Ross-Ade Stadium and Mackey Arena were more familiar to Rylan Hainje than Hinkle Fieldhouse.

The 6-foot-6 Butler forward was born in Lafayette, Ind. Although he moved soon thereafter to Indianapolis, he was a regular visitor at Purdue football and basketball games.

His mother is a Purdue graduate, and Hainje lived with her brother's family for more than a year. He transferred from Lafayette Central Catholic to Cathedral High School in Indianapolis, playing football well enough to be offered a scholarship to Purdue.

Hainje loved both sports, but he had to make a decision. He chose basketball. He chose Butler.

Yet he always dreamed of playing at Mackey Arena and finally did so on November 27, 2001. Hainje scored 25 points as Butler erased a 14-point deficit and beat the Boilermakers 74–68. It was the Bulldogs' first victory at Purdue since 1954.

"I didn't feel I had to prove anything to anybody," Hainje said afterward. "My teammates know what I can do, and that's all that matters to me."

If not for an injury midway through that year, Hainje might have produced the greatest individual season of the 2000s by a Butler player. He was less

> We played Butler basketball. It's the same system. Coach Collier taught it to Coach Matta, and Coach Lick brought it back to us this year. It's beautiful.
>
> —Butler forward Rylan Hainje in 2001, talking about coaches Barry Collier, Thad Matta, and Todd Lickliter

explosive after he injured an ankle during an upset of Indiana on December 29.

"From the first 13 games, I wasn't the same," Hainje acknowledged.

That impairment notwithstanding, Hainje averaged 15.2 points and 6.0 rebounds, becoming the Midwestern Collegiate Conference player of the year. Evidence of how much his game evolved was his 44 3-pointers and .404 percentage from the arc. As a freshman, he made one 3-pointer all season.

His shooting range, size (235 pounds), and strength (he set a Butler record with a bench press of 335 pounds) made him a difficult matchup even outside the conference.

Hainje was at his best against the best. Over his final two seasons, he averaged 18.4 points in 18 games against teams falling into one of six categories—power conference, NCAA Tournament team, nationally ranked team, or in championship, postseason, or overtime games. In 48 other games, his average was 11.3.

In one measure of offensive efficiency—points per field-goal attempt—Hainje averaged 1.50. That was better than 13 of the 15 players on the Associated Press All-America teams.

The great regret of Hainje's career was the Bulldogs' snub from the 2002 NCAA Tournament. They were 25–4 in the regular season but lost to No. 8-seed Wisconsin-Green Bay in the MCC Tournament.

"To me, not getting in last year was the biggest disappointment that I have ever had occur," he once wrote in an e-mail. "I mean, I am still hurt that the committee did not feel as though we were one of the best 64 teams in the nation after being ranked. That blew my mind."

Hainje had more on his mind than basketball during his senior season. His son, Kyran, was born on March 16, 2001—the same day the Bulldogs beat Wake Forest for their first NCAA Tournament victory since 1962. It's not as if there was a template for Hainje, either. His own father wasn't around much and died when Hainje was eight. As a student, Hainje had custody of his son regularly.

"Not a lot of things have come easy for him," said Rick Streiff, his Cathedral football coach. "And I think that's why he has the work ethic and attitude he does. Rylan has had to overcome things. He's faced some adversity in his life."

That included handling mean-spirited remarks about his biracial background. His mother is white, and his father was black. As a child, Hainje said, he didn't really understand what was being said.

His mother, Kyle, sent him to Lafayette so he could attend a small high school. Hainje was involved in a few scuffles at Central Catholic. He felt out of place there, especially after a racist symbol showed up in his locker one day. He came home to Indianapolis after Thanksgiving in his sophomore year.

At Cathedral, he found his niche. He helped the Irish win state championships in football and basketball. He was the 1998 city player of the year in basketball, averaging 16.8 points a game and leading Cathedral to a 22–4 record.

Ohio State, Michigan, and Michigan State recruited Hainje for football, but he preferred basketball. His college decision represented a breakthrough for Butler, which hadn't landed a scholarship player from Indianapolis since Darrin Fitzgerald in 1983.

Hainje played with a heart flutter that was never precisely diagnosed despite a series of tests. He once acknowledged that a heart-related problem was his biggest fear.

"I'd rather die on the court than any place else," he said.

After college, Hainje considered a return to football as an NFL tight end. The Indianapolis Colts sent him through a private workout. In the end, he stuck with basketball. He was invited to the Indiana Pacers' summer camp and then played two seasons for teams in Hungary and France.

• • •

Joel Cornette

Years: 1999–2003

Hometown: Cincinnati, Ohio

Career Points: 1,100

Career Highlights: Member of Butler's team of the sesquicentennial

Joel Cornette confounded teammates and opponents, either with his play or his outspokenness.

As a Butler senior, he did so with a new 'do. He claimed the hair was all natural. Roommate Mike Monserez found hair all over the bathroom every morning and said it was craziness. Duke fans called Cornette

"Sideshow Bob" after a character from *The Simpsons*. Less charitable were Evansville fans, who chanted, "Chia pet, Chia pet." Cornette's coiffure was a cross between an Afro and dreadlocks, according to his mother.

The hairstyle was a metaphor for Cornette's basketball style. Neither was easy to describe.

Coaches and teammates rolled out the cliches—"he does things that don't show up in a box score"—but then apologized for doing so. He could not be stereotyped.

"Because he's unique," Butler coach Todd Lickliter said.

Cornette once conceded: "I'm not really great at anything."

Instead, he did a bit of everything.

Cornette is the only Butler player ever to be a three-time member of the Horizon League's all-defensive team. At 6-foot-10, he often brought the ball upcourt to relieve pressure on the guards.

He didn't necessarily get the assist but the pass that led to an assist. He might not have secured the rebound, but he blocked out his man so that a teammate did. He scored only if it was imperative—as it was on his game-winning dunk against Indiana on December 29, 2001, and when he had 21 points against Oklahoma in an East Regional semifinal on March 28, 2003.

Not until he was a senior did Cornette average more than 10 points a game (11.6). That season, 2002–03, he and teammate Brandon Miller were Butler's co-athletes of the year for all sports. Cornette rarely posted fancy figures. He left that to younger brother Jordan, who played at Notre Dame.

There was one number that interested Cornette: 100. That's the total victories by his senior class, the most ever for a four-year Butler player. Each year, the Bulldogs tied or exceeded the school record for wins.

Cornette was fiercely competitive, as Monserez knew before he arrived at Butler. They were stars at rival Cincinnati high schools, Cornette at St. Xavier and Monserez at Moeller. After Moeller upset St. Xavier in a sectional final, their exchange was heated.

So when Monserez transferred from Notre Dame, he wondered about residual friction. Cornette treated him like a long-lost relative.

"You walk around this campus with Joel, he's saying hi to so many people, you instantly meet friends because you're associated with Joel," Monserez said. "Everyone who knows Joel likes Joel."

When Cornette was a high school freshman, he was a 5-foot-11 guard. The next year he stood 6-foot-5. When he committed to Butler, he was 6-foot-7. When he arrived on campus, he was 6-foot-10.

St. Xavier coach Scott Martin said Cornette improved more in high school than anyone he had ever seen. The player's parents remembered an uncoordinated son who looked out of place among the more than 90 boys trying out for the freshman team.

"My husband and I often look in amazement at each other and say, 'Remember when he was a freshman? He couldn't walk and chew gym at the same time,'" Christi Cornette said.

Cornette grew into a leadership role at Butler. So there *was* one thing at which he was great: growing.

He would pull teammates aside in warm-ups if he sensed a lack of concentration. He broke the tension of a huddle by cracking jokes. After the Bulldogs' 10–0 start was ended at Hawaii in overtime in December 2002, he gathered teammates together. Win with class, he said, and lose with dignity.

"He's definitely our team spokesman," teammate Darnell Archey said.

It was Cornette who influenced the Bulldogs to set the highest possible goals. Not just to make the NCAA Tournament, he told teammates, but to win there. Not just to make the Sweet Sixteen, but the Final Four ... even the national championship. Cornette embraced the Butler Way and Butler experience.

You want a team player?

After the Bulldogs reached the 2003 Sweet Sixteen, he helped sell NCAA Tournament tickets from a folding table inside Hinkle Fieldhouse. To those unfamiliar with the historic fieldhouse, he gave informal tours.

It was a special time not only for him but the entire Cornette family. In the first and second rounds of that tournament, Jordan's Notre Dame team played on a Thursday and Saturday in Indianapolis and Joel on Friday and Sunday in Birmingham, Ala. Their parents made the eight-hour drive back and forth, even with a stop in Cincinnati to watch a third son, Jonathan, in a high school game.

Cornette knew he would miss his college days. He went on to become a student assistant coach at Butler and played two pro seasons, one in Australia and one with the Nebraska Cranes of the U.S. Basketball League. He rejoined the Butler staff and then followed Lickliter to the University of Iowa as an assistant coach.

Yet it was not the same as striving for a collective goal with the Butler Bulldogs.

"Just all the time I spend with these guys will be what I miss about the whole thing," he said late in his senior season. "Regardless of what I do in the future, I know I'm not going to be able to do it with the guys I do it with here.

"I love all of them. They're like brothers."

• • •

Brandon Miller

Years: 2000–2003

Hometown: New Castle, Ind.

Career Points: 1,121

Career Highlights: Member of Butler's team of the sesquicentennial; Chip Hilton Award for character and leadership, 2003; Horizon League's Cecil Coleman Medal of Honor, 2003

Brandon Miller isn't sure how he acquired his bulldog appearance.

He might have broken his nose in a scrap with older brother Scott. It's hard to identify a single incident.

When he was four or five, his legs were too short to reach the brake pedals of a bicycle he rode downhill and into a neighbor's house. While practicing baton exchanges on a blacktop in junior high track, he ran into a basket support. Miller's head was so bloody that his father thought there had been a drive-by shooting.

"He's had a number of injuries," Roger Miller said of his son. "Most of them are going full tilt."

Brandon Miller knew no other way. The Butler Bulldogs wouldn't have had him any other way. He was the soul of a team that was 77–20 in three seasons and won three NCAA Tournament games.

He played under three head coaches—Barry Collier, Thad Matta, and Todd Lickliter—at Butler. He was "the common denominator" of the three-year run, former athletic director John Parry said.

In Miller's senior year, as the point guard, he was Butler's top scorer (11.9 points), passer (3.4 assists), and defender. In the clutch, he was Chip Hilton right out of a Clair Bee novel. Fittingly, he received the 2003 Chip Hilton Award that season for character and leadership.

Miller made winning or go-ahead baskets against Western Kentucky, Detroit, Cleveland State, and Mississippi State. He was only slightly less dramatic in other games.

Brandon Miller's bulldog tenacity was in evidence against Oklahoma and other opponents during the 2003 NCAA Tournament (Butler University Archives).

Former Butler enforcer Mike Marshall, who later became an assistant coach, graduated before Miller played for the Bulldogs. Marshall said Miller was the only player he ever wished could have been a teammate.

"Because we had the same mind-set," Marshall said.

Duke coach Mike Krzyzewski compared Miller to Steve Wojciechowski, a gritty Blue Devils guard. When Butler played at Duke, Coach K gave future NBA player Chris Duhon one assignment: guard Miller. Duhon didn't score a point, but he guarded Miller in Duke's 80–60 victory.

Wisconsin-Green Bay coach Tod Kowalczyk called him the Horizon League's MVP, even though Miller did not make the all-league first team in 2003.

"He runs his team better than any point guard that I've seen over a long time at any level, be it the Big East or Conference USA," said Kowalczyk, a former Rutgers and Marquette assistant.

Coach Charlie Coles of Miami (Ohio) said he "fell in love" with Miller when the RedHawks once scrimmaged Butler in the preseason. Coles said that with Miller, the Bulldogs played basketball the way it was designed.

"It's damn near comical the way they play," Coles said.

If circumstances of Miller's nose were a mystery, the source of his fierce competitiveness was not. Credit nature and nurture.

As a child, he was infuriated that he couldn't beat his father at checkers. More than once, Butler teammates were awakened on a bus trip by Miller's shouts during a card game.

Winning superseded sleep or health.

Miller broke his arm playing quarterback in youth football. That didn't keep him off the basketball court, where he dove for a loose ball and rebroke the arm. In his final game of high school, he tore an anterior cruciate ligament . . . and kept playing. In his sophomore season at Butler, he hurt his shoulder in November, played all season, and then had off-season surgery. In a 2001 photo published by *Sports Illustrated* that effectively summarized his career, he is diving to the floor in an attempt to secure a loose ball in an NCAA Tournament game against Wake Forest.

Competition was all Miller had known. He was a coach's son influenced by the basketball community of New Castle, Ind. He was raised one block from 9,325-seat Chrysler Fieldhouse, the nation's largest high school arena. He had a key and would shoot alone at 10 or 11 o'clock on summer nights.

Indiana basketball icon Steve Alford and his future wife, Tanya, spent their first date babysitting for little Brandon. Brandon's father was a longtime assistant to coach Sam Alford, Steve's father, at the high school.

The two Miller sons developed such a fractious rivalry that their father intervened to prohibit one-on-one games. But they were as committed to winning together as they were playing against each other. When Scott was a senior and Brandon a freshman, they helped New Castle beat Alexandria 81–74 in overtime in the semi-state at Hinkle Fieldhouse.

"If people ask me what my favorite games are to look back on, that ranks up there as one of the top," Brandon said.

Scott Miller went on to become the No. 3 all-time scorer and 3-point record-holder at Marian College in Indianapolis. Yet toughest of all the Millers, according to their father, was daughter Lindsey. Despite tearing both ACLs, she excelled in track (she was a sectional champion in the 800 meters) and basketball.

It was widely assumed that Miller, who first went to Southwest Missouri State to play for Steve Alford, didn't follow the coach to Iowa because neither believed Miller could make it in the Big Ten. Alford told colleagues that not bringing Miller to Iowa was one of the biggest mistakes of his coaching career.

But Miller missed home, and home was not Missouri or Iowa. Home was Indiana.

"I was missing out on my sister's high school career. I never got to see her, never got to see her play, never got to see my brother anymore," he said. "I was just missing out on my family."

Miller's longtime friend and teammate, Darnell Archey, was already at Butler. When Southwest Missouri played at Butler in Miller's first college game, he noticed how much young talent the Bulldogs had. He also remembered the tireless efforts of Matta, who was a Butler assistant when Miller played for a summer team.

So Miller went to Butler. And waited to play. Transfer rules required that he wait, so practices became his games. Miller turned practices into spectacles and Thomas Jackson into a great point guard. In turn, Miller became a better point guard playing against Jackson every day. Matta said the only player in the country that the Bulldogs couldn't guard was Miller.

Miller's style was uncommon. He dribbled recklessly toward the goal but finished by arching one-handed shots high off the glass and through the hoop. Such a shot beat Mississippi State 47–46 in the first round of the 2003 NCAA Tournament. Miller's trademark was the stare-down of a defender and a quick release beyond the 3-point arc. Through 2009, Miller ranked fourth on Butler's all-time list for 3-pointers made (189), trailing A.J. Graves (303) and New Castle alumni Bruce Horan (314) and Archey (217).

Miller's value was underscored in defeat. After he was ill with the flu for a week, he contributed just four points and one assist in the Bulldogs' 69–52 loss to Milwaukee in the 2003 league championship game. Restored to health, in the Bulldogs' next two games, he helped them beat No. 20 Mississippi State and No. 14 Louisville to reach the NCAA East Regional. He didn't make a field goal against Louisville but withstood the Cardinals' relentless pressure.

After graduation, he rejoined Matta on the coaching staffs of Xavier and Ohio State, interrupted by one year on Brad Stevens' Butler staff.

It was no coincidence that in 11 seasons from 1999 through 2009 at four different schools, Miller's teams played in nine NCAA Tournaments.

•••

Brandon Polk

Years: 2004–2006

Hometown: Wichita, Kan.

Career Points: 975

Career Highlights: Horizon League player of the year, 2006; All-Horizon League first team, 2006

Brandon Polk never won a championship at Butler nor played in an NCAA Tournament game. But the 6-foot-6 post player was a transitional figure who helped restore winning ways.

After reaching the Sweet Sixteen in 2003, the Bulldogs were 16–14 and 13–15 in the next two years. Polk played on the team that had Butler's only losing record since 1993. He led the Bulldogs in scoring (13.6) and rebounding (4.6) despite a shoulder injury that restricted his motion.

"I knew it was a big problem, but I wasn't really excited about missing a whole season," Polk said. "I figured I'd use this brace and make it through and get surgery after the season. Luckily, I was able to make it through."

Polk was unaccustomed to losing.

When he was a senior at Wichita (Kan.) North High School, he scored 36 points in the opening round of the Class 6A tournament and led his team to third place in the state.

"He had an incredible attitude and an incredible work ethic on the court," Wichita North coach Michael Keimig said.

From there, Polk attended Redlands Community College in El Reno, Okla., helping the Cougars to a two-year record of 67–5. In his final season, he averaged 14 points and led Redlands to a 35–2 record and runner-up finish in the national junior-college tournament.

Despite his injury, Polk was a force at the end of his junior season, scoring 24, 27, and 24 points in Butler's final three games. That extended into his senior year, especially against top opponents. Polk scored 23 at Michigan, 26 against Tulane, and 23 against Indiana. Tulane coach Dave Dickerson called Polk one of the best players in the country. Polk said he had "virtually no problem at all" with his shoulder.

The problem was Butler's won-loss record. After a dispiriting 64–62 loss at Youngstown State, the Bulldogs fell to 9–8. It was time for a reality check, Polk said.

"We started to have some pride and tried to salvage what we could that senior year of mine," he said. "We tried. It could have been better. But it was better than the season before."

After Youngstown, the Bulldogs won six in a row, featuring a 63–60 upset of Wisconsin-Milwaukee at Hinkle Fieldhouse. The ordinarily expressionless Polk bounced around the fieldhouse afterward, joining fans who stormed the court. His two free throws with 5.3 seconds left in OT had given Butler a three-point lead.

The Bulldogs reached the 2006 Horizon League Tournament championship game, this time at Milwaukee. They lost the rematch 87–71, despite Polk's 27 points. In an otherwise poor game by Polk, his rebound basket with 2.5 seconds left lifted Butler over Miami of Ohio 53–52 in the first round of the NIT. That supplied the Bulldogs a 20th victory in a season that was once going nowhere.

Polk averaged 18.0 points and totaled 593, the most by a Butler player since Darin Archbold scored 770 in 1991–92. Polk finished his career with a .581 field-goal percentage, third in Butler history. He was voted Horizon player of the year over Milwaukee star Joah Tucker and league scoring leader Quin Humphrey of Youngstown State. Butler coach Todd Lickliter said Polk was patient and unselfish and utilized an array of post moves.

"Most of the time, player of the year is a guy who scores," Lickliter said. "And he does it as efficiently as anybody I've ever seen."

Because his teams didn't win with the regularity of others, Polk's name doesn't come up immediately during discussions of the best Butler players of the 2000s. However, his numbers speak eloquently, even if he was an unconventional center. Almost all of his field goals came close to the basket against taller defenders. How did he manage that?

"I don't really know how to answer that," Polk said. "Just being able to use both hands well around the basket is an advantage. I'm not the best jumper, but I can jump pretty well. Even to this day, playing in Europe, I'm the smallest post player on the floor.

Polk played a season of pro basketball in Switzerland in 2007 but sat out the next year because of a knee injury. In 2009, he averaged 16.6 points in Finland for Karhut Kauhajoen, which won the regular season and playoffs. Moreover, after being chided throughout his Butler days for inadequate defense, Polk was the league's defensive player of the year.

• • •

A.J. Graves

Years: 2004–08

Hometown: Switz City, Ind.

Career Points: 1,807.

Career Highlights: First team All-Horizon League, 2007, 2008; out-standing player of NIT Season Tipoff, 2006; Academic All-American, 2007, 2008; Horizon League's Cecil Coleman Medal of Honor, 2008; Indiana Mr. Basketball runner-up, 2004

Norbert Graves' truck stands as a memorial to the business he created, Graves Plumbing, near the intersection of State Road 67 and S.R. 54 in Switz City, Ind.

The 1988 Ford pickup rests on metal supports about 10 feet off the ground, or the height of a basketball hoop. Plumbing is the family business. Basketball is the family passion.

The latest branch of the family tree—Graves' grandson A.J.—became one of the best college basketball players of his era and one of the greatest in Butler history.

A.J., for Adam James, was never coerced to play basketball. It wasn't necessary. He emulated three older brothers.

"There isn't much to do in Greene County," brother Andrew Graves said. "Most people here are hunters or fishermen. Everywhere he went, he took a ball with him."

A.J. would dribble along the sideline during his brothers' games. He had to be told about his older brothers' exploits for White River Valley High School. That's because he was too young to remember. The oldest, Matthew, is 11 years older than A.J. Mark is nine years older and

Andrew seven years. The three oldest were in a 1993 high school game all at the same time.

Matthew and Andrew played for Butler before A.J. They became the first trio of brothers ever to become Indiana All-Stars.

Family involvement in basketball runs as deep as the gene pool.

A.J.'s uncle, Rusty Miller, led the state in scoring for Switz City in 1974–75 with a 39-point average. Miller had a high game of 60 points against Vincennes Rivet.

A.J.'s father, Rick, made the winning basket in the final Wabash Valley Tournament in 1970. Rick and Andrew coached junior high teams. A.J.'s mother, Melonie, kept detailed statistics in the scorebook she took to every game.

"I'm not hollering at the refs or anything," she explained. "I concentrate on my book."

A.J. Graves, dribbling against Notre Dame, sank eight 3-pointers against the Fighting Irish to launch the Bulldogs' run through the 2006 NIT Season Tipoff (Butler University Archives).

Switz City (pop. 311) has no stoplight, just a flashing light. There's a tavern, fire station, bank, post office, and hunting store. The gas station closed.

A.J.'s parents raised him at a home that features nearly a full blacktop court and five basketball hoops. It was the only asphalt within a square mile. The shooting background was cornfields. The coal mine down the hill made the ground shake once in a while.

Convenient entertainment was to shoot the basketball, maybe some free throws. A.J. once counted 169 made in a row.

He missed out on the sometimes-bloody backyard games of his brothers. When A.J. was in high school, his father said A.J. "might be a little soft" because of that. Not too soft, though.

In one high school game, he took a spill, was knocked unconscious, and required stitches in his chin. The next night, he scored 31 points. In college, A.J. played with chronic sore feet. It was only six weeks after his senior season ended that he could walk without discomfort.

In one college game, he was set to have bothersome wisdom teeth removed. Before oral surgery, he scored 31 points—29 after halftime—and nearly rallied Butler to an overtime victory at Illinois-Chicago.

His brothers were among his biggest supporters. A.J. broke Matthew's high school record for career points with 2,041. Andrew said A.J. had the height of a Graves and the quickness of a Miller.

"He's more of an athlete than we were," Andrew said.

Three Graves families lived in separate houses on 200 acres of property. Mark and Andrew lived there and worked for the plumbing business inherited by their father.

Considering the proximity of the generations, the work ethic, and the rural environment, the Graves family could be basketball's version of *The Waltons*. The difference was prosperity. *The Waltons* was set during the Depression. Graves Plumbing, which began in the mid-1960s as a $10,000-a-year company, grossed millions.

•••

Norbert Graves died in 1994. As for his grandson, suffice it to say that plumbing was not his pleasure. The summers in which A.J. dug ditches took care of that.

"I've already made it clear I want nothing to do with the family business," A.J. said.

In high school, A.J. made it his business to inspire hope for White River Valley, a consolidation of about 300 students. One of the schools absorbed was L&M (Lyons and Marco), which reached the semi-state final in 1985. White River Valley, led by Matthew Graves, made it that far in 1993 before losing to eventual state champion Jeffersonville 61–59. White River Valley lost in the 2002 Class A semi-state to Barr-Reeve 62–57 in overtime.

In 2004, when A.J. was a senior, the Wolverines had a group that had been unbeaten from the fourth through the eighth grade. A.J. set a Hall of Fame Classic record by scoring 45 points in an 80–78 victory over Class 4A Northview at New Castle. White River Valley won the sectional. In the regional, A.J. had 37 points—one more than Tecumseh's team. But in the semi-state, one victory away from the Class A championship game, White River Valley lost to unbeaten Waldron 82–76.

Graves committed early to Butler but not because he didn't think about other options. Southern Illinois, Xavier, and Indiana State showed interest. Indiana University and Purdue had no interest in someone from such a small school and with such a small frame (6-foot-1, 160-pounds).

White River Valley coach Steve Vandeventer once stopped by IU's Assembly Hall to ask if the Hoosiers knew about Graves, whose home was 35 miles from the Bloomington campus. An assistant coach replied, "We already have our guards." Graves went on to finish second in Mr. Basketball voting behind A.J. Ratliff, an IU recruit. In four seasons for the Hoosiers, Ratliff totaled 544 points—or fewer than Graves had in one year at Butler.

• • •

Sometimes, the attention he received in college was embarrassing to A.J. Graves, who was shy and a little quirky.

Facebook, a social networking site on the Internet, had two groups of more than 500 members each devoted to him. One was "A.J. Graves is the clutchest person alive." The other was "Chuck Norris had a son, and his name is A.J. Graves."

Norris, an action star who appeared in the TV series *Walker, Texas Ranger*, became a cult icon credited with absurdly heroic (and fictional) feats.

At least Graves had an authentic résumé. During his final two seasons, he became the face of the Butler Bulldogs.

Reporters nationwide loved writing about his small-town roots and wispy stature. They called him a "Popsicle stick" or someone with an "Olive Oyl body." An NCAA Tournament program published a story about him, referring to his hometown as "Swish City."

He was someone out of the movie *Hoosiers*, a real-life Jimmy Chitwood. Graves once estimated he had seen the film 100 times. Coaches and teammates loved him as much for his humility as his ability. He could have done without all the fuss.

"I have very few friends," Graves said. "I keep to myself, yes. I'm not all about being out there, being real social. Not to be mean or anything. I just like to stay home."

He was not a hoops homebody. Most of his game-deciding plays came away from Hinkle Fieldhouse. It's no wonder his No. 4 black road jersey became a hot seller in Indianapolis.

In November 2006, he was the MVP of the NIT Season Tipoff in New York and the next night led Butler to a double-overtime comeback victory over Kent State in Indianapolis. He showed up for medical treatment on Monday wearing Butler sweats. When asked if he was going straight to class, he said he wanted to go home first and change into jeans, a shirt, and a baseball cap so no one would recognize him.

"He's a little uncomfortable with all the attention and talking to the media, and that sort of goes back to how he was raised in a small town," said brother Matthew, a Butler assistant coach.

• • •

Over Graves' final two seasons, he averaged 19.9 points in 14 games played in the NIT Season Tipoff, Great Alaska Shootout, Wooden Tradition, or NCAA Tournament. The opponents were virtually all from major conferences or nationally ranked. That average was significantly higher than his career figure of 13.9.

Graves called his sequence of game-deciding plays a coincidence.

"You just get put in those positions," he said. "You've just got to make plays, and I just happened to be in the right place and the right time and made it."

• • •

Graves was twice an Academic All-American and finished third on Butler's all-time scoring list with 1,807 points. Because he slumped in January of his senior season, at a time when he was trying to relieve foot soreness, it's easy to forget how spectacularly he played in the other months of the two years in which Butler won 59 of 70 games.

As a junior, he shot .948 on free throws, making 145 of 153. He sank 63 consecutively in 12 games from November 25, 2006 to January 20, 2007. It was the fourth-longest streak in NCAA Division I history.

Graves was the perfect complement to dive-and-dish point guard Mike Green. Graves was a sure ball-handler and clever offensive player who had the shooting range and speed, if not the size, to play in the NBA.

As the numbers revealed, he was also at his best against the best competition.

He pondered a pro career, playing in the predraft camp at Portsmouth, Va., in April 2008. Later, he abandoned that idea and instead accepted a job as a business analyst at AIT Laboratories, an Indianapolis lab science firm. His degree was in actuarial science.

"I don't know, physically, if I could hold up another year," he said.

After a year away from the sport, he changed his mind. He resumed serious workouts in the summer of 2009, hired an agent, and signed with a pro team in Poland.

•••

Mike Green

Years: 2006–08

Hometown: Philadelphia, Pa.

Career Points: 1,637 (996 at Butler, 641 at Towson)

Career Highlights: Great Alaska Shootout most outstanding player, 2007; Horizon League player of the year, 2008; first team all-league, 2008; league tournament MVP, 2008; Frances Pomeroy Naismith Award as nation's top player 6 feet or under, 2008; Chip Hilton Award for character and leadership, 2008

The Blumberg Projects of North Philadelphia can cause the soul of a young man to erode. Maybe slowly. Not inevitably.

That's where Mike Green grew up, and the depressed inner-city area did not get him down. If anything, everything and everyone around there lifted him up. No one could have foreseen how high.

The season before Green arrived on Butler's campus, the Bulldogs were 13–15, for their worst record in 12 years. The two years in which he directed the Bulldogs as a point guard, they were 29–7 and 30–4, for the two winningest seasons in Butler's history.

"I used to not be able to talk about him without crying because of where he's from," said Cedric Powell, his high school coach. "He's worked hard for his success."

How hard?

His single mother, Elena Day, had to scream at him to come inside when he was out on a basketball court until 4 o'clock in the morning. When it was raining or cold, he wrapped his ball in a plastic baggie and kept at it. While in high school, he earned three varsity letters in cross country, a sport that offers no rewards without work. He was so distressed while watching the 2007 NCAA championship game on TV between Florida, a team that escaped Butler, and Ohio State that he was back in a gym before halftime.

Green was six when his father, Leroy Green, died. Green conceded that he lived in a tough area, the same one in which former Indianapolis Colts receiver Marvin Harrison was raised. Yet Green never experienced real trouble. He had his mother—"she's my best friend"—and the support of coaches, relatives, and neighbors.

As a child, Green lived in a basketball bubble. It was a small world. He didn't know the college game existed until he once saw a Villanova game on TV. Older kids in the neighborhood had the court at 22nd and Jefferson, so Green and his friends created their own court. They nailed a crate to a tree in the playground, and they might as well have been in Madison Square Garden. They divided into teams, keeping their own stats.

His mother nurtured his learning by buying spelling and math games for Christmas instead of toys. His grades and test scores allowed him admission to Franklin Learning Center, a diverse public high school of 700 students. The building is a century old, and home games were played in a rec center.

"I guess I could say I'm kind of a savior at home," Green said. "Everybody embraced me."

Well, not everybody. Big-time colleges never called, even though he played on a high-powered AAU team, the Hunting Park Warriors, with a cast of players who landed at such schools. Mustafa Shakur was the star of that team, but when he and Green were on the court simultaneously, Green played the point. Coach Greg Wright was reluctant ever to take Green out.

"He could control the tempo of the game. That's not new," Wright said. "He just got better at it."

Green was an all-city player at Franklin Learning Center, leading the team to a 22–4 record, including a 13–0 mark in the Philadelphia Public

Mike Green, left, and A.J. Graves gave Butler its greatest backcourt ever and a 30-win season in 2007–08 (Butler University Archives).

League. He averaged 19.7 points, 6.2 rebounds, and 7.0 assists—the kind of numbers that presaged what he would do at Butler.

He was a "classic Philly guard," Powell said. Smart. Tough. Fearless. Green's scrappy high school team—undersized, underfunded, and underpublicized—was much like Butler's.

Green ended up at Towson (Md.) University for a chance to play immediately. He became the first Towson freshman to start every game at point guard, and he made the dean's list. Towson finished 8–21.

Then the coach who recruited him, Michael Hunt, resigned. After Pat Kennedy's first season as Towson's coach ended at 6–23, Green stopped liking basketball. Worse, he stopped working hard. Forty-four losses in two years had a more debilitating effect than the projects. He sought a transfer.

Another coach in the Colonial Athletic Association, Brad Brownell of UNC Wilmington, heard about Green's plight and recommended him to a colleague, Todd Lickliter of Butler. Lickliter watched Green in a summer league. Green visited Butler shortly before fall classes were to start. While on campus, he spoke to the coaches for hours about basketball, and both sides sensed this was a good fit.

During the redshirt year, Green developed a close friendship with Pete Campbell, also a transfer who had to sit out. In practice, they played for the Blue team, or second team, which simulates opponents and applies pressure on the first team. Green's skills, coupled with Campbell's 3-point marksmanship, made the Blue team formidable.

Green was a black player from the inner city and Campbell a small-town white Hoosier, but their love of basketball negated the differences. Campbell's family entertained Green and other players at a lake house to celebrate Green's 22nd birthday.

"He's great on the court, and he might be even better off the court," Campbell said. "He's just a great person . . . a lot of people like him on our team. He's kind of a hard guy not to like."

In his second game as a Butler player, Green had 19 points and 12 assists to help the Bulldogs beat Notre Dame 71–69 in an NIT Season Tipoff opener at Conseco Fieldhouse. That victory propelled Butler toward the championship—where Green finally did play in Madison Square Garden—and restored Butler's place in college basketball's consciousness.

However, it was not that triumph, but two missed free throws in a 65–57 loss to Florida's eventual NCAA champions, that motivated Green after the season ended. What to do about it? What else? Work even harder.

Green shared achievements not only with his teammates, but with those from home. Five Philly friends were at Conseco Fieldhouse for NIT victories over Notre Dame and Indiana, staying in the off-campus house he rented. On senior weekend, his mother and about a dozen other relatives and friends were in Hinkle Fieldhouse.

In his senior season, he was one of the few players in the nation to lead his team in scoring (14.6), rebounds (6.5), and assists (5.1). He was the most outstanding player of the Great Alaska Shootout, Horizon League player of the year, and MVP of the league tournament. He twice willed the Bulldogs to overtime victories, scoring 12 points in OT of an 84–78 win over Virginia Tech and 10 in OT of an 83–75 win at Wisconsin-Milwaukee. He never had a triple-double but often came close.

As a junior, he set a Butler record for free throws made (196). As a senior, he set the record for assists (172). Yet those numbers are perhaps no more relevant than the ones Green charted in the crate-basket league. More relevant was Butler's two-year record: 59–11.

"It's hard to quantify the impact he's had on the program," Stevens said.

Green wasn't selected in the 2008 NBA draft but worked out for many teams and played in summer leagues for the Cleveland Cavaliers in 2008 and Houston Rockets in 2009. He spent his first pro season, 2008–09, playing for a team in Turkey.

•••

Matt Howard

Years: 2007–

Hometown: Connersville, Ind.

Career Points: 902

Career Highlights: Horizon League player of the year, 2009; all-league first team, 2009; Academic All-American, 2009

It is difficult, if not impossible, for a college defender to vex Matt Howard by pushing, grabbing, holding, or scratching him. He had seen and felt it all—from older brothers—before he played a single high school basketball game.

Once Howard got to high school, he endured more of the same from Adam Knotts, an older teammate. Knotts was a senior outweighing freshman Howard by about 40 pounds, and the two competed for playing time.

"He'd back me into the bleachers in open gym, throw me around," Howard said. "I wouldn't say anything. I'd just keep coming back. It was really good for me. He taught me to be tough."

Not that learning came tough to Howard. He became an Academic All-American at Butler. What came harder was leadership.

Yet, if it's true that it takes a good follower to be a good leader, Howard was prepared for the role thrust upon him as a sophomore. He had long been a follower. He was the eighth of 10 children born into his Connersville, Ind., family. He was the newbie on a 30-win Butler team featuring five seniors.

Matt Howard, the eighth of 10 children born to a Connersville, Ind., couple, was the Horizon League player of the year in 2009 (Photo by John Fetcho).

Without a single senior on the 2008–09 roster, the Bulldogs needed someone to follow. So they followed the 6-foot-8 Howard into a surprise appearance in the NCAA Tournament. He was the first sophomore in 17 years to be the Horizon League's player of the year, averaging 14.6 points and 6.7 rebounds. He led the league in field-goal percentage at .548.

Before the season, coach Brad Stevens asked the introverted Howard to lead by example. That doesn't mean chiding teammates or losing your identity, the coach told him. Just make sure everyone pulls in the same direction.

"What's been fun for me is watching him do that all year," Stevens said. "And then as the year's gone on, being more and more vocal."

Numbers come more naturally to Howard than words. He exceeded a 3.7 grade point average while majoring in finance, not communications.

He was bumped so often that he ranked seventh in the nation in fouls drawn per 40 minutes (7.6). Two of those ahead of him were All-Americans Blake Griffin of Oklahoma, the No. 1 pick in the NBA draft, and Tyler Hansbrough of national champion North Carolina.

"He really puts the officials and the defense in a tough position because he really throws himself at the rim," Wisconsin-Milwaukee coach Rob Jeter said. "When he does that, there's going to be contact. He's a terrific player."

It took the Bulldogs awhile to build around Howard in his second season. He was a magnet for defenses. He struggled with scoring and with fouling.

As opponents discovered they had other Bulldogs to guard, Howard found more room to maneuver and responded accordingly. In the final nine games, he averaged 19.8 points and shot .625. He scored 22 points in just 25 minutes in a 75–71 loss to LSU in the NCAA Tournament.

"You take him off that team, it's a whole different team," Cleveland State coach Gary Waters said. "Howard is a unique basketball player, probably one of the most unique players to be in this league in a long time."

Howard's upbringing might not have been unique, but it was unusual. When he was born, his family had one bathroom in their rural home. It was frequently "extreme chaos," Howard said.

He is the youngest of five sons separated by 12 years. His five sisters are separated by 20 years. His parents, Stan and Linda, grew up in Connersville. Stan played baseball at Concordia (Mich.) and Hanover College, and has been a mail carrier for three decades. Linda, an Indiana University graduate, became a stay-at-home mom after her first child was born. Later the family moved into a house with seven bedrooms and two bathrooms.

"We didn't start out thinking we were going to have 10 children," Linda Howard said. "But we're not ones to outguess what God has for us. We just marched through it."

Because he was so much younger, Howard didn't play organized sports with his brothers. He was home-schooled in seventh and eighth grades.

Thereafter, his basketball status increased faster than his considerable height. He became Connersville High School's all-time leader in scoring and rebounding, and he led the state in rebounding (14.4) and was eighth in scoring (23.6).

Summer play earned him a ranking among the nation's top 100 prospects. He was the MVP of the prestigious Bob Gibbons Tournament of Champions and Hoosier Shootout.

Colleges nationwide tried to recruit Howard—his father, as a mail carrier, could tell how many letters poured in—and ultimately chose Butler over Purdue. Several siblings live or work in Indianapolis, so he was always near family.

As a freshman, he was the Horizon League newcomer of the year for the 30–4 Bulldogs in a season ending with an overtime loss to Tennessee in the NCAA Tournament. Howard was so disappointed with his play in that defeat—four points in 23 foul-plagued minutes—that he trained hard enough in the offseason to lose about 10 pounds. At least he didn't have to wait in line to use the bathroom scale.

"There are difficulties that come with being in such a big family," Howard said, "but what I've got from it, it's just been great for me."

•••

Gordon Hayward

Years: 2008–

Hometown: Brownsburg, Ind.

Career Points: 420

Career Highlights: All-Horizon League first team, 2009; league newcomer of the year, 2009; All-Tournament Five at Under-19 World Championship, 2009

This is how Gordon Hayward ending up playing basketball for Butler— and becoming one of the best teenage players in the world—instead of tennis for Purdue.

When Hayward was a 5-foot-11, 125-pound freshman at Brownsburg High School, he was going to focus on one sport: tennis. He was going to play No. 1 singles the next year, and he was junior varsity in basketball. He would stand in front of a mirror, rehearsing the speech he would deliver to his coach to explain why he was quitting basketball.

He and his twin sister, Heather, could both play tennis at Purdue, alma mater of their parents.

"I was just thinking ahead and thinking realistically, 'I probably don't have a good chance to play college basketball right now, and maybe I should concentrate on tennis,'" Hayward said. "But I stuck with it. Somehow, I grew."

And grew. And grew some more. As a junior, he was 6-foot-7. As a senior, 6-foot-8. In college, 6-foot-9.

He led the Brownsburg Bulldogs to a surprising Class 4A state championship in 2008—his buzzer-beating shot beat Marion 40–39— and helped the Butler Bulldogs reach the NCAA Tournament in 2009. He was the Horizon League newcomer of the year and the first freshman in 13 years to make the all-league first team.

Then Gordon went global. He and Butler teammate Shelvin Mack were selected to the national team for the Under-19 World Basketball

Championship in Auckland, New Zealand, in July 2009. The United States won the gold medal for the first time since 1991.

From the third grade on, Hayward played summer basketball on the AAU circuit with Municipal Gardens/Indiana Elite. His teams won two national titles, and many of the players went on to earn college basketball scholarships. Still, he wasn't regarded as worthy of a high ranking by recruiting analysts. After all, he had averaged just 13.6 points as a junior on a 14–9 team.

Then, in the months immediately thereafter, Hayward played so well in front of college recruiters that he drew more attention. Someone that tall who could shoot, rebound, and handle the ball was worth pursuing. Purdue showed interest, as did Michigan. Brad Stevens, newly hired as Butler's head coach, entered the mix. Hayward decided Butler would be the best fit, academically and athletically.

Hayward committed to Butler on June 1, 2007, then spent the summer concentrating on tennis. His aim was to win a state singles championship, but he was eliminated by the eventual state runner-up.

During the subsequent basketball season, the flawed nature of recruiting rankings was revealed. Late-bloomers such as Hayward, who aren't witnessed in the summer, don't fit the template. If he had performed in the summer of 2007, as he did in the winter of 2008, he might have been known to schools such as North Carolina, Kansas, or UCLA.

All this time, Hayward was growing not only in height, but in confidence, skill, and resolve. Brownsburg coach Joshua Kendrick told other players to foul Hayward with impunity during scrimmages.

"I hated it. I just hated it at the time and almost got in fights in practice because they'd just be fouling on purpose," Hayward said. "I think it helps in the long run. You can't be frustrated by it or flustered."

Nor did Brownsburg become flustered during a 15–5 regular season in which it finished with two three-point defeats. Hayward and Julian Mavunga, a Zimbabwean-born post player who was also 6-foot-8, weren't done yet. Hayward called Mavunga "a monster," and Mavunga called Hayward "an athletic freak."

Together, they led Brownsburg on a dizzying seven-game run to a state championship. In the two-games-a-day regional, Hayward had 14 points, 19 rebounds, and nine assists in a 62–58 victory over North Central. Then he came back with 21 points and 11 rebounds in a 63–59 victory over Carmel, which spent most of the season ranked No. 1 in Indiana. Hayward followed that with 24 points and 16 rebounds in a 51–41 victory over No. 1 New Albany, which had been 26–0.

"I'm so proud of him for stepping up," Kendrick said. "He's really improved his game in just this postseason."

Brownsburg appeared beaten in the championship game, trailing Marion 39–38 with two seconds on the clock. Austin Fish threw an inbounds pass three-fourths of the length of the floor, and Mavunga jarred the ball loose from a Marion defender. The ball squirted free to Hayward in the middle of the lane, and he scored as time expired. It hadn't been his best game—he scored 10 points—but it couldn't have had a better outcome. He was also honored as winner of the Trester Mental Attitude Award.

• • •

Gordon Hayward was an all-league player as a freshman, then won a gold medal and made the all-tournament team in the 2009 Under-19 World Basketball Championship (Photo by John Fetcho).

When Hayward was a fifth-grader, he was asked to write a paper about someone who showed good character. He wrote about his twin sister, Heather.

The years did nothing to diminish their close relationship. They were so close that Hayward wasn't going to go to a college where Heather couldn't follow. She was going to go where he did. That's how she became a Butler tennis player. They managed to schedule some classes together.

"She's a great supporter and a good friend to me," Hayward said. "She has been my whole life."

The twins were kept in separate classrooms throughout elementary school because the district believed twins needed individuality. Their mother, Jody, a twin herself, repeatedly asked that they be together. Finally, the district relented.

The twins did not relent in their sibling rivalry. The competed in everything: tennis, soccer, grades...even over who could shut the van door the quickest. They were Brownsburg's male and female athletes of the year in 2008. Both are majoring in engineering at Butler.

Gordon pushed his sister in sports. Heather influenced her brother in his schoolwork and spiritual life. Hayward has followed his sister to meetings of Athletes in Action, the sports ministry of Campus Crusade For Christ.

Heather acknowledged that her brother has been so protective that boys in high school wouldn't ask her for dates because they feared Gordon "would beat them up." On Heather's side, she is concerned about "the different crowd" her brother could someday encounter in the NBA.

In Butler classrooms, few students realize Hayward has a sister enrolled or that Heather is his twin. Heather said there have been no negatives to having a twin and that she was always happy to have someone to share activities with.

"Sometimes I forget how good he is, and I think, 'That's my brother,'" Heather said.

● ● ●

Hayward averaged 13.1 points and 6.5 rebounds in his first college season, shooting 45 percent on 3-pointers. His 420 points were the second-most ever by a Butler freshman. It was a season unusual in two respects: he often forgot his height, and his highest-scoring games all came on the road.

When he watched game films, he wondered why he didn't shoot when he was near the rim.

"Sometimes, I feel I'm still little, underneath with the big guys," he said. "But I'm not little. Especially on offense, it's a weird feeling."

He did not lose his bearings away from Hinkle Fieldhouse. His seven games of 19 or more points all came on opponents' courts—20 at Bradley, 25 at Ohio State (featuring seven 3s), 19 at Xavier, 25 at Illinois-Chicago (with seven 3s again), 22 each at Green Bay and Detroit, and 27 at Davidson.

He was a revelation in the nationally televised game against All-American guard Stephen Curry of Davidson. Curry, impaired by an ankle injury, was limited to 20 points. Hayward scored 20 in a 10-minute span bridging the first and second halves.

Xavier coach Sean Miller couldn't believe how good Hayward was, calling him the best player the Musketeers faced all season. Davidson coach Bob McKillop compared Hayward to NBA player Mike Dunleavy, a former All-American at Duke. Hayward thrived in hostile environments.

"It's almost like the team against the world," he said.

That was true when the team was 7,200 miles away, playing against the world. In the Under-19 World Championship, Hayward scored 20 points in Team USA's 93–73 quarterfinal victory over Canada and 15 in an 81–77 semifinal victory over Croatia. He didn't score in the championship game, an 88–80 victory over Greece, but he had made his mark.

He was selected to the All-Tournament Five along with American teammate Tyshawn Taylor of Kansas, MVP Mario Delas and Toni Prostran of Croatia, and Nikolaos Pappas of Greece. The numbers revealed Hayward's versatility. In nine games in which he averaged 22 minutes, he was third on the team in scoring average (10.0), second in rebounding (5.7), first in free throws made (22) and attempted (31), second in blocked shots (10), third in steals (13), and fifth in assists (16).

He was a clear leader in New Zealand "groupies," young girls who baked cakes for him and held signs with his name. All that resulted in was a few autograph signings and relentless teasing from teammates.

Including the 2008 high school postseason, the 2009 college season, and the world tournament, Hayward's teams went 42–6.

Butler has not had an NBA player since Buckshot O'Brien in 1953. Hayward created a buzz during the USA Basketball training camp in Colorado Springs, Colo., prompting speculation that he would soon end up in the NBA. He was a guard for so long that he modeled his game after NBA playmakers John Stockton and Steve Nash. Hayward was honored to be included in such speculation but said it was hard to see himself in the NBA after one college season.

"Only God knows what the future's going to hold," he said. "You can't really worry about any of that. You just have to focus on being better."

• • •

Shelvin Mack

Years: 2008–

Hometown: Lexington, Ky.

Career Points: 382

Career Highlights: Captain of USA team for Under-19 World Championship, 2009

In his freshman season, 6-foot-3 guard Shelvin Mack was as consistent off the court as he was on it. Repeatedly asked how he and the Butler Bulldogs could so often beat older and more experienced teams, he smiled and always said the same thing:

"It's just basketball. We've been playing it all our lives."

Playing for his high school team, Bryan Station, as an eighth-grader; playing for teammates; playing for victory.

Always playing. Usually winning.

"I would go the park every day; play every day, play late," he said.

Recruiters from two colleges once visited an open gym and left disappointed because Mack didn't dominate the session. His high school coach, Champ Ligon, said Mack didn't take over because he was trying to make teammates better.

Mack played summers for Cincinnati's D-I Greyhounds. He was obscured on that AAU club by future NBA players O.J. Mayo and Bill Walker, along with high school All-Americans William Buford and Darius Miller.

However, Mack caught the attention of then-assistant coach Brandon Miller of Butler. Mack's pal Darius Miller chose the University of

Shelvin Mack was captain of the USA Basketball team that won a gold medal at the Under-19 World Basketball Championship (Photo by John Fetcho).

Kentucky, which later expressed some interest in the hometown boy. Mack kept a commitment to Butler.

As a high school senior, he averaged 23.7 points for a 30–3 team that reached No. 1 in the state. It was unusual for Mack to be cast in such a starring role. He had been content to be part of the cast.

If you want tattoos, behind-the-back passes, spectacular dunks, or animated gestures, Mack is not your man. He's just fundamental basketball. Just fitting in.

"Here at Butler, everybody takes care of each other," he said. "We're like a big family."

His personal characteristics, as well as skills, allowed him to join Gordon Hayward on Team USA for the Under-19 World Basketball Championship in New Zealand, in July 2009. Mack went to the tryouts only because other candidates were injured or declined invitations, and he wasn't a standout there. But Syracuse coach Jim Boeheim, chairman of the selection committee, said Mack was better than he showed.

The observation proved prescient. Mack became the team captain, point guard, and steadying influence on the first USA team to win the gold medal since 1991. In nine games, Mack averaged 5.9 points and 1.9 assists in 19 minutes.

"Shelvin on the team, too, really made me proud," Hayward said. "It kind of shows where Butler's going as a program."

Mack averaged 11.9 points and a team-leading 3.5 assists during the Bulldogs' 26–6 season in 2008–09. He scored 22 points in a 72–68 comeback victory over Alabama-Birmingham and 18 each in the final two games against Cleveland State in the Horizon League Tournament and LSU in the NCAA Tournament.

Before the careers of Mack and Hayward end, ESPN analyst Fran Fraschilla said, they could become two of the most important players in Butler history.

Best Coaches

There were 12 head basketball coaches at Butler before 1920 and nine thereafter. Here are six who have stood out.

•••

Harlan "Pat" Page

Born: March 20, 1887

Died: November 23, 1965

Hometown: Watervliet, Mich.

Education: University of Chicago

Butler Record and Years: 98–30, .765 (1920–26)

Best Teams: 11–7 (AAU national champions), 1923-24; 20–4, 1924–25

Harlan "Pat" Page is credited with bringing energy to Butler at a time when the school was becoming more serious about athletics. He also brought in Tony Hinkle.

The left-handed Page was a three-sport star at the University of Chicago, playing for coach Amos Alonzo Stagg. Page was a quarterback in football and a guard for three national-championship teams in basketball. He once averaged 10.3 points a game, then an astounding figure, and was chosen as national player of the year by the Helms Foundation in 1910.

When Page arrived at Butler, basketball was not as prominent as football. He changed that, coaching the Bulldogs to a 16–4 record in his first season, 1920–21, including a victory over Page's alma mater, Chicago. He led Butler to a national championship in basketball in 1924, winning the AAU Tournament in Kansas City, Mo. Hinkle, also a

Chicago graduate, was lured to Butler by Page and was an assistant coach on that team.

The Page era ended abruptly. He resigned before Butler's final basketball game in 1926. Students protested, but the administration said he was not forced out. Page significantly increased the athletic budget, and there was speculation he quit because he was going to have to relinquish control of the fund.

Page left Butler to coach football at Indiana University, where he had a 14–24–3 record from 1926 to 1930. He also coached basketball at the College of Idaho and Chicago.

•••

Paul "Tony" Hinkle

Born: December 19, 1898

Died: September 21, 1992

Hometown: Logansport, Ind.

Education: University of Chicago

Butler Record and Years: 560–392, .588 (1926–42, 1945–70)

Best Teams: 19–3, 1927–28; 17–2 (national champions), 1928–29; 17–2, 1930–31; 18–5, 1948–49; 22–6 (NCAA Sweet Sixteen), 1961–62

In August 2009, the *Sporting News* ranked the 50 greatest coaches of all time. It was a flawed list, but the publication might have been correct on No. 1: John Wooden. The native Hoosier won 10 NCAA basketball championships at UCLA from 1964 to 1975, and no other team in a major American sport has been so dominant.

Wooden was not on the panel of 118 experts making the selections. If he had been, his vote might have gone to Paul D. "Tony" Hinkle. At least that's what Wooden once told Buckshot O'Brien, who played basketball and baseball under Hinkle.

"He said coach Hinkle is perhaps the greatest coach that ever lived," O'Brien recalled. "Because he coached baseball, football, and basketball and was athletic director. Mr. Wooden only coached one sport."

Hinkle himself would have been disinterested in such a list. He just wanted to coach. It was his life. He was 93 when he died, and if Butler had allowed it, he might have coached up until then. After all, Hinkle's football coach at the University of Chicago, Amos Alonzo Stagg, was coaching until age 98. As it was, after retiring in 1970, Hinkle continued

Tony Hinkle, (center) probably would have coached well into his 70s if the university had allowed it (Butler University Archives).

to serve Butler as a special assistant to the president, "working for my pension," as he described it.

So Hinkle's career at Butler spanned 71 years, from 1921 to 1992. That in itself would be an achievement. Yet coaching at a small liberal arts college in Indiana—even producing winners there—does not qualify one to be a national figure. And Hinkle did win one national championship, in basketball in 1929. With a 560–392 record, he was the seventh-winningest coach in college basketball history when he retired. Including all three sports, he won more than 1,100 games.

Better measurements of a coach are whether he influenced lives or a sport. Hinkle did both. At one time, more than 50 of his former players and assistant coaches were employed as coaches in Indiana alone.

Moreover, perhaps Hinkle's greatest coaching triumph came not at Butler and not in basketball. When he was at the Great Lakes Naval Station during World War II, he coached its football and basketball teams.

In 1943, Great Lakes was a huge underdog against a 9–0 Notre Dame football team coached by Frank Leahy. In the last minute, Hinkle's sailors came from behind to beat Notre Dame 19–14. The Fighting Irish were so strong that they were consensus national champions anyway.

Of course, basketball is the sport with which Hinkle is associated. He was enshrined in the Naismith Basketball Hall of Fame in 1965 not as a coach, but as a contributor. The fieldhouse that bears his name, when built in 1928, was the largest in the country and remains a memorial to its namesake. Hinkle was a member of the national rules committee in the mid-1930s when the center jump was removed and continued to serve on the panel, including two years as chairman.

He also originated the orange-colored basketball. Until the late 1950s, basketballs were dark brown. Hinkle wanted a ball that could be better seen by players and fans. He worked with the Spalding Company to come up with a new ball, which was tested at the 1958 Final Four in Louisville, Ky., and approved by the NCAA.

In the late 1940s, he introduced the Hoosier Classic, a two-day doubleheader involving Butler, Indiana University, Purdue, and Notre Dame. Although Butler was a small university, the coach developed such a reputation that larger schools agreed to play against the Bulldogs and the so-called Hinkle system. For instance, in the first 10 games of the 1959–60 season, Butler played eight Big Ten opponents and Wooden's UCLA Bruins (who lost to the Bulldogs 79–73). Because of Hinkle's friendship with football coach Knute Rockne, Notre Dame became a regular on Butler's basketball schedule.

Through it all, Hinkle's favorite sport might have been baseball. If the spitball hadn't been banned in 1921, he might have become a major league pitcher. He is reported to have been offered contracts by both the Chicago Cubs and New York Giants. He was so devoted to the game that he often went to the Butler diamond himself to rake the infield or tend to the grass.

"The phone didn't ring down there," was his explanation.

•••

Paul Daniel Hinkle was born near Logansport., Ind., on a farm owned by his mother's parents. In the biography written by Howard Caldwell, *Coach for All Seasons*, Hinkle told the author that his father, Edgar, grew up a "waif" in the Logansport area. Edgar's mother died when he was

6. Edgar's father, Lewis, remarried, but Edgar never felt accepted and ran away from home.

Despite such beginnings, Edgar Hinkle pursued education, became a math teacher, and passed on high standards to his son. Edgar and wife Winnie lived on the farm early in their marriage because teaching pay was so low. The family moved around—to Goshen, Ind.; Winona, Minn.; and Elgin, Ill.—before settling in Chicago.

The family spent summers on the farm until young Hinkle was about to enter high school. The farm was sold in 1912 after both of his grandparents died. Just before Hinkle's 11th birthday, sister Florence was born, and the two remained close despite being separated by so many years.

At Chicago's Calumet High School, Hinkle played basketball, baseball, and golf. He also played soccer because the school had dropped football. When he was a senior, Calumet won the city soccer championship.

Hinkle's father directed him toward the University of Chicago, whose campus was four miles from his home. Stagg was the football coach and athletic director, and Harlan "Pat" Page coached basketball and baseball. Page, Hinkle, and Fritz Crisler, who became the Michigan football coach, were the only University of Chicago athletes ever to win three letters each in football, basketball, and baseball.

In his sophomore year, Hinkle acquired the nickname that stayed with him. On a road trip, he came out of a restaurant carrying an extra serving of spaghetti and meatballs, and Page called him "Tony," as if he were Italian. The Hinkle family never accepted the nickname and continued to call him Paul.

College was interrupted in the fall of 1918, during World War I, when Hinkle reported to Camp McArthur in Waco, Texas, to begin officer training. The war ended a few weeks later, and he returned to the University of Chicago in time for basketball season. He was an all-conference guard in 1918–19, and the next season he helped Chicago win the Big Ten championship. He had two seasons of football eligibility left after returning from military service, and had courses to complete for graduation, so he finished his college athletic career in the fall of 1920.

By that time, Page had left Chicago to take over athletics at Butler. Stagg appointed himself acting basketball coach at Chicago, and Hinkle assisted him as he finished courses for a degree in oil geology. Page asked Hinkle to join him at Butler in February 1921, and to Stagg's surprise, Hinkle left for the Indianapolis campus.

• • •

Hinkle arrived at Butler in an era when a new attitude was developing about athletics.

He began as head baseball coach and an assistant in other sports. He was Page's aide when the Bulldogs won the 1924 AAU Tournament in Kansas City, Mo., for their first national championship in basketball. Page unexpectedly resigned before Butler's final basketball game in 1926.

Hinkle took over as acting head coach in football and basketball and served as athletic director. Butler hired George "Potsy" Clark as football coach and athletic director, so Hinkle was removed from those two jobs. He stayed as basketball coach, however, a post he held for 41 seasons. He ranks fifth on the all-time list for seasons coached behind Phog Allen of Kansas, Jim Phelan of Mount St. Mary's, Ed Diddle of Western Kentucky, and Ray Meyer of DePaul.

Hinkle, who never had much of a social life, met his future wife, Jane Murdock, in 1927. The only other woman anyone remembered him dating was Eleanor Twitchell, who became the wife of baseball slugger Lou Gehrig.

Hinkle wed Jane on June 30, 1928, in Indianapolis. Jane shared her life not only with a husband, but also with countless practices, ballgames, and ballplayers. Their home on West 46th Street was two blocks from the fieldhouse. The couple had two daughters, Barbara and Patty. Jane died in 1959 at age 52.

• • •

Hinkle was successful coaching basketball from the beginning. He won 100 of his first 126 games, reaching that milestone faster than all but 14 coaches in major-college history. In his third season, at age 30, he led Butler to a second national title. The Bulldogs were recognized as national champions by the Veterans Athletic Association of Philadelphia after a 17–2 record in 1928–29.

Crisler tried, unsuccessfully, to lure Hinkle to Michigan as its basketball coach in 1931. Herb Schwomeyer, a Hoosier basketball historian who served Butler in various capacities for 38 years, speculated on why Hinkle stayed.

"He loved to coach all three sports," Schwomeyer said.

Schwomeyer described the Hinkle system of basketball as constant ball movement between pairs of players, using 14 basic plays. Those would be called picks and screens in the modern game. All players were expected to move, handle the ball, and shoot—a template, coincidentally, that Butler has used in recruiting players in the 21st century.

"He was a precise guy, fundamentally sound," Schwomeyer said of Hinkle.

Players were assigned roles and were expected to fulfill them, according to Billy Shepherd, the high-scoring guard who played on Hinkle's final team in 1970. Hinkle substituted infrequently, finding a lineup he liked and sticking to that.

"He didn't try to keep a bunch of guys happy," Shepherd said. "If you were in the rotation, top eight, you knew you were going to get your minutes."

Recruiting wasn't as intense when Hinkle coached, and he never enjoyed it. According to Schwomeyer, Hinkle seriously pursued just four basketball players: Oscar Robertson, twins Tom and Dick Van Arsdale, and Lou Unseld. None enrolled at Butler.

A prospect would know Hinkle was offering a scholarship if the coach asked what size shoe he wore. After the teenager replied, Hinkle would say, "We have that size at Butler."

There were few black athletes participating in college sports before World War II, although there were exceptions such as Jesse Owens at Ohio State. Another was Butler's Tom Harding, a graduate of Crispus Attucks High School, the alma mater of Robertson. Harding was a standout in football, baseball, and track. Hinkle called him the best athlete he ever coached and said that if the Brooklyn Dodgers had not chosen Jackie Robinson to break the major leagues' color barrier in 1947, that player could have been Harding.

In 1989, Hinkle supplied his all-time all-star teams at Butler, with the caveat that they not be revealed until after his death. The following are the Hinkle All-Stars, along with year of graduation:

Football

Al Sporer, 1939; Tom Harding and Vic Lanahan, 1940; John Schuesler, 1952; Leroy Thompson, 1956; Paul Furnish, 1959; Don Benbow, 1963; Lee Grimm, 1964

Basketball

Archie Chadd, 1929; Frank Baird, 1934; Jerry Steiner, 1940; Bob Dietz, 1941; John Barrowcliff and Bill Shepherd, 1949; Ralph "Buckshot" O'Brien, 1950; Bobby Plump, 1958; Ken Pennington, 1960; Dick Haslam and Gerry Williams, 1962; Tom Bowman, 1963; Jeff Blue, 1964

Baseball

Oral Hildebrand, 1929; Inmon Blackaby, 1938; Tom Harding, 1940; Paul O'Connell, 1951; Norm Ellenberger, 1955

• • •

During Hinkle's first nine basketball seasons, he never had a record worse than 12–8. The Bulldogs endured a decline in the mid-1930s with successive seasons of 6–15 and 6–14. The downturn didn't last long. Led by Bob Dietz, who later became Hinkle's longtime assistant coach, and guard Jerry Steiner, the Bulldogs produced a 17–6 record in 1939–40. One of the losses was 40–33 to Indiana's Hoosiers, who went on to win their first NCAA championship.

Hinkle's last pre–World War II team opened the season on December 6, 1941, the night before Japanese warplanes attacked Pearl Harbor. By the time that season was over, Hinkle was leaving for military service. He was commissioned as a lieutenant at the Great Lakes Naval Training Center, north of Chicago on Lake Michigan. He was assigned to do what he did best: coach.

In two seasons, his teams were 16–5–1 in football, featuring that upset of Notre Dame. He was 64–6 in basketball, including a 59–34 victory over his own Butler Bulldogs. He took a brief respite from coaching when was assigned to be the recreation director at the U.S. Navy base on Guam in the South Pacific.

• • •

Hinkle rarely called athletes by name, usually referring to them as "kid" or calling them by their hometown. When Geoffrey Bannister became president of the university in 1989, he prepared an organizational chart. Soon thereafter, Hinkle, then a special assistant to the president, came to Bannister's office and asked to see him. Hinkle's simple message:

"Kid, you left me off the chart!"

Bannister loved that incident.

"I already knew and respected him, but now that he had called me 'Kid,' I felt like family," Bannister said.

Even though Hinkle's family accompanied him to Great Lakes during the war, it didn't feel like the family was intact until he returned to campus. Less than four months after the war ended, he was preparing for another Butler basketball season.

Hinkle's first postwar football team was 7–1, but there were some lean years thereafter. The student newspaper called for him to resign, and in 1952 a petition circulated to have him removed as football coach.

Hinkle's basketball credentials were not questioned in such a way. His fourth postwar team, in 1948–49, was 18–5 and climbed into the Top 20 of the inaugural Associated Press poll. The Bulldogs, led by the backcourt of Ralph "Buckshot" O'Brien and Jimmy Doyle, finished the season 18th in the nation. Butler didn't make it into the national rankings again until December 2001, more than a half-century later.

As for football, Hinkle didn't turn out to be the dunce critics thought he was. Beginning in 1956, Butler had successive records of 6–2, 7–2, 8–1, 9–0, 8–1, 9–0, 5–2–2, and 8–1—a cumulative record of 60–9–2 and a winning percentage of .859. The Bulldogs won seven straight Indiana Collegiate Conference titles from 1958 to 1964.

Granted, Butler could not match up to college football's powers. It was not possible in that sport. It was in basketball.

Butler beat Indiana and Purdue so regularly in the Hoosier Classic that the tournament was discontinued after 1960. Butler was chosen for the NIT, for the first time in 1958 and again in 1959. The latter season featured an 81–66 upset of No. 5-ranked Tennessee and an 81–76 victory over Indiana. No. 2-ranked Bradley barely survived, 71–65, in a 1960 visit to the fieldhouse.

Considering how much the sport had changed since the 1929 national title, Butler's Sweet Sixteen appearance in the 1962 NCAA Tournament might have been a comparable achievement. Butler, one of only 25 teams in the tournament, knocked off No. 8 Bowling Green 56–55 in the first round under the direction of its 63-year-old coach.

The 1969–70 season was to be the last for Hinkle in a move that created controversy. Yes, he was turning 71. No, he wasn't ready to go.

Schwomeyer said the university president, Alexander Jones, pushed for the change because "he was totally jealous of Hinkle." Steve Norris, a guard on Hinkle's final team, said the university wronged the coach.

"Just to throw him out because he's 70 years old. I mean, he was a legend," Norris said. "He knew his basketball. He would teach you fundamentals without you realizing you were being taught that."

Prominent Butler sports alumni circulated a petition to have Hinkle retained as basketball coach, but he resigned himself to the fact that the university wanted him out.

"Nobody wants to work for somebody who doesn't really want him," Hinkle said. "This kind of thing could cause all kinds of trouble. I love Butler and wouldn't want that to happen."

A crowd estimated to be about 17,000—exceeding the capacity of Hinkle Fieldhouse—turned out for Hinkle's final game, February 23, 1970, against Notre Dame. A pregame ceremony honored Hinkle, and it included a standing ovation lasting 2½ minutes. The action befitted the occasion, with the No. 14 Fighting Irish pulling out a 121–114 victory in what was then the highest-scoring game in the history of the fieldhouse.

Bannister delivered the eulogy at Hinkle's 1992 funeral, held inside the fieldhouse where the coach toiled tirelessly. The Butler president said Hinkle was a Hoosier hero whose love of place triumphed over love of self.

"He was from and of an Indiana that we long to see again," Bannister said. "He was a bridge to our own better times and better values. Because of this, his very presence was a constant physical reminder of who we should be."

Hinkle was buried in Crown Hill Cemetery. Among others interred there are Civil War generals, bank robber John Dillinger, poet James Whitcomb Riley, President Benjamin Harrison, and university founder Ovid Butler.

•••

Barry Collier

Born: July 16, 1954

Hometown: Atlanta, Ga.

Education: Miami-Dade (Fla.) Community College, Butler University, Indiana State University (M.S.)

Butler Record and Years: 196–132, .598 (1989–2000)

Best Teams: 23–10 (NCAA Tournament), 1996–97; 22–11 (NCAA Tournament), 1997–98; 23–8 (NCAA Tournament), 1999–2000

Barry Collier was born in England and raised in Atlanta, Ga.; Birmingham, Ala.; and Miami, Fla. He lived in five different cities as a college basketball assistant coach and spent six years in Lincoln, Neb., as the University of Nebraska's head coach.

Yet Butler University is the place that always seemed like home—even though Collier played basketball there just two years and once left as coach for a higher-paying job. He returned to Butler as athletic director in August 2006, bringing the Butler Way full circle.

Collier is credited for building the system that allowed Butler to reach eight NCAA Tournaments between 1997 and 2009. He never won in the tournament himself. Upon returning, he labored to help successors exceed his coaching achievements.

None of it might have happened had it not been for a conscientious dean of education, Joseph Nygaard. Collier, a transfer student, was less than three weeks into his first semester as a business major at Butler. He felt miscast, and that reinforced his long-held ambition to teach and coach.

He went to the education office and was surprisingly ushered in to see the dean. The student explained the dilemma and wondered if it was too late to enroll in education. It was near the end of the school day, so the dean told him to see him the next morning.

When Collier reported back, Nygaard handed him a revamped schedule and told him his next class was in a half-hour. Any problems, the dean said, check back with him. The incident changed Collier's life and almost certainly would not have occurred at a large university.

"I'm sure that has a lot to do with why I think so much of Butler," Collier said.

It wasn't the first time Collier was steered in a different direction. Growing up, he wanted to be a pilot.

Barry was the third of four sons born to Walter and Nancy Collier on a Royal Air Force base near Norfolk, England. The father was an Air Force navigator who earned a law degree while in the military. The oldest brother, also Walter, was a pilot who flew in the Vietnam War. The youngest, Courtney, flew missions in Iraq and Afghanistan. Courtney and Greg both graduated from the Air Force Academy. All three brothers eventually became commercial pilots.

Barry Collier resurrected a Butler program that declined after Tony Hinkle's retirement, then returned to his alma mater as athletic director (Butler University Archives).

At Miami-Dade Junior College, Barry joined an ROTC unit and was selected the outstanding freshman cadet. He was grounded when a physical exam revealed that his vision wasn't good enough, and his height, 6-foot-6, disqualified him from being a pilot.

He was a latecomer to basketball, as evidenced by his playing career. He was cut from the freshman team at Palmetto High School in Miami. That prompted him to get more serious about the sport. He began dribbling a basketball a mile to a park where he played all day or after school, until it was too dark or the lights were shut off. Then he would dribble home in the dark, unable to see the ball.

"You can get the feel, and it was great training at night," Collier said.

Collier's high school experience influenced him because he liked his teachers, including basketball coach Dale Collins. Collier learned about Butler from Stan Evans, his junior college coach. Evans and Butler's George Theofanis met at a coaches' gathering, and Theofanis began recruiting the tall forward. Collier said he was "a border-line Division I player" whose only other offers were from Georgia State and Division

II Florida Southern. He visited the Indianapolis campus, liked the school and fieldhouse, and decided to go with the Bulldogs.

"They signed me sight unseen," Collier said.

At Butler, he made friends with teammates such as Bill Lynch and John Dunn. Lynch, who was a co-captain with Collier, became the head football coach at Butler, Ball State, and Indiana University. Dunn was later president of Butler's board of trustees.

Collier joined Lambda Chi, where several teammates were fraternity brothers. He moved out of the fraternity house before his senior year after wedding the former Annette Gaines, a Miami-based flight attendant, on June 14, 1975. They are parents of three sons, Casey, Brady, and Clay.

Collier averaged 15.2 points and 7.5 rebounds in 1975–76, when he and Wayne Burris were team co-MVPs. Collier was later selected to Butler's team of the 1970s. Even as a player, Theofanis said, Collier was a student of the sport.

"He was a good team man," Theofanis said. "He did what we practiced. Barry was not selfish in any way. He wanted to win."

The Bulldogs lost more than they won. They were 10–16 and 12–15 in Collier's two seasons. He relocated to play basketball but said what he came to appreciate about his undergraduate days were the people at Butler.

"The thing I remember most vividly about Barry was his ability to get along with people," Lynch said. "He's always been a very considerate person who relates well to people and who's very much at ease with those in all age groups."

After graduation, Collier started the requisite apprenticeship for coaches, serving as an assistant at Rose-Hulman Institute, Seattle Central Community College, Idaho, Oregon, and Stanford. His driven nature and disciplined lifestyle once manifested itself in training for a marathon—he ran a respectable time of 3 hours, 25 minutes in the Big Surf Marathon along the Pacific Coast Highway.

He sought head coaching jobs at Idaho (twice) and University of the Pacific but was rebuffed. He was with Stanford at the Pac-10 Tournament when he heard Butler was seeking a successor for Joe Sexson and immediately applied. The best thing that ever happened, Collier said, was not getting one of the other jobs.

On April 4, 1989, at the age of 34, Collier became the Bulldogs' coach. His 45-page proposal on how to revive the program was persuasive to Geoffrey Bannister, the university president.

Collier did not begin auspiciously. The Bulldogs were 6–22 that first season, tying a school record for defeats. He told a Butler administrator that he was so bad that he probably should have been fired. After that season, he was invited to a meeting with university leaders and wondered if he would be retained. Instead, he was awarded a four-year contract.

The next season, led by Midwestern Collegiate Conference player of the year Darin Archbold, the Bulldogs were 18–11 and made the NIT. Collier earned the first of four awards as conference coach of the year. But he yearned for the Bulldogs to be in the NCAA Tournament, and after a few more good but unsatisfying seasons, he became convinced his up-tempo style would not get them there.

In the 1995 off-season, Collier and Bowling Green coach Jim Larranaga spent two days with Dick Bennett, who had left Wisconsin-Green Bay for Wisconsin. Collier admired the way Bennett's teams played but didn't think he should ask for trade secrets from a coach in the same league. Bennett was no longer in the MCC, and Collier no longer wanted business as usual. If that retreat didn't produce an epiphany in the Butler coach, it was something close to that. Collier called it a turning point.

"I had the pieces of the puzzle," he said. "I didn't put them together."

In basketball terms, the Bulldogs became better defensively and recruited more efficiently. More personally, Collier found that his Christian principles—humility, passion, unity, servanthood, and thankfulness—coincided with winning basketball. Maybe age and maturity would have led him to such spiritual growth anyway, Collier said, but he became renewed in his faith and coaching.

"I wasn't perfect. Far from it," he said. "But that helped."

Butler made it to the NCAA Tournament in 1997 and 1998, and after an NIT bid in 1999, won 15 straight heading into the NCAAs in 2000. That year the Bulldogs lost a late lead and then lost to Florida 69–68 in overtime in one of the most momentous games in Butler history.

Collier does not like to revisit that game—his last as Butler's coach—but conceded that "our team played the way you want Butler teams to play." The Butler Way.

He recalled that when Butler first won the MCC Tournament, over Illinois-Chicago, 69–68, in 1997, his immediate thought was: "Is that it? I don't know what it was I had been expecting."

More important than winning, he said, is playing in such a way as to win. The path walked is more important than the destination, he added. That's right out of 1 Corinthians 9:24:

"You know that in a race all the runners run but only one wins the prize, don't you? You must run in such a way that you may be victorious."

Over the years, Collier had been mentioned as a coaching candidate at several schools, including SMU and Minnesota, and he finally left Butler for Nebraska. In six seasons at Nebraska, from 2000 to 2006, he was 89–91 and never had a winning record in Big 12 play. The best the Cornhuskers could do was the NIT in 2004 and 2006.

However, Collier was held in high regard by peers such as Rick Barnes of Texas. Barnes once called Collier one of the best coaches in the country, placing him in a category with Texas Tech's Bob Knight and Oklahoma State's Eddie Sutton.

Collier's military bearing and restrained persona disguised his wit and sense of humor. When he returned to Butler as athletic director on August 1, 2006, he was as aggressive in attempts to elevate all teams as he had been in trying to win in basketball. Not all moves were popular. He dropped men's lacrosse and swimming and raised basketball ticket prices. He was so hands-on that when it became hot inside Hinkle Fieldhouse, he climbed to the top himself and opened the windows.

When he once surveyed graduating athletes to ask whether they would attend Butler if they had to do it all over again, he was "sickened" by the fact that more than half said no. Above all else, he said, his aim was to make the student/athlete experience at Butler a good one.

"The constant improvement that we're striving for is an essential part of the Butler Way," Collier said. "Sitting still doesn't seem to be a really good option. I think we can get a lot better here in a lot of ways."

• • •

Thad Matta

Born: July 7, 1967

Hometown: Hoopeston, Ill.

Education: Butler University

Butler Record and Years: 24–8, 2000–01

Best Teams: 24–8, 2000–01

One day in 2001, Thad Matta was sitting in the basketball office at Hinkle Fieldhouse, looking at a Tony Hinkle photograph hanging on the wall. Matta was speaking on the phone to Barry Collier. Although Matta took Butler to the NCAA Tournament in his only season as head coach, he referred to his predecessors with reverence.

Matta regretted not spending more time with Hinkle, who died in 1992. Matta's aim was to add layers to the foundation laid by Collier from 1989 to 2000. Matta had a style all his own, a blend of passion and compassion. Foremost, he was a student with many teachers.

The coach is the son of a coach. The coach's father-in-law was a coach. Matta was raised in school buses and gymnasiums, listening to chalk talk.

"You wouldn't trade those moments for anything," he said. "That was a great learning opportunity for a young kind."

Matta's last season as a Butler player, 1989–90, was Collier's first as a Butler coach. Matta said it was the worst year of their respective lives.

The Bulldogs were 6–22, tying a school record for defeats. Matta was team captain but lost his starting job. He was ultimately sidelined by an ailing back that had required surgery at Mayo Clinic when he was in high school.

Still, Matta was convinced Collier was on the right road. As it turned out, so was Matta. There was nearly a detour in which Matta pursued a sales job in medical supplies, but Collier kept him at Butler as an administrative assistant.

"I learned, probably first and foremost, how to run a program from top to bottom," Matta said

Matta was the one who coined the phrase "The Butler Way," the team-oriented style of play for which the Bulldogs became known. Butler's program was shaped by Hinkle, resurrected by Collier, and maintained by Matta.

In his only season as the Bulldogs' head coach, 2000–01, Matta led them to a 24–8 record and their first NCAA Tournament victory since 1962. Butler built a 33-point halftime lead and beat Wake Forest 79–63 in the first round. Matta's staff included Todd Lickliter, John Groce, Mike Marshall, and administrative assistant Brad Stevens.

Matta's first position as an on-the-floor assistant was under Herb Sendek at Miami (Ohio) in 1994–95. The team went to the NCAA Tournament, an achievement that became a pattern for Matta. As an assistant coach, he went to the NCAA Tournament with Western Carolina in 1996, Miami again in 1997, and Butler in 1998 and 2000. After leading Butler to the tournament in 2001, he took Xavier in 2002, 2003, and 2004.

Matta's Xavier run ended but not his string of NCAA appearances. Ohio State was ineligible for the postseason in 2005, but the Buckeyes were 20–12 and upset a No. 1-ranked Illinois team that was 29–0. In his third season at Ohio State, in 2007, the Buckeyes won Big Ten regular-season and tournament titles, and Matta was conference coach of the year. That's a triple crown he achieved at Butler in 2001 and Xavier in 2002. The Buckeyes, led by Indianapolis products Greg Oden and Mike Conley, lost to Florida in the 2007 NCAA championship game.

Through 2009, Matta's record was 229–77, a percentage of .748. Only three coaches in Division I history won more games in their first nine seasons: Roy Williams (1989–97), Kansas, 247–58; Everett Case (1947–55), North Carolina State, 241–56; and Mark Few (2000–08), Gonzaga, 236–60.

On all of Matta's stops, he took notes. When Collier left Butler for Nebraska, he wanted Butler's job search to stop with Matta. So did Butler's players, most of them recruited by Matta. Athletic director John Parry interviewed two other candidates, former Butler assistant Jay John and recently fired Air Force coach Reggie Minton. Parry ultimately agreed with the players.

"I said to them, 'OK. Show that I made the right decision,'" Parry said.

They did. The personal relationships that Matta developed with the players weren't undermined by a new title. Players said the coach was still himself.

Matta's coaching style developed over many years around coaches. His father, Jim, remembered an eight-year-old Thad watching games intently and not running around the gym with the other children. Thad noticed how the players tied their shoes and asked about nuances his father hadn't detected.

"When there was a game on TV, he saw everything," Jim Matta said. "It's just a knack that he has."

Matta's hometown is Hoopeston, Ill., located seven miles west of the Indiana state line. As a player, he led Hoopeston-East Lynn High School to the Elite Eight of Class A state tournaments in 1984 and 1985. He was so absorbed in the sport that after a date one night, he didn't realize he had been shooting for two hours until his parents awakened to the sound of a ball bouncing on the driveway at 1:30 a.m.

"You can beat Thad, but you'll never outwork him," his father said.

Matta played one college season at Southern Illinois, then transferred to Butler. He led Butler in assists (100) and 3-point percentage (.433) in 1987–88 and in free-throw percentage (.872) in 1988–89. Through 2009, he was fourth at Butler and fifth in the Horizon League in career 3-point percentage (.444).

•••

Todd Lickliter

Born: April 17, 1955

Hometown: Indianapolis, Ind.

Education: Butler University, Central Florida Community College

Butler Record and Years: 131–61, 2001–07

Best Teams: 26–6, 2001–02; 27–6 (NCAA Sweet Sixteen), 2002–03; 29–7 (NCAA Sweet Sixteen and NIT Season Tipoff champion), 2006–07

It was not Todd Lickliter's manner to blaze like an oil fire. He was a campground log whose embers burned into morning.

Too calm? Too meek? Too intense, maybe. Or too caring.

Or, for Butler opponents, too often victorious.

"He has an unbelievable fire burning, a competitive fire inside," Butler forward Mike Monserez once said.

Butler players were fiery in defense of Lickliter, who was in his third stint as a Bulldogs assistant when he was promoted to head coach in 2001. They wanted Lickliter to succeed Thad Matta. They were outspoken in 2003, complaining that Lickliter wasn't coach of the year

Todd Lickliter, left, twice guided Butler to the Sweet Sixteen before being succeeded by assistant coach Brad Stevens (Butler University Archives).

in the Horizon League after Butler won the regular-season championship.

Lickliter didn't plunge into tirades when Butler lost. What he did stung worse than words.

"If you come in the day after a loss, you can just see where it's taken so much out of him," Joel Cornette said. "You can see he hasn't got any sleep. It just makes you want to go out and perform for him and do what you can the next time out.

"I never want to let that man down."

Cornette was on Butler's staff in 2006–07, then went to Iowa as an assistant when Lickliter took the job there. Cornette was on the 2003 team that reached the NCAA Sweet Sixteen, one of two times the Bulldogs did so under Lickliter. Butler also advanced to the Sweet Sixteen in 2007, a season featuring the NIT Season Tipoff championship.

That year Lickliter was honored as national coach of the year by the National Association of Basketball Coaches.

Lickliter was 53–12 in his first two seasons. Through 2009, only three men in Division I won more games in their first two years as a head coach: Bill Guthridge (1997–99) at North Carolina, 58–14; Brad Stevens (2007–09) at Butler, 56–10; and Everett Case (1946–48) at North Carolina State, 55–8.

When Lickliter became Butler's head coach, everyone called it his dream job. Yet he didn't need that to achieve fulfillment. He already had that in faith and family.

He found contentment when he converted to Orthodox Christianity, which identifies historically with the holy Catholic Church founded by Jesus Christ and the apostles. He remembered ruining one birthday party by debating theology for hours with younger brother Rhet. Later, they both worshiped at Orthodox churches.

"We walked in and said, 'We are *home*,'" Lickliter said.

Home provided the only hobby he required. He spent spare time with his wife, Joez, a pharmacist, and three basketball-playing sons. Relationships endure long after the memory of victory and defeat, and Lickliter nurtured them in his personal and professional lives.

His mother, Jimmye Sue, worked at the Oxford Shop, a clothier a few blocks from Butler's campus. While Lickliter was at Butler, three of his four siblings lived in the Indianapolis area, including youngest sister Beth Anne, who lived in the house where he grew up.

Teammates hung out at the house when his father, Arlan, was the coach at North Central High School. Todd continued to bring players home when he was on the Butler team, and he did so at all of his coaching stops.

"He cared a great deal about his players, both on and off the court," said John Groce, who played for Lickliter at Danville (Ind.) High School and was on the Butler staff with him. "It was very genuine, and everyone who played for him felt that way."

Earl Boykins sure did. The former NBA guard and Lickliter developed a mutual admiration during days at Eastern Michigan. Lickliter was so moved by Butler players' support of him that his voice broke while expressing gratitude at a news conference announcing his appointment as head coach.

It was inevitable that Lickliter would become a coach. He accompanied his father to the gym, went on scouting trips, and watched reels of taped games.

As a player, Lickliter wasn't particularly strong or quick. After he scored poorly on fitness tests while at Butler, a coach told him he was the worst athlete ever to play Division I basketball.

Todd Lickliter, as the point guard, helped North Central win a sectional championship in 1973, during a one-class era when a sectional title in Indiana was a major achievement. His mother has a newspaper clipping that underscored her son's ability and humility. After Lickliter scored 24 points for North Central in a 93–74 victory over New Castle, his father said it was the first time he let Todd go one-on-one.

"He was surprised," Arlan Lickliter said at the time. "He said, 'Dad, I don't want to do that.'"

Todd Lickliter spent summers at an all-sports camp run by his father in Cloverdale, Ind. The rest of the year was devoted to basketball. If it took zeal just to be a three-year starter in high school, that was no struggle at all compared to the tests ahead.

Lickliter delayed enrollment in college and worked for a bricklayer, toting bricks through mud and up ladders. It was honest labor. It was menial, boring, and exhausting. And it was invaluable. He learned from the bricklayer, Robert E. Lee, to look on the bright side of any task.

Lickliter spent one year at the University of North Carolina-Wilmington, then one at Central Florida Community College. When he transferred again, to Butler, he was back in his element. He returned to Hinkle Fieldhouse and played in the 1978 game commemorating the building's 50th anniversary, an 87–86 upset of Ohio State.

Lickliter's first test in coaching came at Park Tudor, a private Indianapolis school.

He coached there for eight years and another four at Danville. He recommended against others doing likewise. No one, he said, should be a head coach before he is an assistant.

"Those 12 years were like being in a laboratory," Lickliter said. "I'm sure with the great inventors, every experiment didn't work. So those led to something else. The only thing I would say to those who were involved during those years: forgive me.

"What I needed was to get to this level. Once I got there, I thought, 'I'm *home.'*"

Division I basketball was a sanctuary compared to the months in 1993–94 in which he coached a team in Saudi Arabia, decoding language and cultural barriers. He returned to Butler, where he had been an assistant in 1988–89, for the 1996–97 season under Barry Collier. That season launched the Bulldogs' run of NCAA Tournament appearances.

Lickliter left at the end of that season, spent two years at Eastern Michigan, and returned to Butler. He did so at the urging of Matta, who succeeded Collier.

Lickliter acknowledged that his methods differed from those of his father. Arlan Lickliter, who died in 1990, was old-school. He laid down rules and demanded discipline. On the other hand, Arlan was organized and a perfectionist. Like Todd.

Lickliter retained control of his teams, even if he held the reins looser than his father might have. In his third and fourth seasons, Butler's records declined to 16–14 and 13–15. After that losing record in 2004–05, four players left the program.

After that? Butler was 20–13 and won a game in the NIT. Then came the landmark 29–7 season that ended with a loss to eventual national champion Florida in the 2007 NCAA Tournament.

Lickliter's style could be summarized by poet Ralph Waldo Emerson, whose words once hung in the coach's office:

"Trust men and they will be true to you. Treat them greatly, and they will show themselves great."

Lickliter was 13–19 and 15–17 in his first two seasons at Iowa. Coincidentally, four players left the Hawkeyes' program after the 2008–09 season. When the same thing happened at Butler, Lickliter led the Bulldogs to unprecedented heights.

•••

Brad Stevens

Born: Oct. 22, 1976

Hometown: Zionsville, Ind.

Education: DePauw University

Butler Record and Years: 56–10, 2007–09

Best Teams: 30–4, 2007–08; 26–6, 2008–09

Brad Stevens is an only child. Yet he was rarely lonely growing up.

Whether it was touch football, backyard basketball, or home-run derby, he was the kid who brought everyone together.

Those who know Stevens cite his intelligence, organizational skills, and competitive nature. Mostly, though, they call him a people person.

"His activity always involved lots of people," said Jan Stevens, his mother. "He thrived on and got a lot of energy from people."

Stevens was 30 when he became Butler's head basketball coach on April 4, 2007. After seven years on the Bulldogs' staff, he succeeded Todd Lickliter. The promotion surprised some because of Stevens' age. He looked younger than some of his players.

Moreover, basketball was not his original career path. He became a marketing associate at Eli Lilly and Co., the Indianapolis pharmaceutical giant, after graduating with an economics degree from DePauw University.

Chris Koumpouras, a pharmacist, was not surprised. He was Stevens' manager at Lilly. After Lickliter left for Iowa, Koumpouras correctly predicted Stevens would be Butler's next coach.

"If passion and desire and drive are anything, they made the right choice," Koumpouras said. "I know I'd work for him."

If wins and losses are anything, Butler made the right choice.

He was 30–4 in his first season, 2007–08, setting a Butler record for victories. Only three coaches in major-college basketball ever won more games in their first season. Stevens was the youngest coach in more than a half century to win 30 games and the third-youngest ever.

The Bulldogs, starting three freshmen, were 26–6 in Stevens' second season, 2008–09. That's a two-year record of 56–10. Only one NCAA Division I coach, North Carolina's Bill Guthridge (58–14 from 1997 to 1999), had more victories in his first two years.

Though not Indiana-born, Stevens has long had a passion for Indiana's sport.

When he was three, his family moved from Greenville, S.C., to Zionsville, Ind. Stevens' father, Mark, was a football player at Indiana University. Football was the sport of choice for most Zionsville youths.

Not Brad. He played soccer and baseball, and he ran the 400 meters in track. He took church mission trips to Texas and Louisiana, and his father took him fishing in Canada. Those were all secondary to basketball.

Stevens was more riveted by basketball videos than video games. One treasured memory is of going into the home of Jim Rosenstihl, who coached Rick Mount at Lebanon (Ind.) High School, and listening to the coach narrate film of Mount's games from the 1960s.

"I never got sick of the game," Stevens said, "I never thought it wasn't the best game in the world."

Matt Broughton, a DePauw teammate, said Stevens traveled in basketball circles and could always find a pickup game. Anywhere they played, Stevens knew someone or someone who knew someone.

"He was always kind of interconnected in that loop," Broughton said.

Stevens was a star player in high school and a role player in college. Through it all, he wasn't just playing the game. He was thinking the game. That was evident during summers with Municipal Gardens, an AAU team that attracted some of Indiana's top talent.

In one state championship game, Municipal Gardens was down to four players because of injuries, foul-outs, and absences. Municipal Gardens employed a triangle-and-one defense in which Stevens chased the opponent's top guard. Municipal Gardens won.

Stevens said he was a spectator. That's not the way the coach remembered it.

"Brad's smarts really came through and his basketball IQ," coach Red Taylor said. "He was a coach on the floor at that particular point."

Stevens' coach at Zionsville High School, Dave Sollman, said Stevens had the respect of teammates even as a freshman. Stevens finished with several school records, including season scoring average (26.8) and career points (1,508). He scored 97 points in three games in leading Zionsville to a sectional championship in 1995. Zionsville hasn't won one since.

Stevens was never a full-time starter at DePauw. He averaged fewer minutes (15.2) and points (5.4) as a senior than he did as a freshman. In his senior year, he mentored freshmen Mike Howland and Joe Nixon, according to coach Bill Fenlon. Three years later, Howland and Nixon led DePauw to the NCAA Division III Elite Eight. Stevens left DePauw with a leadership award, the only basketball honor the school gives.

"He was always more concerned with how the group was doing than how he was doing," Fenlon said.

Not all of Stevens' games were confined to the hardcourt. A Zionsville teammate, Brian Flickinger, was such a close friend that the two developed a virtual sibling rivalry. They competed in everything, from golf to Monopoly. If there was no game, one would be created.

"Walking to the next room, 'OK, who can get there first?'" recalled Flickinger, a former La Salle University player.

Stevens' wife, Tracy, coped with her future husband's competitiveness on a Florida trip with his parents. Everything was a contest—laps in the pool, shuffleboard, tennis, and miniature golf.

"At that point, I realized I would have to put my competitive nature aside if we were going to make it in the long run," Tracy said.

After college, family and friends considered it a natural progression for Stevens to move into business. He won a coveted Lilly internship and then accepted a position there. Stevens said the months at Lilly were exciting and rewarding. A Lilly director gave him what he considers the best advice he ever received—do your best on the job you have, and good things will happen.

Still, Stevens conceded he was "itching to be a part of basketball." He shocked his parents and some friends by quitting Lilly to become a volunteer in Butler's basketball office in the summer of 2000. Tracy, who had been dating Brad since they were DePauw sophomores and who married him in 2003, remembered the dinner at which he told his parents.

They were scared, Tracy recalled. His father said he "about flipped out." His mother reasoned that whatever he lost financially could be recouped over the rest of his life. Tracy said she was enthusiastic. Brad acted like a different person thereafter, she said.

"He couldn't be in a profession he wasn't passionate about," Tracy said. "It just wouldn't work."

Stevens was sharing a rented house with friends in 2000. He made ends meet by working at various basketball camps. He was going to wait tables until then-coach Thad Matta hired Stevens as Butler's director of basketball operations, an administrative post. Stevens didn't reveal what the job paid, but it was far less than what he made at Lilly.

"It wasn't even necessarily chasing a dream of being a head coach," he said. "It was about being part of the game, competing on a daily basis and really looking forward to that, and being around a team, being part of a team."

The years, and Stevens' rise, came quickly. Matta left Butler after one season in 2001 for Xavier, and successor Lickliter promoted Stevens to assistant coach. Stevens' methods so closely resembled those of Lickliter that some Bulldog players called him "Little T," as in Little Todd. Stevens absorbed all he could from all the coaches he had been around.

"He's been as dedicated to his job as any intern to the art of learning medicine," said Stevens' father, an orthopedic surgeon.

Tracy Stevens, an attorney, said her husband is so absorbed with what he's doing during summer recruiting that he eats breakfast at 7 a.m. and forgets about eating the rest of the day. In the days before he became head coach, he stayed up until 4 a.m. answering e-mails from home, slept a couple of hours, and returned to Hinkle Fieldhouse.

It would be hard work, except that it's not work to him, his wife said. Their respective schedules don't allow much free time, and the hours they do have are spent together or with their young children, Brady and Kinsley. The guy who once organized ballgames plans family outings.

"I call him my own cruise director," Tracy said.

That Stevens would be steering Butler's ship surprised those who thought he had too much earnings potential to go into coaching. Butler will have difficulty retaining him because bigger schools can pay him so much more. Not that it has ever been about money.

After all, Stevens worked one summer for nothing. He said his most valued possession is a key to Hinkle Fieldhouse.

He has been young enough to interact comfortably with players, such as playing Nintendo or exchanging text messages. He has been old enough not to be the players' pal. He has been around the program long enough to teach and embrace the Butler Way.

The Best Games

Out of more than 2,400 games, it would be presumptuous to select 40 and declare them the best in Butler basketball history. But these top 40 are representative, if you forgive a predisposition to choose games from recent decades. Games were selected not only for their quality or drama, but also for their significance.

Games are listed chronologically, with three exceptions: Butler's 65–57 loss to No. 3 Florida on March 23, 2007, in the NCAA Midwest Regional at St. Louis; the 79–64 upset of No. 3 Michigan on December 22, 1965, at Indianapolis; and the 36–22 upset of Franklin College on February 28, 1924.

The author votes for those three as the best games in Butler history.

March 23, 2007:
No. 3 Florida 65, No. 21 Butler 57

With less than four minutes left, the Bulldogs led 54–53 over Florida, the defending NCAA champion whose roster had six future NBA players. The winner of the game, played before 26,037 at St. Louis' Edward Jones Dome, would be one victory from the NCAA Tournament's Final Four.

The Gators made the necessary plays down the stretch to blunt Butler's valiant attempt. The Bulldogs came closer than any team in the tournament to preventing Florida from winning a second straight national championship.

The Gators went ahead for good when 6-foot-10 Al Horford backed down Butler's Brandon Crone, who fouled out on the play. Horford's basket and free throw sent Florida ahead 57–54 with 2:34 left.

"They have a unique style, and I think the one thing about their team that maybe goes unnoticed is they're extremely physical," Florida

---

coach Billy Donovan said. "They're as good as anybody we've played against dislodging the post and banging you off the post."

Butler led by as many as nine points in the first half. The Gators ended the half on a 13–0 run to go ahead 35–29 but never seized control until the last minute.

Guard Taurean Green and Horford scored 17 and 16 points, respectively, for Florida. Pete Campbell came off the bench to lead Butler with 14. Mike Green added 12. A.J. Graves scored 11, all in the second half.

"I think we played them as tough as anybody can," Campbell said. "I think we fought, we played hard, we played smart. We played Butler basketball most of the game."

December 22, 1965:
Butler 79, No. 3 Michigan 64

Jim Petty knew what coach Tony Hinkle was going to ask him to do. Actually hearing it was something else.

You chase "this Russell guy," the coach told him.

"My heart jumped in my throat," Petty recalled. "I thought, 'Here's a chance in front of 10,000 people to make of fool of myself.'"

Michigan's Cazzie Russell was not only one of the greatest college basketball players of the 1960s; he has been ranked among the top 10 college players of all time.

The Bulldogs came into the game at Butler Fieldhouse with a 2–5 record. Besides Petty, their key figure was Ed Schilling, a transfer from Cincinnati who had 26 points and 13 rebounds. Schilling's memory was not only of the game, but of the warm-ups. The Wolverines, at a time when the dunk was disallowed, put on a spectacular dunking display before the game.

"They were just so athletic," Schilling said.

So was Petty. He was better in track and field, once finishing fourth in the NAIA long jump, than in basketball. The 6-foot Petty had defensive help against the 6-foot-5 Russell, whose 22 points were nine less than his season average.

The Wolverines, coming of an NCAA-runner-up finish, lost to No. 1 Duke 100–93 in overtime at Detroit the night before. They were also without future Indiana Pacers forward Oliver Darden, who had the flu. Michigan fell behind 20–8 and never recovered.

It would have hard for any team to beat Butler, which shot 58 percent. Larry Shade scored 16 points on 6-of-8 shooting. Schilling, who was 10-of-16, remembered taking off on the wrong foot for a hook shot and making it anyway.

"And I thought, 'Hey, this is pretty good,'" Schilling said.

Petty started a construction business in Fortville, Ind., after teaching and coaching for 21 years. He said beating Michigan was so unexpected that an account of the game was published in a Paris newspaper.

"We kind of took them to school that night," Petty said.

February 28, 1924: Butler 36, Franklin 22

Franklin High School's "Wonder Five" is one of the most storied basketball teams in Indiana history, having won three successive state championships (1920, 1921, and 1922). Players on the team stayed in town, about 20 miles south of Indianapolis, and enrolled at Franklin College to follow their coach, Griz Wagner.

Franklin was unbeaten in 1922–23 and was proclaimed college basketball's national champion. Franklin beat Butler 25–17 and 26–22 that season and again in December 1923, 35–19. Coach Pat Page's 6–7 Bulldogs visited Franklin to finish the season. The Wonder Five, led by Robert "Fuzzy" Vandivier, had won 36 in a row over two college seasons.

"Even the most enthusiastic Bulldog backer entertains but little hope for a victory over the apparently invincible Baptist combination," reported the *Indianapolis Star*. (Franklin was nicknamed the Fighting Baptists.)

Three special cars took Butler fans and the school band to Franklin. Unexpectedly, Butler built a 13–12 halftime lead. Still, 20 minutes remained for the Baptists to bop the Bulldogs.

It never happened. Butler extended the margin to 22–15 and, shockingly, led 33–17 with two minutes left.

"It was one of those exceptional cases where fight and determination overcome versatility and basketball cunning," the *Star* reported.

Robert Nipper and Haldane Griggs scored 11 points each for Butler. Vandivier was held to eight on a single field goal and six three throws.

"My boys were 'off' tonight, and Butler was definitely 'on,'" Wagner said. "It's bound to happen."

Despite a 7–7 record, that victory earned Butler an invitation to the AAU Tournament in Kansas City, Mo. The Bulldogs won four games there to claim the 1924 national championship.

Here are the best of the rest, in reverse chronology:

November 24, 2007: Butler 81, Texas Tech 71

At a banquet preceding the Great Alaska Shooout, Bob Knight and Brad Stevens were separated by three feet—and by 889 victories. However, it was the 31-year-old Stevens who had a veteran Butler team, while Knight, 67, brought a younger Texas Tech quintet.

When their teams met for the championship in Anchorage, the Bulldogs used clinical precision to beat Texas Tech. After leading 34–32 at halftime, Butler shot 65 percent in the second half and 75 percent (9-of-12) on 3-pointers. The Bulldogs didn't commit a turnover in the second half until two minutes remained.

Butler finished 16-of-24 from the arc and set title game records for 3s made and percentage (.667). A.J. Graves tied the title game record with six 3-pointers, and Pete Campbell and Mike Green added four each. Butler's three-game total of 3s made (47) exceeded the former record of 34 set by California-Irvine in 1990. Green, voted the tourney's outstanding player, had 23 points and seven assists.

Knight said he wished his team played as smart as Butler did. Stevens said Knight set the standard in the sport for doing things right.

"For him to say that to us, it means a lot to me personally," Stevens said.

Among those congratulating the Bulldogs at the postgame ceremony was Sarah Palin. About nine months later, the Alaska governor became the Republican running mate for Sen. John McCain in the 2008 presidential race.

March 17, 2007:
No. 21 Butler 61, No. 18 Maryland 59

The Bulldogs were long shots to begin this season. They made long shots to keep it going.

In an NCAA Tournament game in Buffalo, N.Y., the Bulldogs sank 12-of-26 from the 3-point line in eliminating the bigger Terps.

A. J. Graves scored 19 points to help Butler reach the Sweet Sixteen for the second time in five years and set a school record with a 29th victory. Graves sank four 3s, and Pete Campbell and Brandon Crone three each.

"It's an indescribable feeling," said Butler's Julian Betko, who played despite injuring his shoulder in a first-round victory over Old Dominion.

November 25, 2006:
Butler 83, Kent State 80 (2 OT)

Was Butler expecting to win the NIT Season Tipoff? No, because the day after beating Gonzaga to win the tournament, the schedule showed the Bulldogs were to play Kent State. Their charter flight from New York didn't arrive in Indianapolis until 3:00 a.m.

The Bulldogs never led in the opening 35 minutes and trailed by as many as eight points. They were on the verge of defeat at the end of regulation and overtime. Brian Ligon's tap-in tied the score at 57 to end regulation, and A.J. Graves' 3-pointer tied it at 67 with 5.5 seconds left in the first OT.

Mike Green played all 50 minutes and scored 16 points. Graves scored 22 of his 26 points after halftime and played 48 minutes.

"It was the toughest thing I've ever done," Graves said.

November 14, 2006: Butler 60, Indiana 55

The Hoosiers were favored to reach the semifinals of the NIT Season Tipoff, and there was no reason to think otherwise when they led by 12 points with less than 10 minutes left at Conseco Fieldhouse.

Butler's A.J. Graves kept missing from the field, but he changed course and began driving to the basket. He sank six free throws during a 9–0 run that trimmed Indiana's lead to 47–44. With Butler ahead 57–55 and the shot clock expiring, Graves banked in a 3-pointer with five seconds left. Before that, he had missed 14 of 17 shots.

The backcourt of Graves (20 points) and Mike Green (17) booked the Bulldogs a trip to New York.

"The guys pulled me together," Green said. "I believe in the Butler Way."

November 13, 2006: Butler 71, Notre Dame 69

At Butler, it should be called "The Shot." It was as meaningful to the Bulldogs as "The Catch" was to the San Francisco 49ers. Dwight

Clark's touchdown catch gave the 49ers a 28–27 victory over the Dallas Cowboys in the NFC Championship on January 10, 1982, and prefaced the first of the 49ers' four Super Bowl victories of the 1980s.

The Shot was by A.J. Graves. His long 3-pointer from the right corner with 1:28 left—the game's final points—delivered a victory over Notre Dame in the NIT Season Tipoff. That started the Bulldogs toward a run of success continuing well into the decade and maybe longer.

The 3-pointer was Graves' eighth, the most of his career. It came after a pass from Mike Green, whose assist was his 12th, the most of his career in only his second game in a Butler uniform.

"It helps to play with a player like him," Graves said. "He drives to the basket, and he gets the defense looking at him."

March 23, 2003:
Butler 79, No. 14 Louisville 71

When the Bulldogs fell behind 24–9, the second-round NCAA Tournament game in Birmingham, Ala., didn't look like it could hold a TV audience. But, hold on. Butler did.

Freshman guard Avery Sheets sank a shot from the arc to momentarily hold back the tide, and that signaled a change in the weather. It was raining 3s.

Butler outscored Louisville 12–0—a run that began and ended on 3s by Mike Monserez—to climb to within two, 26–24. Darnell Archey's 3-pointer and Joel Cornette's basket closed the half, and Butler led 34–33.

Butler made its first four 3-point attempts of the second half, two by Archey, and led 50–39. Although the Cardinals soon tied the score at 52, Butler never trailed in the second half. Archey sank all six of his 3-pointers in the second half, was 8-of-9 overall from the arc, and finished with 26 points. The Bulldogs shot 14-of-23 (64 percent) on 3-pointers in a victory that propelled them to the Sweet Sixteen for the first time in 41 years.

All over the Indianapolis area, fans watched TV sets in admiration, including a group gathered at a girls basketball tournament in Shelbyville, Ind.

"The crowd made up of referees, other girls AAU teams, coaches, parents, and volunteers clapped and cheered like we were all in Birmingham," Doug Maier wrote in an e-mail.

Maier, a sales manager for a pharmaceutical company, had an interest in the outcome because Rob Walls was a summer intern at his company and an assistant coach for Catholic youth teams in Westfield, Ind. When Cornette crashed into the sideline and had his shoes ruined by a spilled liquid, the quick-thinking Walls took off his size 15s and handed them to his teammate.

Walls' gesture became a metaphor for Butler basketball. Maier, a North Carolina native, said the Bulldogs made him "proud to call central Indiana my home."

March 21, 2003:
Butler 47, No. 20 Mississippi State 46

The NCAA Tournament is littered with No. 12 seeds knocking off No. 5s. However, in this pairing, fifth-seeded Mississippi State was being projected as a possible Final Four team and not a first-round casualty of Bulldogs vs. Bulldogs.

Butler led 12–3 early, and its patient tempo was unfamiliar to Mississippi State. Butler led 28–25 at halftime, and then Mississippi State controlled most of the second half. Mississippi State built its biggest lead, 42–38, with eight minutes left.

Mississippi State went ahead 46–45 on two free throws with 1:33 left. After that, Butler guard Brandon Miller was caught in the air with the shot clock expiring and passed out of bounds. But Mississippi State missed on its possession, and Miller grabbed the ball. He kept it.

Miller, with seconds ticking away, had an opening in the lane for a running one-hander. He made the shot with 6.2 seconds left, giving Butler another 12-over-5 upset. Afterward, he ran around the court pumping his fist in the air.

"To hit a shot in that situation is definitely the biggest shot of my career," Miller said.

March 1, 2003:
Butler 76, Wisconsin-Milwaukee 74

Without this victory, Butler probably would not have been selected to the NCAA Tournament as an at-large entry. Before a home sellout of 11,043, the Bulldogs won on a 3-pointer by freshman Avery Sheets as time expired. The outcome gave Butler a fourth straight regular-season Horizon League title.

Milwaukee erased a 16-point deficit to go ahead 74–73 with four seconds left. Butler and Milwaukee were tied for first in the league at 13–2.

December 29, 2001:
No. 23 Butler 66, Indiana 64

Joel Cornette rebounded Thomas Jackson's miss with 3.4 seconds left, then dunked the ball to hand Indiana its first loss after 39 straight victories in the Hoosier Classic. For 16,471 fans at Conseco Fieldhouse, the game was a classic.

The Bulldogs thus defeated Purdue and Indiana in the same season for the first time since beating both in 1948 in the original Hoosier Classic hosted by Butler.

The Bulldogs trailed by nine points with fewer than 12 minutes left and won even though top scorer Rylan Hainje went down with an ankle injury early in the second half. Indiana coach Mike Davis was whistled for a technical foul with 2:10 left, and two technical free throws by Darnell Archey and one free throw by Jackson sent Butler ahead 62–60.

Tourney MVP Jackson scored 14 points. Jared Jefferies led the Hoosiers with 18.

March 16, 2001:
Butler 79, No. 23 Wake Forest 63

This was one of those rare occasions that defied credulity. In Kansas City, Mo., the Bulldogs built a 43–10 halftime lead in achieving their first NCAA Tournament victory in 39 years.

Butler led 17–2, 25–3, and 30–5. Before nine minutes had elapsed, Butler had seven 3-pointers.

"They came out of the gate with all barrels loaded," Wake Forest coach Dave Odom said. "It is easy to concentrate on the early made 3s, but you need to look at the great spacing, good ball handling, and unselfish play that made those possible."

Wake Forest's 10 points were the fewest in one half of an NCAA Tournament game since 1941. Brandon Miller scored 18 points, Rylan Hainje and LaVall Jordan 15 each, and Thomas Jackson 14 for Butler.

January 30, 2001:
Butler 58, No. 10 Wisconsin 44

For the only time in its history, Butler beat a top 10 team on the opponent's court. The Badgers fell behind by seven in Madison, Wis., but tied the score at 20 by halftime.

Joel Cornette twice scored on dunks early in the second half, and Butler pulled away. Led by guards Thomas Jackson and Brandon Miller, the Bulldogs spread the floor and used superior quickness to neutralize Wisconsin's size. Jackson scored 17 points and Miller 14.

The outcome ended Wisconsin's streak of 20 consecutive home victories over nonconference opponents. The Badgers, who reached the Final Four the year before, were ranked in the top 10 for the first time since December 1962.

November 28, 1997:
Butler 73, No. 19 Oklahoma 63

Jon Neuhouser scored 21 points and grabbed nine rebounds to lead the Bulldogs to an upset in the first round of the Big Island Invitational in Hilo, Hawaii. Oklahoma was coached by Kevin Sampson.

Butler went on to beat Pacific 73–67 in overtime of a semifinal before losing to No. 15 Stanford 99–86 in the championship game.

March 4, 1997: Butler 69, Illinois-Chicago 68

The Bulldogs' victory in the Midwestern Collegiate Conference championship game in Dayton, Ohio, sent them to the NCAA Tournament for the first time in 35 years. Tourney MVP Kelsey Wilson and Jon Neuhouser scored 18 points each.

Noting how long it had been since the Bulldogs had been in the NCAA field, coach Barry Collier said: "My parents were buying a black and white TV, and I was learning cursive writing in the third grade."

November 27, 1993:
Butler 75, No. 11 Indiana 71

Butler fans probably framed the *Indianapolis Star*'s headline from the next day: "Trice 'n Guice Put Indiana on Ice."

The Hoosiers came to Hinkle Fieldhouse off a Big Ten championship and 31–4 season. Butler, which was 11–17 the season before, opened with a 90–72 loss at Cincinnati in the Preseason NIT. The sellout crowd was dominated by Indiana fans.

Travis Trice scored 24 points, including seven 3-pointers, and Jermaine Guice added 19 and stern defense. The victory was Butler's first victory over the Hoosiers in 35 years.

"I thought they really took it to us," Indiana coach Bob Knight said.

January 27, 1992:
Butler 87, No. 17 UNC Charlotte 84

Tim Bowen sank a 3-pointer at the buzzer, then proceeded to do backflips to the opposite end of the Hinkle Fieldhouse floor in celebration of the Bulldogs' victory. Charlotte had tied the score on Delano Johnson's 3-pointer with four seconds left. It was Butler's first victory over a nationally ranked opponent under Collier.

November 26, 1991: Butler 67, Notre Dame 60

Jermaine Guice and John Taylor each scored 18 points to lead the Bulldogs to victory in South Bend, Ind. It was Butler's first victory at Notre Dame in 30 years, snapping a streak of 14 consecutive losses on the Fighting Irish's home court.

February 9, 1991:
Evansville 136, Butler 128 (2 OT)

Butler rallied from a 16-point deficit to send the game into overtime and led 116–109 with fewer than two minutes left in the first extra period. Successive 3-pointers by Billy Reid helped Evansville force another overtime.

Little-used Chris Westlake scored 13 of his 15 points in the second OT for the Purple Aces. Reid finished with 34 and Butler's Darin Archbold with 31. The game remains the highest-scoring in Hinkle Fieldhouse history.

"This is one you'll look back at years down the road and say, 'That was unbelievable,'" Butler's Brett Etherington said.

December 28, 1987:
Butler 78, No. 16 Iowa State 76

Darren Fowlkes didn't appear for the Bulldogs' scheduled departure to Toledo, Ohio, for the Blade Classic. His roommate drove him to Toledo, and Fowlkes showed up at the next day's pregame meal. Coach Joe Sexson told him he might as well head back to Indianapolis because he wasn't playing.

Afterward, team captain Chad Tucker told the coach that the Bulldogs had come to win the tournament and that the players felt Fowlkes had made amends and should be allowed to contribute, even if that meant just sitting on the bench.

Fowlkes stayed but did not start. With 13:03 left in the half and Iowa State ahead 18-13, he entered the game and scored 10 points to push Butler into a 38–37 halftime lead. His basket tied the score at 76, and he passed to Tucker for the winning basket with 57 seconds left. Fowlkes finished with 26 points, shooting 10-of-10 on free throws, in 27 minutes.

Toledo beat Butler 52–50 for the championship the next night.

February 9, 1987: Butler 88, Detroit 77

When the NCAA introduced the 3-point line this season, no one used it more effectively than Darrin Fitzgerald. His average of 5.6 field goals a game from the arc remain the NCAA record. Against Detroit, he set Butler and Hinkle Fieldhouse records with 12 3-pointers and 54 points.

"I was just trying to get the win, basically," Fitzgerald said.

February 28, 1985: Butler 70, Notre Dame 69 (OT)

Mike Burt scored eight of his 20 points in overtime for Butler, which ended a streak of 12 successive losses to Notre Dame dating back to 1966. Burt helped limit Notre Dame's David Rivers to 21.

Many in the crowd of 13,222 ran onto the floor at the finish. The victory enabled Butler to secure its first NIT berth in 26 years.

November 25, 1978: Butler 87, Ohio State 86

Butler marked the 50th anniversary of its fieldhouse by introducing coach Tony Hinkle and eight members of the 1929 national championship team. But it didn't look like the Bulldogs' day.

Ohio State, featuring future NBA players Herb Williams and Kelvin Ransey, built a 60–40 lead. The Bulldogs rallied with a full-court press and foul shooting by Joe Maloney, who was 16-of-18 from the line in the second half. Tom Orner's shot from the corner with two seconds left was the game winner.

Among the Butler heroes was point guard Todd Lickliter, who later became the Bulldogs' coach.

January 3, 1973:
No. 3 Marquette 67, Butler 66

Marquette was 8–0 and Butler 6–4. There was little indication the game would become so taut, especially after Marquette led by 12 points with 15 minutes left.

The Bulldogs, bolstered by a home crowd of 11,000, came all the way back to lead by five inside the three-minute mark. Two baskets by Allie McGuire, son of coach Al McGuire, brought Marquette to within one, 66–65. Dale Delsman sank a one-and-one to put the Warriors ahead with 1:24 left, and they held on after neither team could score.

Coach McGuire was so incensed at Marquette's play that he was heard upbraiding his players afterward. He did not speak to reporters.

"I think maybe the pros are around, troubling the kids like they did last year," Marquette assistant Hank Raymonds said. "The coach wants to get to this problem before it becomes one."

Larry McNeill led Marquette with 21 points, and Maurice Lucas had 16 points and nine rebounds.

Kent Ehret led Butler with 22 points. Daryl Mason had 15 points and 11 rebounds.

"These kids kept coming back, and I think we outplayed them," Butler coach George Theofanis said.

Theofanis had no issues with McGuire. The Butler coach offered Marquette a $10,000 guarantee to play at Indianapolis, and McGuire declined. McGuire proposed to keep all the gate receipts, play at Marquette next year, and take part of that gate.

"Now, that's class," Theofanis said.

Butler lost at Marquette 73–54 the next season.

February 23, 1970:
Notre Dame 121, Butler 114

Before a record crowd of 15,000—and maybe more—in Hinkle's final game as coach, the Irish won what was then the highest-scoring game in fieldhouse history. Austin Carr scored 50 points, a fieldhouse record, and Collis Jones 40 for Notre Dame. Billy Shepherd scored 38 for Butler.

December 20, 1967: Butler 76, Purdue 59

A fight late in the first half resulted in the ejection of two Butler players, Bill Mauck and Gary Cox, and one from Purdue, Roger Blalock, at Hinkle Fieldhouse. Mauck's nose was broken.

Also gone was Rick Mount's shooting touch. The Purdue guard scored 23 points but was only 8-of-25 from the field. Teammate Herm Gilliam missed the game with a thigh bruise. Doug Wininger led Butler with 18 points.

February 23, 1963: Butler 79, Evansville 74

Butler ended Evansville's school-record 17-game winning streak and prevented the Purple Aces from becoming the Indiana Collegiate Conference's first unbeaten champion.

The Bulldogs, who had two players sick with the flu, were led by Tom Bowman's 19 points. For Evansville, Buster Briley had 21 and future NBA player and coach Jerry Sloan added 18.

March 12, 1962:
Butler 56, No. 8 Bowling Green 55

In the Bulldogs' first game ever in the NCAA Tournament, played in Lexington, Ky., they upset a Bowling Green team that had future NBA stars Nate Thurmond and Howard Komives.

Butler took a 56–53 lead on Gerry Williams' two free throws with 33 seconds left. The 6-foot-10 Thurmond had 21 points and 14 rebounds for Bowling Green.

December 10, 1960:
No. 2 Bradley 71, Butler 65

Bradley was coming off a 27–2 season and NIT championship. The second-ranked Braves were led by Chet Walker, an All-American forward who had recently scored 50 points in a game.

The outsized Bulldogs were outrebounded 44–27, and Bradley maneuvered inside to shoot 59 percent. Butler, playing before a home crowd of 8,550, stayed close with outside shooting in an era before the 3-point line. Gerry Williams sank successive shots from the left corner, tying the score at 63.

Bradley scored the next eight points—two baskets each by Tom Robinson and reserve guard Mack Herndon—to escape defeat. Coach Hinkle never substituted until the 36th minute.

Robinson scored 24 points and Walker 16 for Bradley. Butler's Williams and Tom Bowman, both sophomores, scored 27 and 19, respectively.

December 28, 1960: Butler 65, Purdue 63

This was the final game of the Hoosier Classic, a two-day event that began with Butler, Indiana, Purdue, and Notre Dame. Indiana, perhaps weary of losing to Butler, pulled out and was replaced by Illinois.

A day after the Bulldogs beat Illinois 70–68, they beat Purdue on Gerry Williams' jump shot with nine seconds left. All-American Terry Dischinger of Purdue scored 34 points and broke or tied five classic records.

February 16, 1959:
Butler 92, Notre Dame 89 (3 OT)

Butler's campus was thrown into such upheaval that M.O. Ross, the university president, called off classes for the next morning.

Bill Scott scored 23 points for the Bulldogs, including the basket that sent them ahead 91–89 in the third overtime. All-American center Tom Hawkins scored 36 for Notre Dame. Hawkins was the first black basketball star at Notre Dame and became vice president of the Los Angeles Dodgers.

December 20, 1958:
Butler 81, No. 5 Tennessee 66

This was supposed to be a homecoming for Tennessee coach Emmett Lowery, an Indianapolis native who had starred at Tech High School and Purdue. After all, the fifth-ranked Vols were 5–0 and Butler an unimposing 1–5.

The Vols' trip began poorly when they missed a train connection in Cincinnati and had to charter a bus to Indianapolis, arriving at 3:30 p.m. for that night's game. The Vols missed a planned morning practice at the fieldhouse. Circumstances then worsened.

Tennessee trailed 36–32 at halftime, and its position was more precarious than the score reflected. Four starters had three fouls each.

In the opening nine minutes of the second half, Butler extended its lead to 15, and the Vols were doomed. Butler finished 31-of-38 on free throws.

Tennessee captain Gene Tormohlen, a 6-foot-8 native of Holland, Ind., scored 19 points before fouling out. Bill Scott scored 17, Ken Pennington 16, and Larry Ramey 11 for Butler.

January 5, 1957: Butler 86, Notre Dame 84

The Bulldogs were 4–6, had lost 20 in a row at Notre Dame, and were without Hinkle. The coach was hospitalized, recovering from prostate surgery that would sideline him the rest of the season.

Longtime assistant coach Bob Dietz took over, and he made an unusual decision on the bus trip to South Bend. Instead of using the motion offense and man-to-man defense that Hinkle always employed, Dietz opted for a freewheeling offense and zone defense.

With Ted Guzek scoring 38 points and Bobby Plump 33, the Bulldogs shocked a Notre Dame team that later reached the NCAA Sweet Sixteen.

The next morning, Dietz walked into Hinkle's hospital room and said, "It's not too tough to win up there if you know how to coach."

January 6, 1954: Rio Grande 81, Butler 68

To address dwindling attendance, coach Hinkle scheduled Rio Grande, a tiny Ohio college with a traveling show named Bevo Francis. Attempts were made to discredit Francis, a 6-foot-9 forward who as a freshman in 1952–53 averaged 50.1 points against junior colleges, military bases, and seminaries. He scored 116 in one game.

Francis scored 48 against Butler, a "legitimate" opponent, on 17-of-31 shooting. The crowd numbered 11,593.

"I never saw a better shooter anywhere," Hinkle said afterward.

A month later, against Hillsdale (Mich.), Francis scored 113, which the NCAA recognized as its all-division record. His 46.5 average is still a collegiate record.

Francis, with a wife and family, soon dropped out of school. He later played for the Boston Whirlwinds, one of the white teams that barnstormed with the Harlem Globetrotters. He eventually went to work loading trucks at an Ohio steel mill.

January 2, 1948: Butler 64, Indiana 51

In the inaugural Hoosier Classic, Butler claimed a state championship by beating Purdue and Indiana on successive nights.

Jimmy Doyle scored 17 points for the Bulldogs, who recovered from a 17–9 deficit. Buckshot O'Brien, one night after scoring 18 in a 52–50 victory over Purdue, was just 3-of-17. But Butler's 5-foot-8 sparkplug left to an ovation from the crowd of 13,000.

December 23, 1939: Indiana 40, Butler 33

Butler built a 14–5 lead but couldn't hold off a Hoosier team that went on to win the second NCAA Tournament ever played. Bob Dietz scored 11 points for Butler, and Bob Dro had 11 for Indiana.

Indiana, despite finishing second to Purdue in the Big Ten, was selected for the NCAA Tournament by a committee that included Hinkle. Indiana coach Branch McCracken had misgivings about it, but Purdue coach Piggy Lambert supported the Hoosiers because they had beaten Purdue twice.

December 21, 1929: Butler 36, Purdue 29

Butler held one of Purdue's two All-Americans, Charles "Stretch" Murphy, without a field goal. The other, John Wooden, never made it to the game.

Wooden, waiting for a cab to take him to the train station, hailed a passing truck when the cab didn't arrive. As he started to climb on, another truck rear-ended the first one. Wooden was caught between the trucks. Fortunately for college basketball, his only injuries were bruises.

December 13, 1928: Butler 35, Pittsburgh 33

The season-opening victory started Butler toward a 17–2 record and national championship. Pittsburgh, which had a 27-game winning streak, was the acknowledged national champion from the previous season and had averaged a staggering 49 points a game.

The game attracted so much attention that floodlights were used to facilitate parking. The Indianapolis Street Railway Co. arranged car and bus service from Circle Monument to the fieldhouse.

Future major league pitcher Oral Hildebrand scored 18 points for the Bulldogs. "Hilde" used a fake pivot within the foul circle for most of his scoring. Dana Chandler added 11 points. Butler's captain, Frank White, went to the bench with a knee injury.

Pittsburgh led 23–17 before the Bulldogs went ahead with six minutes left and stayed ahead.

March 15, 1924: Butler 30, Kansas City Athletic Club 26

The Bulldogs completed their run through the AAU Tournament by beating the host team before a crowd of 10,000 in Kansas City, Mo. It was Butler's first basketball national championship.

"The Butler boys won the honor fairly in a game that, for wonderful teamwork, marvelous individual performance, and all-around brilliance, probably never has been equaled on any basketball court," reported the *Blue Diamond*, a publication of the K.C. Athletic Club.

Bob Nipper scored the go-ahead basket, and Haldane Griggs added another after the center jump. Griggs scored 12 points, Paul Jones eight, and Nipper six for Butler.

Sources

Books

Caldwell, H. (1991). *Tony Hinkle: Coach for All Seasons*. Bloomington, IN: Indiana University Press.

Denny, D. (2006). *Glory Days: Legends of Indiana High School Basketball*. Champaign, IL: Sports Publishing.

Gould, T. (1995). *Pioneers of the Hardwood: Indiana and the Birth of Professional Basketball*. Bloomington, IN: Indiana University Press.

Guffey, G. (2006). *The Golden Age of Indiana High School Basketball*. Bloomington, IN: Quarry Books/Indiana University Press.

Heller, B. (1995). *Playing Tall*. Chicago: Bonus Books.

Johnson, G. K. (2008). *Official 2009 NCAA Men's Basketball Records Book*. Chicago: Triumph Books.

Johnson, G. K. (2009). *Official 2009 NCAA Men's Final Four Records Book*. Chicago: Triumph Books.

Krider, D. (2009). *Indiana High School Basketball's 20 Most Dominant Players*. Bloomington, IN: AuthorHouse.

Nored, R. (1999). *Reweaving the Fabric: How Congregations and Communities Can Come Together to Build Their Neighborhoods*. Montgomery, AL: Black Belt Press.

Newspapers

Anchorage Daily News

Atlanta Journal-Constitution

Butler Collegian

Chicago Tribune

Cincinnati Enquirer
Indianapolis News
Indianapolis Star
New York Times
Omaha World-Herald
Peoria Journal-Star
Philadelphia Inquirer
St. Petersburg Times
Topeka Capital-Journal
USA Today

Web Sites

Basketballreference.com
CBSsports.com
ESPN.com
FIBA.com (international basketball governing body)
Foxsports.com
IHSAA.org (Indiana High School Athletic Association)
NBA.com
Rivals.com
Sportsillustrated.cnn.com
USAbasketball.com
Wikipedia.org

College Media Guides and Web Sites

Bradley University
Butler University
Cleveland State University
Franklin College
Gonzaga University
Horizon League
Indiana University
Loyola University, Chicago

University of Arizona
University of Detroit/Mercy
University of Illinois
University of Illinois-Chicago
University of Notre Dame
University of Pittsburgh
University of Wisconsin-Green Bay
University of Wisconsin-Milwaukee
Valparaiso University
Wabash College
Wright State University
Youngstown State University

Other

Amateur Athletic Union
Butler University Archives
Helms Foundation
Indiana Basketball Hall of Fame
Kansas City Athletic Club
Naismith Memorial Basketball Hall of Fame
Sports Illustrated
Time

 **David Woods** has been covering Butler basketball for the *Indianapolis Star* since 2001. He is a native of Urbana, Ill., and a University of Illinois journalism graduate. He has reported from five Olympic Games for the *Star*. He and his wife, Jan, have two daughters.